Footprint Handbook

Western Brazil

ALEX & GARDÊNIA ROBINSON

This is
Western Brazil

Western Brazil covers a continental area, stretching from the Iguaçu Falls in the far southwest to the northern reaches of the Amazon on the borders of Colombia and Venezuela. This is Brazil at its wildest and most magnificent, with a variety of terrain and scenery awe-inspiring in its scale. Iguaçu is a waterfall as wide as a London borough, while the Pantanal is a wetland bigger than most European countries. It's the Serengeti of South America and should not be missed by anyone with even a passing interest in wildlife.

Then there's the Amazon basin itself: more than twice the size of India, with mountains over 3 km high, sweeping savannahs and the largest tracts of tropical rainforest on Earth. The whole area is cut by myriad rivers, including three of the 10 biggest in the world by water volume. And with such expanse comes great variety, from powdery white sand (and mosquito-free) beaches of the Tapajos river and Marajó island, to the remote forests of the upper Rio Negro and Anavilhanas archipelago. There are some great jungle lodges, the best at Mamirauá near Tefé, and a string of cities to base yourself in before exploring the forest; including the lively state capitals of Manaus and Belém.

The vibrant city of São Paulo is the best international gateway for Iguaçu Falls and the Pantanal.

Alex Robinson
Gardênia
Robinson

Best of
Western Brazil

❶ São Paulo

Although not in Western Brazil, São Paulo is the gateway to the region. It's South America's biggest city and the best place in Brazil for great food, gallery art, nightlife and high-end shopping. Page 24.

❷ Iguaçu

The world's most spectacular waterfalls drop in a 3-km-wide tier of thundering water in the middle of a huge rainforest park. Be sure to visit both the Brazilian and Argentinian sides. Page 72.

❸ Fazendas around Miranda

Stay in a *fazenda* farmhouse in the heart of the southern Pantanal, set in the savannah and *cerrado* forest. Spot wildlife, learn how to lasso a steer and enjoy a barbecue grill under a canopy of stars. Page 97.

❹ A jaguar safari from Porto Jofre

Search for jaguars, giant anteaters and caiman in the rivers around Porto Jofre, the best place in the world to see South America's most elusive big cat. Page 111.

❺ Amazon jungle lodges

Get into the heart of the Amazon at Cristalino Jungle Lodge in northern Mato Grosso, Mamirauá Ecological Reserve west of Manaus or one of the other jungle lodges around Manaus (the best for budgeteers) and see rainforest wildlife close-up.
Pages 121, 137 and 149.

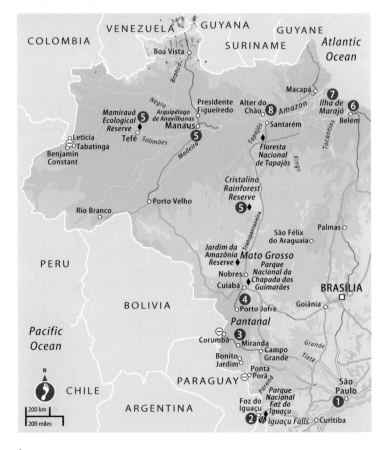

7

❻ Belém

Wander the old colonial Portuguese streets and shop in one of South America's most exotic markets. You'll also find some of Brazil's finest food and one of its liveliest music scenes in this vibrant Amazon port city. Page 155.

❼ Ilha de Marajó

Stay in a belle époque rubber-boom mansion, herd water buffalo on a *fazenda*, laze on white-sand beaches and spot wildlife in the rainforest creeks and mangroves on the world's largest river island located near Belém. Page 166.

❽ Alter do Chão

Swim in the glassy blue Tapajos river, fringed with pepper-fine sandy beaches. You can also visit the pristine Floresta Nacional do Tapajós (FLONA) rainforest reserve and the indigenous *caboclo* riverine communities around the Amazon village of Alter do Chão. Page 170.

A Pantanal cowboy and his cattle in Mato Grosso do Sul

Route planner

Western Brazil – including the Iguaçu Falls, the Pantanal and the Amazon – covers a vast area, so you'll need to fly. Consider buying an air pass (see page 180) before leaving for Brazil, and allow plenty of time to take in the sights. It's good to plan at least one full day for Iguaçu Falls, three to four days for the Pantanal and three days for anywhere in the Amazon.

One to two weeks
city sights, waterfalls and wildlife

With one to two weeks you'll have to sample highlights from this long itinerary. Allow a day for São Paulo and be sure to see the city lights from the top of the Banespa building. Then fly to Foz do Iguaçu for a whistle-stop day trip of both the Brazilian and Argentinian side of the waterfalls. From here take a plane to Cuiabá and spend a few days in a *fazenda* in the northern Pantanal, one of the best places in the Americas for wildlife spotting. If you have more than a week then take the short flight north to Alta Floresta and spend two to three days at Cristalino Jungle Lodge, one of the top spots to see Amazon wildlife in South America. Then return from Cuiabá to São Paulo for the flight home.

Three to four weeks
fashion capital, rainforests and safaris

A three- to four-week trip will allow you to enjoy the route at a more leisurely pace. Spend a couple of days in São Paulo to see the museums and sights, shop in the best fashion boutiques in South America, and enjoy a gourmet meal in a São Paulo restaurant.

A full day is enough to see the Iguaçu Falls themselves. Two days will allow you to see the bird park as well, and to take a helicopter flight over both the falls and the rainforest.

It's a long bus ride (or a flight via São Paulo) from Foz do Iguaçu to Campo Grande, the access point for the southern Pantanal. Allow three days for a Pantanal safari or a stay in a traditional Pantaneiro *fazenda* ranch house, or take a boat safari. You'll need two days to see the crystal-clear streams, caverns and bird-filled forests around Bonito, one of the best family-friendly wildlife destinations in Brazil. Alternatively, fly to Cuiabá and the northern Pantanal, with a three to four day jaguar safari in Porto Jofre, the best location to see the cats in South America. Consider taking a side trip to the table-top mountains of the Chapada dos Guimarães whose vertiginous cliffs drip with beautiful waterfalls. Or visit the clear-water rivers in Nobres which are filled with brightly coloured freshwater stingrays.

Another flight from Cuiabá will bring you to Manaus in the heart of the Brazilian Amazon. Allow a day to see the city. Wander the handsome centre which is crowned with the imposing and opulent Teatro Amazonas opera house and take a boat trip to the Museu Seringal, a reconstruction of an old rubber baron mansion set on a creek just north of the city. Spend a few days at a jungle lodge, on a river cruise, or in a homestay with *caboclo* people. If you have enough time and money journey up the jet-black Rio Negro to swim with bubble-gum pink Amazon river dolphins.

Fly to Belém (for return flights to Europe or the USA). Allow four days for the city and its environs. Take a day for the sights, which include another opulent opera house and the Ver-o-Peso market which overflows with Amazon produce, from energy berries to bizarre fish and medicinal herbs. Then spend a few days on the Ilha de Marajó, a vast sand island in the mouth of the Amazon River with extensive tracts of rainforest and broad, white-sand beaches. Or take an optional stopover in Santarém for the fabulous forests and beaches around Alter do Chão.

When to go

... and when not to

Climate

São Paulo is wet and windy between December and March and dry for much of the rest of the year. See page 26 for a weather chart.

The best time to visit Iguaçu Falls is May or September, when the water flow is fairly strong and the crowds are thinner. See page 73 for a weather chart.

The best time to visit the Pantanal is during its dry season, which runs from May to September; see page 105 for a weather chart. The Amazon can be visited at any time of year, both when it floods (February to July) and when it recedes (August to January). The climate is warm and humid all year round. Rain can come at any time and wildlife is always tough to spot. See page 125 for a weather chart.

Festivals

Carnaval dates depend on the ecclesiastical calendar. The party begins on the Friday afternoon before Shrove Tuesday, officially ending on Ash Wednesday and unofficially on the following Sunday.

Carnival dates
2017 23 February-1 March
2018 8-14 February
2019 28 February-6 March

January

New Year's Eve (Reveillon). Big parties in São Paulo and on the beach in Manaus.

April

Festa do Açaí, Festa da Castanha and **Festa do Cupuaçu**, Codajás, Tefé and Presidente Figueiredo, Amazonas. Three festivals devoted to three of the best Amazonian foods: the açai energy berry, *cupuaçu* and the Brazil nut.
Cuiafolia. The biggest festival of the year in Mato Grosso. The capital, Cuiabá, erupts into a mock-Bahian carnival powered by cheesy Bahian *axé* acts.

June

Boi Bumba, Parintins, Amazonas. A huge spectacle re-enacting the Boi story, with enormous floats and troupes of dancers. See www.boibumba.com.
Festas Juninas (Festas do São João), throughout Brazil. Everyone dresses up as a yokel, drinks hot spiced wine and dances *forró*.

October

Círio de Nazaré, Belém. One of the largest religious celebrations in Brazil. Huge crowds, long processions and many live music and cultural events. See www.ciriodenazare.com.br.

Improve your travel photography

Taking pictures is a highlight for many travellers, yet too often the results turn out to be disappointing. Steve Davey, author of Footprint's *Travel Photography*, sets out his top rules for coming home with pictures you can be proud of.

Before you go
Don't waste precious travelling time and do your research before you leave. Find out what festivals or events might be happening or which day the weekly market takes place, and search online image sites such as Flickr to see whether places are best shot at the beginning or end of the day, and what vantage points you should consider.

Get up early
The quality of the light will be better in the few hours after sunrise and again before sunset – especially in the tropics when the sun will be harsh and unforgiving in the middle of the day. Sometimes seeing the sunrise is a part of the whole travel experience: sleep in and you will miss more than just photographs.

Stop and think
Don't just click away without any thought. Pause for a few seconds before raising the camera and ask yourself what you are trying to show with your photograph. Think about what things you need to include in the frame to convey this meaning. Be prepared to move around your subject to get the best angle. Knowing the point of your picture is the first step to making sure that the person looking at the picture will know it too.

Compose your picture
Avoid simply dumping your subject in the centre of the frame every time you take a picture. If you compose with it to one side, then your picture can look more balanced. This will also allow you to show a significant background and make the picture more meaningful. A good rule of thumb is to place your subject or any significant detail a third of the way into the frame; facing into the frame not out of it.

This rule also works for landscapes. Compose with the horizon two-thirds of the way up the frame if the fore-ground is the most interesting part of the picture; one-third of the way up if the sky is more striking.

Don't get hung up with this so-called Rule of Thirds, though. Exaggerate it by pushing your subject out to the edge of the frame if it makes a more interesting picture; or if the sky is dull in a landscape, try cropping with the horizon near the very top of the frame.

Fill the frame
If you are going to focus on a detail or even a person's face in a close-up portrait, then be bold and make sure that you fill the frame. This is often a case of physically getting in close. You can use a telephoto setting on a zoom lens but this can lead to pictures looking quite flat; moving in close is a lot more fun!

Interact with people

If you want to shoot evocative portraits then it is vital to approach people and seek permission in some way, even if it is just by smiling at someone. Spend a little time with them and they are likely to relax and look less stiff and formal. Action portraits where people are doing something, or environmental portraits, where they are set against a significant background, are a good way to achieve relaxed portraits. Interacting is a good way to find out more about people and their lives, creating memories as well as photographs.

Focus carefully

Your camera can focus quicker than you, but it doesn't know which part of the picture you want to be in focus. If your camera is using the centre focus sensor then move the camera so it is over the subject and half press the button, then, holding it down, recompose the picture. This will lock the focus. Take the now correctly focused picture when you are ready.

Another technique for accurate focusing is to move the active sensor over your subject. Some cameras with touch-sensitive screens allow you to do this by simply clicking on the subject.

Leave light in the sky

Most good night photography is actually taken at dusk when there is some light and colour left in the sky; any lit portions of the picture will balance with the sky and any ambient lighting. There is only a very small window when this will happen, so get into position early, be prepared and keep shooting and reviewing the results. You can take pictures after this time, but avoid shots of tall towers in an inky black sky; crop in close on lit areas to fill the frame.

Bring it home safely

Digital images are inherently ephemeral: they can be deleted or corrupted in a heartbeat. The good news though is they can be copied just as easily. Wherever you travel, you should have a backup strategy. Cloud backups are popular, but make sure that you will have access to fast enough Wi-Fi. If you use RAW format, then you will need some sort of physical back-up. If you don't travel with a laptop or tablet, then you can buy a backup drive that will copy directly from memory cards.

Recently updated and available in both digital and print formats, Footprint's Travel Photography by Steve Davey covers everything you need to know about travelling with a camera, including simple post-processing. More information is available at www.footprinttravelguides.com

What to do

Bird- and wildlife watching

Brazil has the greatest terrestrial biodiversity of any country on Earth, with more primates, insects, reptiles, amphibians and freshwater fish than anywhere else. Almost a fifth of the world's bird species are Brazilian. The country is home to some 1750 species, of which 218 are endemic, the highest number of any country in the world. Brazil also has the largest number of globally threatened birds: 120 of 1212 worldwide. This is accounted for partly by the numbers of critically threatened habitats that include the *caatinga*, which has lost Spix's macaw, and the *cerrado* on the edges of the Amazon, which is being cut at an alarming rate to feed the demand for soya.

The Pantanal and the Amazon offer some of the best birding and wildlife spotting in the world and the finest guiding in Brazil. Serious birders looking for many rare species should head to Cristalino Jungle Lodge or Mamirauá Ecological Reserve. Those eager to see an anaconda should visit the Southern Pantanal with **Explore Pantanal** (see page 98). Jaguars are best seen from Porto Jofre with **Pantanal Nature** (see page 109). Booking directly with these operators is always far cheaper than

booking through a safari company back home and all the safari companies use pretty much the same local guides. Manaus, Alter do Chão and the Ilha do Marajó also offer plenty of wildlife opportunities and by far the most beautiful scenery in the Amazon region, but are not as good for dedicated wildlife lovers looking for high species diversity. Two comprehensive websites are **www.worldtwitch.com** and **www.camacdonald.com**.

Climbing and hill walking

There is good light hill walking in the Serra do Bodequena in the Southern Pantanal (organize through **Explore Pantanal**, page 98), in the Chapada dos Guimarães in the Pantanal and in the hills around Alter do Chão in the Amazon.

Cycling and mountain biking

Brazil is well suited to cycling, both on and off-road. On main roads, keep on the lookout for motor vehicles, as cyclists are very much treated as second-class citizens. There are endless roads and tracks suitable for mountain biking, and there are many clubs in major cities which organize group rides, activities and competitions. The Chapada dos Guimarães in the Pantanal is a particularly good area.

Diving

Cave diving can be practised in many of the underwater grottoes in Bonito and Mato Grosso do Sul in the Pantanal.

Fishing

Western Brazil is great for sport fishing. Officially, the country's fish stocks are under the control of Ibama (www. ibama.org.br) and a licence is required for fishing in any waters. As states often require permits too it is easiest to organize a trip through an agency. The best areas are the Amazon, the Pantanal and Rio Araguaia. Be aware

Shopping tips

Arts and crafts

Western Brazil has some enchanting arts and crafts. Best buys include bead jewellery and indigenous weave work, which are available in the Amazon at excellent shops in Alter do Chão and Manaus. Avoid feather items as these will be confiscated on arrival back home. The Terena indigenous people near Miranda in the Pantanal make beautiful ochre ceramics, and locals in Marajó produce fine rustic jewellery and pottery to age-old Marajoaora designs. Browse Belém's Ver-o-Peso for foodstuffs, herbal remedies and fabulous aromatic resins and incenses from the rainforest. Brightly coloured fabric hammocks are sold throughout Amazônia (be sure to buy hooks – *ganchos para rede* – for hanging your hammock at home).

Cosmetics and herbal remedies

For those who know how to use them, medicinal herbs, barks and spices can be bought from street markets. Coconut oil and local skin and haircare products (including fantastic conditioners and herbal hair dyes) are as good though far and cheaper than in Europe. Natura and O Boticário are excellent local brands, similar in quality to the Body Shop.

Fashion

Brazil has long eclipsed Argentina as the fashion capital of Latin America. Brazilian cuts, colours and contours are fresh and daring by US and European standards. Quality and variety is very high, from gorgeous bags and bikinis to designer dresses, shoes and denims.

São Paulo is the epicentre of the industry, with the best labels and the widest choice. Outside the US there is simply nowhere better to fashion shop in the Americas and if you love your clothes, dedicate some money and time to exploring what's on offer.

In São Paulo city the best area for fashion shopping is Jardins (around Rua Oscar Freire); the three big high-end malls, **Iguatemi** on Avenida Faria Lima, **Shopping Cidade Jardim** in Morumbi and **Shopping JK** in Itaim. Labels to look out for include **Dorothy Campolongo**, **Cris Barros**, **Adriana Barra**, **Herchcovitch**, **Amir Slama**, **Carina Duek** and that many Brazilians do not keep best practice and that rivers are quickly becoming over-fished.

Whitewater rafting

Whitewater rafting started in Brazil in 1992. Tour companies listed in the text under locations like Foz de Iguaçu offer trips in the southeast.

Carlos Miele. The city has a string of mid-range quality clothing brands, comparable to **GAP** or **Jigsaw**, with branches in most malls (the aforementioned three being a few of many). They include **Zoomp**, **Sidewalk**, **Hering**, **Forum** and **Iodice**, Bargain fashion – featuring Brazilian and international styles – is available in bewildering array on Rua 25 Março near the centre. Dedicated shoppers should consider hiring a personal shopper like **Ale Ribeiro** (see page 64) – if only for the huge discounts they can offer.

Jewellery

Gold, diamonds and gemstones are good buys and there are innovative designs in jewellery. For something special and high quality, buy at reputable dealers such as **H Stern** or **Antonio Bernado**. Cheap, fun pieces can be bought from street traders. There are interesting furnishings made with gemstones and marble – some of them rather cheesy – and huge slabs of amethyst, quartz and crystal at a fraction of a New Age shop price. More interesting and unusual is the seed and bead jewellery, much of it made with uniquely Brazilian natural products, and based on original indigenous designs and available in Manaus and Alter do Chão in the Amazon.

Music and instruments

Music is as ubiquitous as sunlight in Rio and browsing through a CD shop anywhere will be sure to result in at least one purchase.

Musical instruments are a good buy, particularly Brazilian percussion items. For example: the *berimbau*, a bow with a gourd sound-bell used in *candomblé*; the *cuica* friction drum, which produces the characteristic squeaks and chirrups heard in samba; assorted hand drums including the *surdo* (the big samba bass drum); and the *caixa*, *tambor*, *repinique* and *timbale* (drums that produce the characteristic Brazilian ra-ta-ta-ta). The most Brazilian of hand drums is the tambourine, a misnomer for the *pandeiro* (which comes with bells), as opposed to the *tamborim* (which comes without). There are many unusual stringed instruments too: the *rabeca* (desert fiddle), the *cavaquinho* or *cavaco* (the Portuguese ancestor of ukulele), the *bandolim* (Brazilian mandolin), with its characteristic pear shape, and many excellent nylon-strung guitars. São Paulo is the best place to source all these items.

Then there's Brazilian music itself. Only a fraction of the best CDs reach Europe or the USA. In São Paulo city, **FNAC** on Avenida Paulista is a good place to look; see page 60.

Where to stay

from *pensões* to *pousadas*

There is a good range of accommodation options in Western Brazil. An *albergue* or hostel offers the cheapest option. These have dormitory beds and single and double rooms. Many are part of **Hostelling International (HI)** ⓘ *www.hihostels.com*; **Hostel World** ⓘ *www.hostelworld.com*, **Hostel Bookers** ⓘ *www.hostelbookers.com*, and **Hostel.com** ⓘ *www.hostel.com*, are all useful portals. **Hostel Trail Latin America** ⓘ *T0131-208 0007 (UK), www.hosteltrail.com*, managed from their hostel in Popayan, is an online network of hotels and tour companies in South America. A *pensão* is either a cheap guesthouse or a household that rents out some rooms.

> **Tip...**
> Be sure to book hotels in advance over the busy Carnival, New Year and July Brazilian school holiday periods.

Pousadas

A *pousada* is either a bed-and-breakfast, often small and family-run, or a sophisticated and often charming small hotel. A *hotel* is as it is anywhere else in the world, operating according to the international star system, although five-star hotels are not price controlled and hotels in any category are not always of the standard of their star equivalent in the USA, Canada or Europe. Many of the older hotels can be cheaper than hostels. Usually accommodation prices include a breakfast of rolls, ham, cheese, cakes and fruit with coffee and juice; there is no reduction if you don't eat it. Rooms vary too. Normally an *apartamento* is a room with separate living and sleeping areas and sometimes cooking facilities. A *quarto* is a standard room; *com banheiro* is en suite; and *sem banheiro* is with shared bathroom. Finally there are the *motels*. These should not be confused with their US counterpart: motels are used by guests not intending to sleep; there is no stigma attached and they usually offer good value (the rate for a full night is called the '*pernoite*'), however the decor can be a little garish.

Hidden Pousadas Brazil ⓘ *www.hiddenpousadasbrazil.com*, offers a range of the best *pousadas*.

Luxury accommodation

Much of the best private accommodation sector can be booked through operators. **Angatu** ⓘ *www.angatu.com*, offers bespoke trips. **Matuete** ⓘ *www.matuete.com*, has a range of luxurious properties and tours.

Camping

Those with an international camping card pay only half the rate of a non-member at **Camping Clube do Brasil** sites ⓘ *www.campingclube.com.br*. Membership of the club itself is expensive: US$70 for six months. It may be difficult to get into some Camping Clube campsites during high season (January to February). Private campsites charge about US$6-8 per person. For those on a very low budget and in isolated areas where there is no campsite available, it's usually possible to stay at service stations. They have shower facilities, watchmen and food; some have dormitories. There are also various municipal sites. Campsites tend to be some distance from public transport routes and are better suited to people with their own car. Wild camping is generally difficult and dangerous. Never camp at the side of a road; this is very risky.

Homestays

Staying with a local family is an excellent way to become integrated quickly into a city and companies try to match guests to their hosts. **Couch surfing** ⓘ *www.couchsurfing.com*, is a free, backpacker option.

Quality hotel associations

The better international hotel associations have members in Brazil. These include: **Small Luxury Hotels of the World** ⓘ *www.slh.com*; the **Leading Hotels of the World** ⓘ *www.lhw.com*; the **Leading Small Hotels of the World** ⓘ *www.leadingsmallhotelsoftheworld.com*; **Great Small Hotels** ⓘ *www.greatsmallhotels.com*;

Price codes

Where to stay	Restaurants
$$$$ over US$150	$$$ over US$12
$$$ US$66-150	$$ US$7-12
$$ US$30-65	$ US$6 and under
$ under US$30	
Price of a double room in high season, including taxes.	Prices for a two-course meal for one person, excluding drinks or service charge.

---

and the French group **Relais et Chateaux** ⓘ *www.relaischateaux.com*, which also includes restaurants.

The Brazilian equivalent of these associations are **Hidden Pousadas Brazil** ⓘ *www.hiddenpousadasbrazil.com*, and their associate, the **Roteiros de Charme** ⓘ *www.roteirosdecharme.com.br*. Membership of these groups pretty much guarantees quality, but it is by no means comprehensive.

Online travel agencies (OTAs)

Services like **www.tripadvisor.com** and OTAs associated with them, such as **www.hotels.com**, **www.expedia.com** and **www.venere.com**, are well worth using for both reviews and for booking ahead. Hotels booked through an OTA can be up to 50% cheaper than the rack rate. Similar sites operate for hostels (though discounts are far less considerable). They include the Hostelling International site, **www.hihostels.com**, **www.hostelbookers.com**, **www.hostels.com** and **www.hostelworld.com**.

Food
& drink

from a *chope* with *churrasco* to a *pinga* with *pesticos*

Food

While Brazil has some of the best fine dining restaurants in Latin America and cooking has greatly improved over the last decade, everyday Brazilian cuisine can be stolid. Mains are generally heavy, meaty and unspiced. Desserts are often very sweet. The Brazilian staple meal generally consists of a cut of fried or barbecued meat, chicken or fish accompanied by rice, black or South American broad beans and an unseasoned salad of lettuce, grated carrot, tomato and beetroot. Condiments consist of weak chilli sauce, olive oil, salt and pepper and vinegar.

The national dish – which is associated with Rio – is a heavy campfire stew called *feijoada*, made by throwing jerked beef, smoked sausage, tongue and salt pork into a pot with lots of fat and beans and stewing it for hours. The resulting stew is sprinkled with fried *farofa* (manioc flour) and served with *couve* (kale) and slices of orange. The meal is washed down with *cachaça* (sugar cane rum). Most restaurants serve the *feijoada completa* for Saturday lunch (up until about 1630). Come with a very empty stomach.

Brazil's other national dish is mixed grilled meat or *churrasco*, served in vast portions off the spit by legions of rushing waiters, and accompanied by a buffet of salads, beans and mashed vegetables. *Churrascos* are served in *churrascarias* or *rodízios*. The meat is generally excellent, especially in the best *churascarias*, and the portions are unlimited, offering good value for camel-stomached carnivores able to eat one meal a day.

In remembrance of Portugal, but bizarrely for a tropical country replete with fish, Brazil is also the world's largest consumer of cod, pulled from the cold north Atlantic, salted and served in watery slabs or little balls as *bacalhau* (an appetizer/bar snack) or *petisco*. Other national *petiscos* include *kibe* (a deep-fried or baked mince with onion, mint and flour), *coxinha* (deep-fried chicken or meat in dough), *empadas* (baked puff-pastry patties with prawns, chicken, heart of palm or meat), and *tortas* (little pies with the same ingredients). When served in bakeries, *padarias* or snack bars these are collectively referred to as *salgadinhos* (savouries). You'll find *feijoada*, *churrascaria* and *bacalhau* throughout Western

Brazil, together with some fabulous regional cooking. Fish, local vegetables like *pequi* (a tart cooked fruit with lethal spines at its heart, so don't bite down) and meaty stews are popular in the Pantanal.

The Amazon has some of the best food in Brazil. The superb river fish here are delicious, especially the firm-fleshed pacu and tambaqui. The piracururu is an endangered species and should only be eaten where it is farmed or fished sustainably, from reserves such as Mamirauá (see page 149). The most celebrated regional dish in the Amazon is *tacacá no tucupi* (prawn broth cooked in manioc juice and jambu leaf). The soup is infused with an alkaloid from the jambu that numbs the mouth and produces an energetic rush to the head. Other dishes include tart *maniçoba* and spicy *pato no tucupi*. Try the superb **Remanso do Bosque** restaurant in Belém for a gourmet take on these local flavours.

There are myriad unusual, delicious fruits in Western Brazil – particularly the Amazon – including many with unique flavours. They include the pungent, sweet cupuaçu, which makes delicious cakes, the tart camu-camu, a large glass of which holds a gram of vitamin C, and açaí – a dark and highly nutritious berry from a *várzea* (seasonally flooded forest) palm tree, common in the Amazon. Açaí berries are often served as a frozen paste, garnished with *xarope* (syrup) and sprinkled with *guaraná* (a ground seed, also from the Amazon, which has stimulant effects similar to caffeine). Brazil also produces some of the world's best mangoes, papayas, bananas and custard apples, all of which come in a variety of flavours and sizes.

Eating cheaply

The cheapest dish is the *prato feito* or *sortido*, an excellent-value set menu usually comprising meat/chicken/fish, beans, rice, chips and salad. The *prato comercial* is similar but rather better and a bit more expensive. Portions are usually large enough for two and come with two plates. If you are on your own, you could ask for an *embalagem* (doggy bag) or a *marmita* (takeaway) and offer it to a person with no food (many Brazilians do). Many restaurants serve *comida por kilo* buffets where you serve yourself and pay for the weight of food on your plate. This is generally good value and is a good option for vegetarians. *Lanchonetes* and *padarias* (diners and bakeries) are good for cheap eats, usually serving *prato feitos*, *salgadinhos*, excellent juices and other snacks.

The main meal is usually taken in the middle of the day; cheap restaurants tend not to be open in the evening.

Drink

The national liquor is *cachaça* (also known as *pinga*), which is made from sugar cane, and ranging from cheap supermarket and service-station firewater, to boutique distillery and connoisseur labels. Mixed with fruit juice, sugar and crushed ice, *cachaça* becomes the principal element in a *batida*, a refreshing but deceptively powerful drink. Served with pulped lime or other fruit, mountains of sugar and smashed ice it becomes the world's favourite party cocktail, caipirinha. A less potent caipirinha made with vodka is called a *caipiroska* and with sake a *saikirinha* or *caipisake*.

Some genuine Scotch whisky brands are bottled in Brazil. They are far cheaper even than duty free; Teacher's is the best. Locally made and cheap gin, vermouth and Campari are pretty much as good as their US and European counterparts.

Wine is becoming increasingly popular and Brazil is the third most important wine producer in South America. The wine industry is mainly concentrated in the south of the country. Reasonable national table wines include Château d'Argent, Château Duvalier, Almadén, Dreher, Preciosa and more respectable Bernard Taillan, Marjolet from Cabernet grapes, and the Moselle-type white Zahringer. There are some interesting sparkling wines in the Italian spumante style (the best is Casa Valduga Brut Premium Sparkling Wine), and Brazil produces still wines using many international and imported varieties. The best bottle of red is probably the Boscato Reserva Cabernet Sauvignon, but it's expensive (at around US\$20 a bottle); you'll get far higher quality and better value buying Portuguese, Argentine or Chilean wines in Brazil.

Brazilian beer is generally lager, served ice-cold. Draught beer is called *chope* or *chopp* (after the German Schoppen, and pronounced 'shoppi'). There are various national brands of bottled beers, which include Brahma, Skol, Cerpa, Antartica and the best Itaipava and Bohemia. There are black beers too, notably Xingu. They tend to be sweet. The best beer is from the German breweries in Rio Grande do Sul and is available only there.

Brazil's fruits are used to make fruit juices or *sucos*, which come in a delicious variety, unrivalled anywhere in the world as well as those sourced from the Amazon (and mentioned above) you'll find *caju* (cashew), *pitanga*, *goiaba* (guava), *genipapo*, *graviola* (chirimoya), *maracujá* (passion fruit), *sapoti*, *umbu* and *tamarindo*,– all of them delicious. *Vitaminas* are thick fruit or vegetable drinks with milk. *Caldo de cana* is sugar-cane juice, sometimes mixed with ice. *Água de côco* or *côco verde* is coconut water served straight from a chilled, fresh, green coconut. The best known of many local soft drinks is *guaraná*, which is a very popular carbonated fruit drink, completely unrelated to the Amazon nut. The best variety is *guaraná Antarctica*. Coffee is ubiquitous and good tea entirely absent.

Menu reader

A
água de côco coconut water
arroz doce rice pudding

B
bacalhau salt cod
bauru sandwich made with melted cheese, roast beef and tomatoes

C
cachaça sugar cane rum
caipirinha cocktail of crushed fruit (usually limes), *cachaça* and lots of sugar and ice
caju cashew
caldo de cana sugar cane juice
caldo de feijão bean soup
chope/chopp draught beer
churrasco mixed grilled meat
churrasqueira restaurant serving all-you-can-eat barbecued meat
côco verde coconut water served from a chilled, fresh, green coconut
comida por kilo pay-by-weight food
coxinha shredded chicken or other meat covered in dough and breadcrumbs and deep fried
curau custard flan-type dessert made with maize

E
empadas or **empadinhas** puff-pastries with prawns, meat or palm hearts

F
farofa fried cassava flour
feijoada hearty stew of black beans, sausages and pork
frango churrasco grilled chicken

K
kibe a petisco deep-fried or baked mince with onion, mint and flour

M
mandioca frita fried manioc root
maracujá passion fruit
misto quente toasted ham and cheese sandwich
moqueca seafood stew cooked with coconut and palm oil

P/Q
padaria bakery
palmito palm heart
pamonha paste of milk and corn boiled in a corn husk
pão de queijo a roll made with cheese
pastéis deep-fried pastries filled with cheese, minced beef, or palm heart
peixe fish
petisco a tapas-style snack
picanha rump, a popular cut of beef
pinga sugar cane rum
prato feito/prato comercial set meal
queijo cheese

R
requeijão ricotta-like cream cheese
roupa velha literally meaning 'old clothes', a dish of shredded dried meat served with rice *mandiocas*

S
salgadinhos savoury snacks such as *empadas* and *tortas*
sortido inexpensive set meal
suco fruit juice

T
tortas small pies filled with prawns, chicken, palm hearts or meat

V
vatapá fish and prawn stew cooked in a creamy peanut sauce
vitaminas fruit or veg drinks with milk

São
Paulo

Essential São Paulo city

Finding your feet

There are three airports. The main international airport at **Guarulhos** in the suburbs, 25 km northeast of the centre, is 40 minutes to one hour by airport bus to the centre, depending on the destination, although journeys can take up to two hours in rush hour. **Congonhas** airport 7 km south of the centre has mainly domestic flights, and buses between here and Guarulhos take around one hour 10 minutes, depending on traffic. São Paulo's third airport is **Viracopos** in the commuter town of Campinas, some 95 km from São Paulo.

There are four long-distance bus terminals: **Tietê**, **Barra Funda**, **Bresser** and **Jabaquara**. All are connected to the *metrô* system. See also Transport, page 64.

Getting around

The best way to get around São Paulo is on the excellent *metrô* system, which is clean, safe, cheap and efficient, and integrated with the overground CPTM light railway. Buses can be slow due to frequent traffic jams. However,

they are safe, clean and only crowded at peak hours (0700-0900 and 1700-1830). White city taxis are easily identifiable by their green lights on the roof and are readily available at taxi stations (*postos*) within five minutes' walk from anywhere in the city.

When to go

It's warm and wet in summer (October to March) on the coast and drier inland with blue skies. Try and avoid January and February when it's very wet. The weather is cool in winter (April to September) with blue skies. Temperatures can drop to below 10°C during a cold spell.

Time required

Two to three days for the city, preferably over a weekend for nightlife.

Useful addresses

Immigration **Federal Police**, Rua Hugo D'Antola 95, Lapa de Baixo, T011-3538 5000, www.dpf.gov.br. Open 1000-1600. For visa extensions; allow all day and expect little English.

Weather São Paulo city

January	February	March	April	May	June
27°C	28°C	27°C	25°C	23°C	21°C
19°C	19°C	18°C	17°C	15°C	13°C
240mm	200mm	140mm	50mm	40mm	30mm

July	August	September	October	November	December
21°C	22°C	22°C	25°C	25°C	26°C
12°C	13°C	13°C	15°C	17°C	18°C
20mm	30mm	50mm	140mm	120mm	190mm

São Paulo city

São Paulo is as famous for its concrete as Rio is for its beaches. However, don't let that put you off. São Paulo may lack those wonderful Rio views, surf and sea, but nowhere in Latin America can compete for the sheer variety of restaurants, shops and nightlife.

The country's great metropolis is peopled by Brazilians from all over the country, who have made São Paulo their home and have left their cultural mark on the city, together with immigrants from the world over. Living here are the greatest numbers of ethnic Japanese, Koreans, Arabs and Italians in Latin America.

A vast city, São Paulo can feel intimidating on first arrival. But this is a city of separate neighbourhoods, only a few of which are interesting for visitors, and once you have your base it is easy to navigate.

Those who are prepared to spend time (and money) here, and who get to know Paulistanos, are seldom disappointed. Nowhere in Brazil is better for concerts, clubs, theatre, ballet, classical music, restaurants and beautifully designed hotels. And nowhere in Brazil has so much of Brazil contained within it.

1 São Paulo

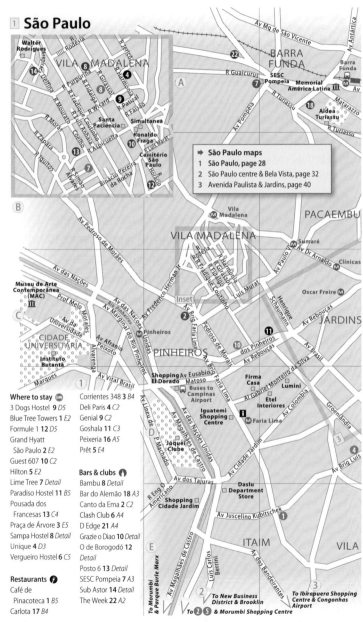

São Paulo maps
1 São Paulo, page 28
2 São Paulo centre & Bela Vista, page 32
3 Avenida Paulista & Jardins, page 40

Where to stay

3 Dogs Hostel 9 *D5*
Blue Tree Towers 1 *E2*
Formule 1 12 *D5*
Grand Hyatt
 São Paulo 2 *E2*
Guest 607 10 *C2*
Hilton 5 *E2*
Lime Tree 7 *Detail*
Paradiso Hostel 11 *B5*
Pousada dos
 Francesas 13 *C4*
Praça de Árvore 3 *E5*
Sampa Hostel 8 *Detail*
Unique 4 *D3*
Vergueiro Hostel 6 *C5*

Corrientes 348 3 *B4*
Deli Paris 4 *C2*
Genial 9 *C2*
Goshala 11 *C3*
Peixeria 16 *A5*
Prêt 5 *E4*

Bars & clubs

Bambu 8 *Detail*
Bar do Alemão 18 *A3*
Canto da Ema 2 *C2*
Clash Club 6 *A4*
D Edge 21 *A4*
Grazie o Diao 10 *Detail*
O de Borogodó 12
 Detail
Posto 6 13 *Detail*
SESC Pompeia 7 *A3*
Sub Astor 14 *Detail*
The Week 22 *A2*

Restaurants

Café de
 Pinacoteca 1 *B5*
Carlota 17 *B4*

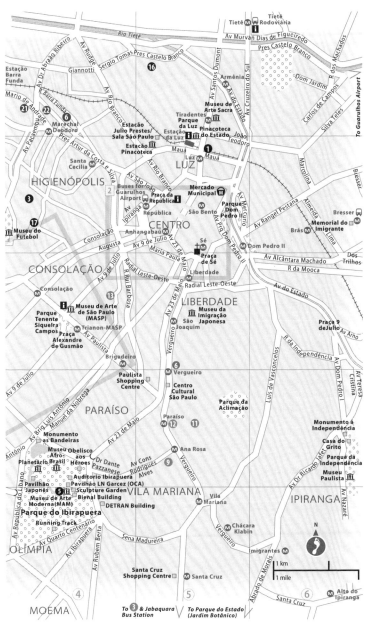

Tietê Rodoviária
Tietê
Rio Tietê
Av Morvan Dias de Figueiredo
Pres Castello Branco
Av Rudge
Av Santos Dumont
Armênia
Av Cruzeiro do Sul
Dom Jardim
Av do Estado
Carlos de Campos
To Guarulhos Airport
Estação
Barra Funda
Giannotti
Sergio Tomas Pres Castello Branco
Av Rio Branco
16
Silva Teles
Marcolina
Bresser
Mario de Andrade
R Barra Funda
Av Pacaembu
21 22 6
Marechal Deodoro
Pres Artur da Costa e Silva
Museu de Arte Sacra
Tiradentes
Parque da Luz
Estação Júlio Prestes/Sala São Paulo
Pinacoteca do Estado
João Teodoro
Estação da Luz
HIGIENÓPOLIS
Santa Cecília
Estação Pinacoteca
Av São João
Mauá
Luz
Mauá
1
Buses for Guarulhos Airport
Av São João
Av Rio Branco
2
Praça da República
República
Mercado Municipal
São Bento
Parque Dom Pedro II
Av Mercúrio
Av Rangel Pestana
Almeida
Bresser
3
Consolação
Av Ipiranga
CENTRO
Sé
Praça de Sé
Av Pq Dom Pedro II
Dom Pedro II
Brás
Memorial do Imigrante
Av Lima
17
Museu do Futebol
Augusta
Av 9 de Julho
Av 23 de Maio
Maria Paula
Liberdade
Av Álcântara Machado
Dos Trilhos
R da Mooca
CONSOLAÇÃO
Av 9 de Julho
R Rui Barbosa
Radial Leste-Oeste
Radial Leste-Oeste
Av do Estado
Consolação
Museu de Arte de São Paulo (MASP)
Trianon-MASP
LIBERDADE
Museu da Imigração Japonesa
São Joaquim
Av 23 de Maio
Verguerio
Praça 9 deJulho
Av Arno
Parque Tenente Siqueira Campos
Praça Alexandre de Gusmão
Av Paulista
Brigadeiro
6
Vergueiro
R da Independência
Av 9 de Julho
Manuel da Nóbrega
PARAÍSO
Paulista Shopping Centre
Centro Cultural São Paulo
Parque da Aclimação
Luis de Vasconcelos
Av Dom Pedro I
Av Teresa Cristina
Av Brig Luis Antônio
Paraíso
12
11
Monumento á Independência
Antônio
Monumento as Bandeiras
Museu Afro-Brasil
Obelisco aos Heróis
Planetário Brasil
Av 23 de Maio
Dr Dante Pazzanese
Ana Rosa
Av Cons Rodrigues Alves
9
Vergueiro
Casa do Grito
Parque da Independência
Av Dr Ricardo Jafet
Museu Paulista
Av Nazaré
Pavilhão Japonês
Auditório Ibirapuera
Pavilhão LN Garcez (OCA)
Sculpture Garden
Bienal Building
5
Museu de Arte Moderna (MAM)
DETRAN Building
VILA MARIANA
Vila Mariana
IPIRANGA
Parque do Ibirapuera
Running Track
Av República do Líbano
Av Quarto Centenário
Sena Madureira
Chácara Klabin
Vergueiro
OLÍMPIA
Av Ibirapuera
Av Rubem Berta
Santa Cruz Shopping Centre
Santa Cruz
Imigrantes
Abraão de Morais
1 km
1 mile
N
4
MOEMA
To 3 & Jabaquara Bus Station
5
To Parque do Estado (Jardim Botânico)
Santa Cruz
6
Alto do Ipiranga

The city centre (altitude 850 m) was once one of the most attractive in South America. English visitors in the 19th century described it as being spacious, green and dominated by terracotta-tiled buildings. There were even macaws and sloths in the trees. Today, most of the historical buildings and former beauty are long gone, and the centre is dominated by concrete: anonymous edifices, towering over a huddle of interesting churches and cultural centres, and criss-crossed by narrow pedestrian streets. These are lined with stalls selling everything from shoes to electronics, second-hand goods and bric-a-brac. Avoid staying after dark, though, as the area is insalubrious.

Praça da Sé and around   *Metrô Sé.*

The best place to begin a tour is at the Praça da Sé, an expansive square shaded by tropical trees and watched over by the hulking Catholic **Catedral Metropolitana** ① *Praça da Sé, T011-3107 6832, Mon-Fri 0800-1900, Sat 0800-1700, Sun 0830-1800, free, Metrô Sé*. This is the heart of the old city and has been the site of Brazil's largest public protests. Crowds gathered here in the late 1980s to demand the end to military rule. And, in 1992, they demanded the impeachment and resignation of the new Republic's second elected president, Fernando Collor – the first in a series of corrupt leaders who, in 1990, had frozen the country's savings accounts and personally pocketed millions. The *praça* is always busy with hawkers, beggars, shoe-shiners and business men rushing between meetings. Evangelists with megaphones proselytize on the steps of the cathedral – a symbol of the war between Christians for the souls of the poor that dominates contemporary urban Brazil. The *praça* is a great spot for street photography though be discreet with your camera and check that you aren't followed after taking your shots.

Like São Paulo itself, the cathedral is more remarkable for its size than its beauty and is a somewhat unconvincing mish-mash of neo-Gothic and Renaissance. A narrow nave is squeezed uncomfortably between two monstrous 97-m-high spires beneath a bulbous copper cupola. It was designed in 1912 by the Kassel-born Maximilian Hehl (a professor at the Escola Politécnica da Universidade de São Paulo), inaugurated in the 1950s and fitted with its full complement of 14 towers only in 2002. The interior is bare but for a few stained-glass windows designed in Germany and capitals decorated with Brazilian floral motifs. In the basement there is a vast, pseudo-Gothic crypt. Hehl was also responsible for the Igreja da Consolação and the Catedral de Santos.

Look out for the striking modernist steel sculpture in front of the cathedral in the Praça da Sé, comprising a symmetrical steel plate cut and seemingly folded in the middle along a curvilinear plane. The play of shadow and light around the work – most notable in the early morning or the late afternoon – are hallmarks of its creator, Mineiro graphic artist and sculptor Amílcar de Castro (1920-2002), who revolutionized Brazilian newspaper design in the 1950s before establishing himself at the forefront of the neo-constuctionist movement in Latin America. Together with simple design productive of complex shadow play, his work is characterized by its interaction with the environment. De Castro's sculptures have no protective cover – rust is their paint,

> **Tip...**
>
> The best way to explore the Centro Histórico is by *metrô* and on foot.

The Centro Histórico lies at the heart of the city. Although undergoing renovation, it remains a place to visit rather than to stay. The old commercial district or Triângulo, bounded by Ruas Direita, 15 de Novembro, São Bento and Praça Antônio Prado (and nowadays to Praça da República), is one of São Paulo's three commercial centres. Another lies immediately southwest of the Centro Histórico along the city's grandest street, Avenida Paulista. Just to the north is the Consolação neighbourhood, centred on tawdry Rua Augusta but undergoing a renaissance.

South of Avenida Paulista are the Jardins, São Paulo's most affluent inner-city neighbourhoods. Next to Jardins, 5 km south of the centre, the Parque do Ibirapuera is the inner city's largest green space. Between Ibirapuera and the river, Itaim, Moema and Vila Olímpia are among the nightlife centres of São Paulo. These areas border São Paulo's third and newest commercial centre, lying on and around Avenida Brigadeiro Faria Lima and Avenida Luís Carlos Berrini.

and they echo the decaying but modern urban environment of late 20th-century Brazil. De Castro was a key figure in post-War Brazilian art. An obituary in the New York Times described him as "a towering figure in Brazil's art scene" who "gained prominence in the postwar period when Brazilian sculptors, painters and architects were imbued with ambition to break away from the grip of European artistic traditions."

There are a few other sights of interest around the *praça*. Next door to the cathedral itself and housed in a 1930s art deco building is the **Conjunto Cultural da Caixa** ① *Praça da Sé 111, T011-3321 4400, www.caixacultural.com.br (in Portuguese only), Tue-Sun 0900-1900, US$2, Metrô Sé*, a gallery that hosts excellent small international art and photography exhibitions by day, and, in the evenings, a boutique theatre. It also has a small banking museum with colonial furniture on one of its upper floors.

Two minutes' walk west of the cathedral, squeezed between ugly modern buildings at the end of Rua Senador Feijó, is the **Igreja da Ordem Terceira de São Francisco** ① *Largo de São Francisco 133, T011-3106 0081, closed at time of publication, Metrô Sé*. This is one of the city's oldest churches, preserving a modest baroque interior (parts of which date to the 17th century) painted in celestial blue. It is quiet and meditative inside. The exterior is largely an 18th-century excrescence. The church is often referred to as 'O Convento de São Francisco' after a beautiful baroque convent that stood here until the 1930s. This was demolished along with vast swathes of the old colonial centre and sadly the Igreja da Ordem Terceira is in danger of undergoing the same fate; it was condemned in 2008 and remains closed pending donations for a restoration project.

There are now only two churches in the centre of one of Brazil's oldest cities that retain any baroque remnants: the Igreja de Santo Antônio (see page 36) and the **Igreja da Ordem Terceira do Carmo** ① *R Rangel Pestana 230, Tue-Sun 0900-2100, free, Metrô Sé*. This church sits just off the far northeastern corner of the Praça da Sé, dates from 1632 and was built by lay brothers, many of whom were former *bandeirantes*, or their children. It preserves much of its baroque interior, including an impressive ceiling painting, stucco work, religious paintings and artefacts, and an 18th-century gilt baroque altarpiece. It is a peaceful place amidst the hustle and bustle, seldom receiving any visitors.

Pátio do Colégio and around *Metrô Sé.*

The site of the founding of São Paulo can be reached by walking north from the bottom of the Praça da Sé (furthest from the cathedral) along Rua Santa Teresa and to the Praça Pátio do Colégio. Here lies the **Pátio do Colégio** and **Museu de Anchieta** ① *Praça Pátio do Colégio, T011-3105 6899, www.pateodocollegio.com.br, museum: Tue Fri 0840-1630, US$1, free on the last Sun of the month, Metrô Sé.* Jesuit priests, led by 18-year-old Padre José de Anchieta, arrived here in 1554, when the area was a tiny clearing on a hill in the midst of a vast forest. They made camp and instructed their domicile indigenous Guaraní to construct a simple wattle and daub hut. They inaugurated the building with a celebration of Mass on 25 January 1554, the feast of the conversion of São Paulo. Their simple hut took the saint's name, the 'Colégio de São Paulo de Piratinga'. The hut became a school for

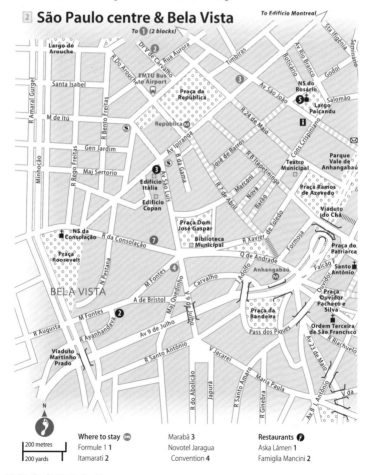

2 São Paulo centre & Bela Vista

	Where to stay 🛏	Marabá **3**	Restaurants 🍴
200 metres	Formule 1 **1**	Novotel Jaragua	Aska Lámen **1**
200 yards	Itamarati **2**	Convention **4**	Famiglia Mancini **2**

converted indigenous Brazilians seduced from the forests around. The school became a church and the church gave its name – São Paulo – to a settlement for *bandeirante* slaving raids into the Brazilian interior. In 1760, the Jesuits were expelled from the city, ironically for opposing the *bandeirantes* – who had established their town around the colegio – and for campaigning in Europe for an end to the indigenous slave trade in Brazil and the Americas, much to the chagrin of the then influential slave and plantation owners in the cities of Salvador, Belém and São Luís. The Pátio do Colégio (as the complex of buildings came to be known) remained, becoming the palace of the fledgling province's Portuguese colonial captains general, and then of its Brazilian imperial governors. The church's tower fell down in 1886 and, shortly after, the whole building was demolished (but for one section of wattle and daub wall). The Jesuits didn't return to São Paulo until 1954 when they immediately set about building an exact replica of their original church and college, which is what stands today.

Most of the buildings are occupied by the **Museu Padre Anchieta**. This preserves, amongst other items, a modernist (and not altogether sympathetic painting) of the priest, by Italian Albino Menghini, bits of his corpse (which is now that of a saint after Anchieta was canonized by Pope John Paul II), a 17th-century font used to baptize the indigenous Brazilians and a collection of Guaraní art and artefacts from the colonial era.

The Pátio has a great little alfresco café with a view, serving good snacks and light meals.

The clergy in the college have long maintained an interest in a 'preferential option for the poor' which, since the suppression of Liberation Theology in Brazil, has been out of fashion. Members of the college joyously celebrated the election of the new Jesuit pope, Francisco, in 2013. After a parade for the poor children of the city's periphery, dozens of children dressed as St Francis climbed on the stage singing the prayer of St Francis with a poster showing the pope's face with the words "Papa Francisco, O Papa dos pobres" written beneath.

The exhibition spaces, cultural centres and concert halls of the **Centro Cultural**

Ponto Chic **5**
Sushi Yassu **6**
Terraço Italia **3**

Clubs 🎵
Clube Royale **7**

BACKGROUND
São Paulo

The history of São Paulo state and São Paulo city were much the same from the arrival of the Europeans until the coffee boom transformed the region's economic and political landscape. There were nearly 200,000 indigenous inhabitants living in what is now São Paulo state at the time of the conquest. Today their numbers have been vastly diminished though of the few who survived, some live in villages within metropolitan São Paulo and can be seen selling handicrafts in the centre.

The first official settlement in the state was at São Vicente on the coast, near today's port of Santos. It was founded in 1532 by Martim Afonso de Sousa, who had been sent by King João III to drive the French from Brazilian waters, explore the coast and lay claim to lands apportioned to Portugal under the Treaty of Tordesillas.

In 1554, two Jesuit priests from São Vicente founded São Paulo as a *colégio* (a mission and school) on the site of the present Pátio de Colégio in the Centro Histórico. The Jesuits chose to settle inland because they wanted access to the indigenous population who they hoped to convert to Catholicism. Expeditions were sent to capture and enslave the indigenous people to work on farms. These marauders were known as *bandeirantes*, after the flag wielder who walked at their head to claim territory. They were made up of culturally disenfranchised offspring of the indigenous Brazilians and the Portuguese, spurned by both communities. São Paulo became the centre of *bandeirante* activity in the 17th century. Yet whilst São Paulo was their headquarters, the *bandeirantes'* success in discovering gold led to the economic

Banco do Brasil ① *R Álvares Penteado 112, T011-3113 3651, http://culturabancodobrasil. com.br (select SP for São Paulo, in Portuguese but it's easy to find what's on information), Wed-Mon 0900-2100, closed Tue, free for exhibitions, US$2.50 theatre performances, US$1 films, Metrô Sé or São Bento,* can be reached by turning immediately west from the front of the Pátio do Colégio along Rua do Tesouro and then right for a block along Rua Álvares Penteado. These are housed in an attractive art nouveau building with a pretty glass ceiling. Many of the galleries are contained within the banks original vaults, some of which retain their massive iron doors. The cultural centre has a diverse programme of art and photography shows, cultural events and, in the evenings, theatre, music and cinema; for details, see the website. The cultural centre is always worth a visit.

Mosteiro do São Bento and around *Metrô São Bento.*
The most beautiful of all the churches in São Paulo is the Benedictine Basílica de Nossa Senhora de Assunção, known as the **Mosteiro de São Bento** ① *Largo São Bento, T011-3228 3633, www.mosteiro.org.br, Mon-Fri 0600-1800, Sat and Sun 0600-1200 and 1600-1800, Latin Mass with Gregorian chant Sun 1000; Latin vespers Mon-Fri 1725, Sat 1700, free, Metrô São Bento.* Benedictines arrived on this site in 1598, shortly after the Jesuits and, like them, proceeded to proselytize the indigenous people. Despite their long history in the city the monastery is a modern church dating from 1914. It was designed by Munich-based architect Richard Bernl in homage to the English Norman style. Its façade is strikingly similar to Southwell cathedral in Nottinghamshire, though with added Rhineland roofs and baroque revival flourishes.

demise of the city in the 18th century. The inhabitants rushed to the gold fields in Minas and the *sertão*, leaving São Paulo to fall under the influence of Rio de Janeiro.

The relative backwardness of the region lasted until the late 19th century when the coffee trade spread west from Rio de Janeiro and Brazil's then richest man – the railway magnate Evangelista de Sousa – established São Paulo as a key city on the newly established railway route to the port of Santos on the coast. Landowners became immensely rich. São Paulo changed from a small town into a financial centre and the industrial powerhouse of the country was born.

Between 1885 and 1900 the boom in coffee and the arrival of large numbers of Europeans transformed the state beyond recognition. By the end of the 1930s more than a million Italians, 500,000 Portuguese, nearly 400,000 Spaniards and 200,000 Japanese had arrived in São Paulo state.

São Paulo now has the world's largest Japanese community outside Japan. Significant numbers of Syrian-Lebanese arrived, too and many of the city's wealthiest dynasties are of Middle Eastern descent. São Paulo also has a large and successful Jewish community. There are two fascinating museums in São Paulo devoted to these immigrants, the Museu da Imigração do Estado de São Paulo in Mooca and the Museu Histórico da Imigração Japonesa in the Japanese-dominated neighbourhood of Liberdade.

By the new millennium metropolitan São Paulo had become the fifth most populous metropolitan area on the planet. Today the city covers more than 1500 sq km, three times the size of Paris and greater São Paulo has a population of around 19.96 million, while almost 22% of all Brazilians live in São Paulo state, some 41.6 million people.

However, few visit São Bento for the exterior. The church preserves a striking Beuronese interior painted by Dom Adelbert Gresnicht, a Dutch Benedictine monk who died in 1956. The style is named after techniques developed by Benedictines in the monastery of Beuron in southwest Germany in the late 19th and early 20th centuries. It finds much inspiration in Byzantine art and is characterized by compressed perspective and iconic, almost exaggerated colours. São Bento is one of the finest Beuronese churches in the world. The stained glass (and much of the statuary) is also by Dom Adelbert. Most of the windows show scenes from the life of St Benedict with the most beautiful, at the far end of the nave, showing Our Lady ascending to heaven guided by the Holy Spirit in the form of a dove. The church has Brazil's finest organ which is given its own festival in November and December every year. This being a Benedictine monastery, there is of course a shop, which sells delicious sweets made by the monks in their bakery.

Immediately in front of the monastery, at the corner of Avenida São João and Rua Libero Badaró, is the **Edifício Martinelli (Martinelli Building)** ① *Av São João 35, not open to the public, Metrô São Bento*. This was the city's first skyscraper and, when it was built, looked out over a sea of terracotta roofs and handsome tree-lined avenues. The building pays homage to New York's Upper East Side but while colonial São Paulo was unique and beautiful, the buildings that replaced it are less original or distinguished than the New York edifices they longed to imitate.

A block south, next to the Viaduto do Chá at the bottom of Rua Dr Falcão Filho, is another early São Paulo skyscraper, the bulky **Edifício Francisco Matarazzo** ① *Dr Falcão Filho 56, Centro, T011-3248 1135, Mon-Fri 1000-1700*, built in 1937 and known locally as

'Banespinha'. The building is now occupied by the mayoral office. While it's not officially open to the public, try and visit if you can to see one of Latin America's finest and largest skyscraper gardens (on the 14th floor), which boasts more than 300 species of flowering plants and towering trees, the largest of which are over 20 m tall. There are terrific views from the perimetral veranda.

A few blocks northeast and just round the corner from the monastery is Banespinha's big brother, the **Banespa building** ① *R João Bricola 24 (Metrô São Bento), T011-3249 7466, Mon-Fri 1000-1500, free, ID is required, visits limited to 10 mins (dusk visits are limited to those with prior appointments), daypacks must be left in reception, no tripods or bags can be taken to the viewing deck*. Officially known as the **Edifício Altino Arantes** or **Santander Cultural**, it's a homage to New York, looking a bit like a wan Empire State Building, small enough to collapse under the weight of King Kong. The view of the city from the observatory is awe-inspiring. A sea of concrete spires stretches to the city limits on every horizon, fringed with vast favelas and new distant neighbourhoods and with hundreds of helicopters whirling overhead like giant buzzing flies.

Tip...
For a bird's eye view of the city, head to the lookout platform at the top of the Banespa tower (see left), preferably at dusk.

Less than 50 m from the Edifício Altino Arantes is the oldest church in São Paulo's city centre, the **Igreja de Santo Antônio** ① *Praça do Patriarca s/n, Mon-Fri 0900-1600, free, Metrô São Bento*, with parts dating from 1592. It was fully restored in 2005 and together with the Igreja do Carmo is the only church in the city centre with a baroque interior – although much of what you see today is from reforms in 1899. It's another tranquil spot in the middle of one of the world's busiest city centres.

The streets between São Bento and Luz offer some of the best people-watching and shopping adventures in the city. The partially covered **Rua 25 de Março** ① *daily 0700-1800, Metrô São Bento shopping complex*, runs north to Rua Paula Sousa and Metrô Luz station and is one of the best places in Brazil to buy quality clothing and electronics at a low price.

Two blocks east of 25 de Marco along Rua Comendador Afonso Kherlakian is the beautiful art deco **Mercado Municipal** ① *R da Cantareira 306, Centro, T011-3326 3401, www.oportaldomercadao.com.br, Mon-Sat 0600-1800, Sun 0600-1600, free, Metrô São Bento or Luz; see Shopping, page 62*. It's an easy walk from the market or Rua 25 de Março to Luz, though caution should be observed at all times. The streets to the west, between the centre and Júlio Prestes station, should be avoided especially after dark. This is a notorious area for crack dealing.

Praça da República *Metrô República.*
This tree-lined square a few blocks northwest of the Viaduto do Chá was the centre of the city's Vanity Fair – the place to see and be seen – in the late 19th century. It was then known as the Largo dos Curros, but was rebranded for the Republic after the overthrow of the monarchy. Wealthy Paulistanos would gather here to watch rodeios and touradas. Like the Praça da Sé it has long been an important centre of public protest. On 23 May 1932, towards the end of the Constitutional Revolution, thousands gathered in front of the old Partido Popular Paulista to protest against the Vargas regime. Many were shot dead as a result. There is a lively arts and crafts market in the square every Saturday and Sunday 0900-1700.

A few interesting buildings and sights lie nearby. These include the **Edifício and Terraço Itália** ① *Av Ipiranga 344, T011-2189 2990 and T011-2189 2929, www.edificioitalia.*

com.br (in Portuguese only), restaurant: www.terracoitalia.com.br/ing, US$3, Metrô
República, a rather unremarkable restaurant (see page 51) in the city's tallest building
with a truly remarkable view from the observation deck (which was closed for
refurbishment as this book went to press). Photographers should aim to arrive half an
hour before sunset for the best balance of natural and artificial light, and bring a tripod,
though you should be prepared for the officials to try and charge you extra for its usage.

The skyscraper immediately in front of the *terraço* is Oscar Niemeyer's **Edifício Copan**
ⓘ *Av Ipiranga 200, not open to the public though some visitors are allowed to go to the*
terraço at the discretion of security, Metrô República, built in 1951 in a spate of design by the
architect, which included the nearby **Edifício Montreal** ⓘ *Av Ipiranga at Cásper Líbero*,
and the **Edifício Califórnia** ⓘ *R Barão de Itapetininga*. Edifício Copan is the setting for *Arca*
sem Noé – histórias do edifício Copan, a series of memorable short stories, dissecting daily
life and class in São Paulo, written by the Paulistano writer Regina Rheda (published in
English as *First World, Third Class and Other Tales of the Global Mix* in 2005). A crypt-like art
space, the **Pivô** ⓘ *Av Ipiranga 200, lj 48, T011-3255 8703, www.pivo.org.br/en*, opened in
2013 in the building's basement, showing contemporary art with past shows including
US sculptor David Adamo.

From the corner of Praça da República, a 10-minute walk south-east along Rua 24 de
Maio brings you back into the main part of the city centre and Metrô Anhangabaú, via
the **Teatro Municipal Opera House** ⓘ *Praça Ramos de Azevedo s/n, T011-3053 2100, http://*
theatromunicipal.org.br, box office Mon-Fri 1000-1900, Sat 1000-1700, tickets from US$3,
guided tours in English Tue-Fri 1100 and 1700, Sat 1200, T011-3053 2092, Metrô Anhangabaú,
República or São Bento. Based on the 1874 beaux-arts Palais Garnier but stunted in
comparison, it is made of dull stone with huge baroque flourishes on the roof which make
it look inelegantly top heavy. It is altogether more impressive within, with its stained glass,
opulent hallways and public areas. Maria Callas, Nureyev and Fonteyn and Duke Ellington
have all graced the concert hall and it is now once again one of Brazil's finest venues
for classical music and dance and the home to a body of performers which include the
Orquestra Sinfônica Municipal, Orquestra Experimental de Repertório, Balé da Cidade de
São Paulo, Quarteto de Cordas da Cidade de São Paulo, Coral Lírico, Coral Paulistano and
the Escolas de Dança e de Música de São Paulo.

Next to the theatre is the **Viaduto do Chá**, a steel bridge riding over the attractive but
scruffy Vale de Anhangabaú park and the traffic-heavy Avenida 23 de Maio and 9 de Julho
urban highways.

North of the centre

historical museums, art galleries and a Niemeyer architecture complex

Luz *Metrô Luz or Metrô Tiradentes, Metrô/CPTM Luz or Júlio Prestes.*

A few kilometres north of the city centre is the neighbourhood of Luz. The area is
dominated by two striking 19th- and early 20th-century railway stations, both in use
today: the **Estação da Luz** ⓘ *Praça da Luz 1, T0800-550121 for information on suburban*
trains, and **Estação Júlio Prestes** ⓘ *Praça Júlio Prestes 51*. The former marked the
realization of a dream for O Ireneu Evangelista de Sousa, the Visconde de Mauá, who
was Brazil's first industrial magnate. A visit to London in the 1840s convinced de Sousa
that Brazil's future lay in rapid industrialization, a path he followed with the founding
of an ironworks employing some 300 workers from England and Scotland. It made him
a millionaire and in 1854 he opened his first railway, designed and run by the British.

It linked Jundiaí, in the heart of the São Paulo coffee region, with Santos on the coast via what was then the relatively small city of São Paulo. The line is still extant; though passenger trains only run on the Jundiaí to São Paulo section (see Linha 7 Rubi, page 67). The grandness of the Estação de Luz station, which was completed in 1900, attests to the fact that the city quickly grew wealthy by exploiting its position at the railway junction.

By the time the Estação Júlio Prestes was built, Britannia no longer ruled the railways. This next station was modelled on Grand Central and Penn in New York. In 1999 the enormous 1000-sq-m grand hall was converted into the magnificent 1500-seat cathedral-like **Sala São Paulo Concert Hall** ① *Praça Júlio Prestes 51, T011-3337 9573, www. salasaopaulo.art.br, guided visits Mon-Fri 1300-1630, Sat 1330, Sun 1400 (when there is an evening performance) or 1230 (when there is an afternoon performance), US$1.25, English-speaking tours are available Mon-Fri only and must be arranged 5 days in advance on T011-3367 9573, box office T011-3223 3966, Mon-Fri 1000-1800, Sat 1000-1630, concerts from US$10, Metrô/CPTM Luz or Júlio Prestes,* Brazil's most prestigious classical music venue (see page 59) and home to the **Orquestra Sinfônica do Estado de São Paulo** ① *www.osesp. art.br,* and choir, one of the best in South America, conducted by Marin Alsop, who is also the music director of the Baltimore Symphony Orchestra.

The city's finest collection of Brazilian art lies 100 m from the Estação da Luz in the **Pinacoteca do Estado** ① *Praça da Luz 2, T011-3324 0933, www.pinacoteca.org.br, Tue-Sun 1000-1600 (last entry at 1700), US$1.50, free on Sat, Metrô/CPTM Luz, excellent museum shop and café.* Here you will find works by Brazilian artists from the colonial and imperial eras, together with paintings by the founders of Brazilian Modernism, such as Lasar Segall, Tarsila do Amaral, Candido Portinari and Alfredo Volpi. The gallery also contains sculpture by Rodin, Victor Brecheret and contemporary works by artists such as the Nipo-Brazilian painter Tomie Ohtake. The excellent photography gallery in the basement displays some of the world's greatest black-and-white photographers, many of whom are from Brazil.

The museum overlooks the **Parque da Luz** ① *Praça da Luz s/n, Tue-Sun, 1000-1800, free,* a lovely shady fenced-in green space dotted with modernist sculpture and shaded by large tropical figs and palms. This was the city's first park, opening in 1825. It was fully refurbished (down to the lovely wrought iron faux-French bandstand) in the new millennium. Take care in this area after dark.

The Pinacoteca's sister gallery, the **Estação Pinacoteca and Memorial da Resistência Museum** ① *Largo General Osório 66, T011-3335 4990, www.pinacoteca.org.br, http://memorialdaresistenciasp.org.br, Tue-Sun 1000-1730, US$1.50, free for the Memorial da Resistência and for the galleries on Sat, very good café-restaurant, Metrô/CPTM Luz and Júlio Prestes,* is just over 500 m west of the Pinacoteca along Rua Mauá, next to the Estação Júlio Prestes and Sala São. The *estação* preserves 200 of the country's finest modernist paintings from the archive of the Fundação José e Paulina Nemirovsky, including further key pieces by Tarsila do Amaral, Emiliano Di Cavalcanti, Portinari Anita Malfatti, Victor Brecheret and Lasar Segall. International art includes Chagall, Picasso and Braque. The building was once the headquarters of the Departamento Estadual de Ordem Politica e Social do Estado de São Paulo (DEOPS/SP), the counter-insurgency wing of the Policia Militar police force. Thousands of Paulistanos were tortured and killed here between 1940 and 1983, during the Vargas years and the military dictatorship. The Memorial da Resistência de São Paulo Museum on the ground floor tells their story in grisly detail – through panels, documents and photographs – and shows how the CIA supported the oppression.

Across the Praça da Luz to the south of the Pinacoteca and housed in the Estação da Luz railway station is the **Museu da Língua Portuguesa** ① *Praça da Luz, T011-3322 0080,* *www.museulinguaportuguesa.org.br (in Portuguese only), Tue 1000-2200, Wed-Sun 1000-1800 (last visit 1700), US$2, free Sat, Metrô/CPTM Luz, when this book went to press the museum was temporarily closed following a major fire in early 2016.* This excellent little museum has captivating interactive and audiovisual exhibits in tastefully laid-out galleries devoted to everything Portuguese – from high literary art (with excerpts from seminal works) to street slang, song and correct grammar.

Diagonally across busy Avenida Tiradentes from the Pinacotaca and some 400 metres to the north, is the **Museu de Arte Sacra** ① *Av Tiradentes 676, T011-3326 3336, www. museuartesacra.org.br, Tue-Fri 0900-1700, Sat-Sun 1000-1800, US$1.50, free on Sat, Metrô Tiradentes, Metrô/CPTM Luz.* This superb little museum is often overlooked by visitors, yet it is one of the finest of its kind in the Americas. The collection is housed in a large wing of one of the city's most distinguished colonial buildings, the early 19th-century Mosteiro da Luz. Parts of the monastery are still home to Conceptionist sisters and the entire complex is imbued with a restful sense of serenity. Even those who are not interested in church art will find the galleries a delightfully peaceful haven from the frenetic chaos of São Paulo.

The collection is priceless and of international importance. Rooms house objects and artefacts from lavish monstrances and ecclesiastical jewellery to church altarpieces. Of particular note is the statuary, with pieces by many of the most important Brazilian baroque masters. Amongst objects by Portuguese sculptor and ceramicist Frei Agostinho da Piedade (1580-1661), his Brazilian student, Frei Agostinho de Jesus (1600-1661), Mineiro master painter Manuel da Costa (Mestre) Athayde (1762-1830), and Mestre Valentim (1745-1813), is a wonderful Mary Magdalene by Francisco Xavier de Brito, displaying an effortless unity of motion and melancholy contemplation. There are sculptures by (anonymous) Brazilian indigenous artists, a majestic African-Brazilian São Bento (with blue eyes) and an extraordinarily detailed 18th-century Neapolitan nativity crib comprising almost 2000 pieces, which is the most important of its kind outside Naples.

Barra Funda and Higienópolis *Metrô Palmeiras-Barra Funda, CPTM Barra Funda.*

The Cyclopean group of modernist concrete buildings making up the **Memorial da América Latina** ① *Av Mário de Andrade 664, next to Metrô Barra Funda, T011-3823 4600, www.memorial.org.br, Tue-Sun 0900-1800, free*, were designed by Oscar Niemeyer and built in March 1989. They comprise a monumental 85,000-sq-m-complex of curvilinear galleries, conference spaces, walkways, bridges and squares, broken by an ugly, urban highway and dotted with imposing sculptures. The largest of these is in the shape of an outstretched hand. The complex was built with the grand aim of integrating Latin American nations, culturally and politically, but it is sorely underused. Occasional shows include the annual Latin American art exhibition in the Pavilhão de Criatividade.

A few kilometres west of Barra Funda – a quick hop along the CPTM's Linha Rubi – in the emerging nightlife district of **Água Branca**, is **SESC Pompeia** ① *R Clélia 93, T011-3871 7700, www.sescsp.org.br, CPTM Água Branca, 10 mins' walk southeast or US$2 in a taxi*, an arts complex housed in a striking post-industrial building designed by the Italian-Brazilian Le Corbusier-influenced architect Lina Bo Bardi (who was also responsible for MASP, see page 41). Together with SESC Vila Mariana (see page 55), SESC showcases some of the best medium-sized musical acts in the city, hosting names such as João Bosco, CéU and Otto. It is a vibrant place, with a theatre, exhibitions, workshops, restaurant and café, as well as a gym and areas for sunbathing and watching television.

The upper middle-class neighbourhood of **Higienópolis** lies between Barra Funda and Consolação. It is a favourite haunt of artists and musicians, a number of whom live in the

Bretagne building ⓘ *Av Higienópolis 938, T011-3667 2516*, one of a handful of delightful mid-20th-century blocks of flats. With curved lines, brilliant mosaics and polished stone it looks like a film set for an arty 1960s film. Higienópolis also boasts one of the city's plushest shopping malls, the **Patio Higienópolis** ⓘ *Av Higienópolis 618, T011-3823 2300, www.patiohigienopolis.com.br.*

West of the centre

fashion shopping, hip restaurants, frenetic nightlife and fabulous fine art

Avenida Paulista   *Metrô Vergueiro or Paraíso for the southeastern end of Paulista.*

Southwest of the Centro Histórico, the six-lane Avenida Paulista is lined by skyscrapers, shopping centres and cafés and is home to one of the city's best art galleries. The avenue is one of São Paulo's classic postcard shots and locals like to compare it to Fifth Avenue in New York. In truth, it's more commercial and lined with functional buildings, most of which are unremarkable individually but awe-inspiring as a whole.

Paulista was founded in 1891 by the Uruguayan engineer Joaquim Eugênio de Lima, who wanted to build a Paulistano Champs-Élysées. After he built a mansion on

3 **Avenida Paulista & Jardins** To Higienópolis

Avenida Paulista, many coffee barons followed suit and by the 1930s, Avenida Paulista had become the city's most fashionable promenade. The mansions and rows of stately trees that sat in front of them were almost all demolished in the 1950s to make way for decidedly less beautiful office buildings; these were in turn demolished in the 1980s as banks and multinationals established their headquarters here. A handful of mansions remain, however, including the **Casa das Rosas** ⓘ *Av Paulista 37, T011-3285 6986, www. poiesis.org.br/casadasrosas, Tue-Sat 1000-2200, Sun 1000-1800, free,* one of the last of the mansions to have been built and now a literary centre devoted principally preserving the 35,000-volume library of the poet Haroldo de Campos, which includes a number of rare, autographed first editions by writers such as Otavio Paz and João Cabral de Melo Neto.

The highlight of Avenida Paulista is the **Museu de Arte de São Paulo (MASP)** ⓘ *Av Paulista 1578, T011-3251 5644, www.masp.art.br, Tue-Sun 1000-1800, Thu open until 2000, US$6.25, free on Tue, Metrô Trianon-MASP.* This is the most important gallery in the southern hemisphere, preserving some of Europe's greatest paintings. If it was in the US or Europe it would be as busy as the Prado or the Guggenheim, but here, aside from the occasional noisy group of schoolchildren, the gallery is invariably deserted. Even at weekends, visitors can stop and stare at a Rembrandt or a Velazquez at their leisure.

The museum has a far larger collection than it is able to display and only a tiny fraction reaches the walls of the modest-sized international gallery and as the collection is frequently rotated it's hard to predict what will be on show at any one time. France gets star-billing, with 11 Renoirs, 70 Degas, and a stream of works by Monet, Manet, Cezanne, Toulouse-Lautrec and Gauguin. Renaissance Italy is represented by a Raphael Resurrection, an impeccable Bellini and a series of exquisite late 15th-century icons. The remaining walls are adorned with paintings by Bosch, Goya, Van Dyck, Turner, Constable and many others, cherry-picked from post-War Europe. A gallery downstairs, the **Galeria Clemente de Faria**, houses temporary exhibitions, mostly by contemporary Brazilian artists and photographers. The museum also has a decent and good-value restaurant serving buffet lunches (see page 52) and a small but tasteful gift shop. On Sunday, an antiques fair is held in the open space beneath the museum.

500 metres (approx)
500 yards (approx)

➡ **São Paulo maps**
1 São Paulo, page 28
2 São Paulo centre & Bela Vista, page 32
3 **Avenida Paulista & Jardins, page 40**

There are two more galleries/art centres on Avenida Paulista. **Itaú Cultural** ① *Av Paulista 149, T011-2168 1777, www.itaucultural.org.br (in Portuguese only), Tue-Fri 0900-2000, Sat and Sun 1100-2000, free*, which principally showcases contemporary art, theatre and quality music, and which has a small numismatic museum that was renovated in 2013. **FIESP** ① *Av Paulista 1313, T011-3146 7405, http://www.fiesp.com.br (in Portuguese only), Mon 1100-1930, Tue-Sat 1000-1930, Sun 1000-1830, free*, has free Sunday concerts at midday and a regular theatre programme, including performances for children.

Opposite MASP is the **Parque Tenente Siqueira Campos** ① *R Peixoto Gomide 949 and Av Paulista, daily 0700-1830*, also known as Parque Trianon, covering two blocks on either side of Alameda Santos. It is a welcome, luxuriant, green area located in what is now the busiest part of the city. The vegetation includes native plants typical of the Mata Atlântica. Next to the park is the smaller Praça Alexandre de Gusmão.

Consolação and the Pacaembu Museu do Futebol *Metrô Consolação.*

Consolação, which lies between the northeastern end of Avenida Paulista and the Edifício Italia and Praça República in the city centre, is emerging as the edgiest and most exciting nocturnal neighbourhood in São Paulo. Until a few years it was home to little more than rats, sleazy strip bars, street-walkers and curb-crawlers, but now it harbours a thriving alternative weekend scene. Its untidy streets are lined with graffiti-scrawled shop fronts, the deep velvet-red of open bar doors, go-go clubs with heavy-set bouncers outside, and makeshift street bars. On Friday and Saturday nights hundreds of young Paulistanos down bottles of cooler-fresh Bohemia beer at rickety metal tables, and lines of sharply dressed and well-toned 20- and 30-somethings queue to enter a gamut of fashionable bars, clubs and pounding gay venues.

Just north of Consolação, on the other side of the Sacramento Cemetery and rushing Avenida Doutour Arnaldo, is the beautiful art deco football stadium **Estádio Pacaembu**, which hosts domestic games and big international rock concerts. It sits in a square named after Charles Miller, the Englishman who brought football to Brazil. Inside is the **Museu do Futebol** ① *Estádio do Pacaembu, Praça Charles Miller, T011-3664 3848, www.museudofutebol.org.br, Tue-Sun 0900-1700, US$1.50, free on Sat, under 7s free, restaurants next to the museum in the stadium, the closest station is Metrô Clinicas, but it's safer to go to Metrô Estação Paulista and take a 10-min cab journey*, which cost US$15 million and which was inaugurated by Pelé in September 2008. The story of the FIFA World Cup™, which Brazil has won more often than any other team, is the principal focus. One gallery is devoted to the tournament, profiling the games and what was happening in the world at the time, and telling both stories through video footage, photographs, memorabilia and newspaper cuttings. Music from the likes of Ary Barroso and Jorge Ben forms the soundtrack, along with recordings of cheering fans. A second gallery showcases Brazil's greatest stars, including Garrincha, Falcão, Zico, Bebeto, Didi, Romário, Ronaldo, Gilmar, Gérson, Sócrates, Rivelino, Ronaldo (who is known as Ronaldinho or Ronaldinho Fenomeno in Brazil) and, of course, Pelé. The shirt he wore during the 1970 World Cup final – a game frequently cited as the greatest ever played when Brazil beat Italy 4-1 to take the title for the third time – receives pride of place. A third gallery is more interactive, offering visitors the chance to dribble and shoot at goals and test their knowledge on football facts and figures.

If coming by *metrô* look out for the 44 striking panels showing local people with poems and letters super-imposed on their faces, by Paulistano artist and German resident Alex Fleming. They're situated in the gallery running over Avenida Sumaré.

Jardins *Metrô Consolação*

Immediately west of Avenida Paulista, an easy 10-minute walk from Metrô Consolação along Rua Haddock Lobo, is the plush neighbourhood of Jardins. This is by far the most pleasant area to stay in São Paulo; it has the best restaurants, shops, cafés and tranquil spots for people-watching, or an urban boutique browse. Jardins is, in reality, a series of neighbourhoods, each with its own name. The stretches closest to Paulista are known as **Cerqueira César** (to the northwest) and **Jardim Paulista** (to the southeast). These two areas have the bulk of the boutique shops, swanky hotels and chic restaurants, such as the double Michelin-starred DOM (see page 52). The most self-consciously chic of all is the cross section between Rua Oscar Freire, Rua Bela Cintra and Rua Haddock Lobo, where even the poodles wear collars with designer labels and everyone, from the shop owner to the doorman, addresses each other as '*Querida*' (Darling).

Directly west of Jardim Paulista and Cerqueira César, and separated from those neighbourhoods by a stately city highway preserving a handful of coffee Baron mansions (Avenida Brasil), are three more *jardims*. **Jardim Paulistano** is dominated by Avenida Gabriel Monteiro da Silva, which is lined by very expensive, internationally renowned home decor and furniture stores. Between Jardim Paulistano and Ibirapuera Park are **Jardim America** and **Jardim Europa**, both made up of leafy streets lined with vast mansion houses, almost completely hidden behind towering walls topped with razor wire and formidable electric fencing. Their idyllic seclusion is spoilt only by the stench of raw favela sewage from the nearby Rio Pinheiros.

The **Museu Brasileiro da Escultura** (MUBE) ⓘ *Av Europa 218, T011-2594 2601, www.mube.art.br, Tue-Sun 1000-1900, free, from Metrô Consolação, corner of R Augusta and Av Paulista, take buses 107T-10 or 908T-10 southwest along R Augusta and A Europa*, showcases contemporary Brazilian sculpture through visiting exhibitions. Most are rather lacklustre and the museum merits a visit more for the building itself, which is by Brazil's Prtizker prize-winning architect Paulo Mendes da Rocha. Like many Brazilian architects, Espírito Santo-born Rocha is celebrated for his inventive, minimalist use of concrete. The museum is made up of a series of massive, grey, bunker-like concrete blocks which contrast starkly with the surrounding gardens (by Burle Marx), but which integrate them with the underground exhibition spaces.

The **Museu da Casa Brasileira** ⓘ *Av Brigadeiro Faria Lima 2705, T011-3032 3727, www.mcb.sp.gov.br, Tue-Sun 1000-1800, US$1.75, free on Sat-Sun and holidays; from CPTM Cidade Jardim it's a 10-min walk: from Pinheiros head east along R Professor Artur Ramos to Av Brigadeiro Faria Lima*, devoted to design, architecture and decoration and housed in a stately 1940s mansion, preserves a collection of antique (mostly baroque) Brazilian and Portuguese and contemporary international furniture and examples of iconic Brazilian design. The museum also hosts the annual Prêmio Design MCB design awards, which has become one of the most celebrated in Brazil. Temporary exhibition spaces showcase the winners and the museum has a pleasant garden (with live music on Sundays) and a good café-restaurant.

The **Museu da Imagem de Do Som (MIS)** ⓘ *Av Europa 158, Jardim Europa, T011-2117 4777, www.mis-sp.org.br, Tue-Sat 1200-2200, Sun 1100-2100, free, exhibitions US$2.50, free on Tue, Metrô Faria Lima and Consolação, from Metrô Consolação, corner of R Augusta and Av Paulista, take buses 107T-10 or 908T-10 southwest along R Augusta and Av Europa*, has exciting temporary exhibitions, an arts cinema, sound labs, a huge audio and visual archive and weekly club nights with DJs or live music. **Chez MIS** in the museum is one of the city's best restaurants.

A number of Brazil's most prestigious commercial art galleries lie within Jardins. The prestigious **Galeria Luisa Strina** ① *R Padre João Manuel 755, Jardim Paulista, T011-3088 2471, www.galerialuisastrina.com.br, Mon-Fri 1000-1900, Sat 1000-1700*, shows leading contemporary artists such as Olafur Eliasson, Cildo Meirelles, Leonor Antunes, Pedro Motta and Erick Beltrán. **Dan Galeria** ① *R Estados Unidos 1638, Jardim América, T011-3083 4600, www.dangaleria.com.br, Mon-Fri 1000-1900, Sat 1000-1300*, sells works by some of the most important contemporary and deceased Brazilian including Benedito Calixto, Amelia Toledo, Anita Malfatti, Cícero Dias, Tarsila do Amaral, Volpi, Tomie Ohtake, Candido Portinari and Lygia Clark. The **Galeria Nara Roesler** ① *Av Europa 655, Jardim Europa, T011-3063 2344, www.nararoesler.com.br*, deals with contemporary art since 1975, representing artists including Abraham Palatnik, Antonio Dias, Hélio Oiticica and Milton Machado. **Amoa Konoya** ① *R João Moura 1002, Jardim América, T011-3061 0639, www.amoakonoya. com.br, Mon-Sat 0900-1800*, is devoted to art from Brazil's tribal peoples.

Vila Madalena and Pinheiros *Metrô Madalena or Fradique Coutinho.*

If Jardins is São Paulo's upper East Side or Bond Street, Vila Madalena and neighbouring Pinheiros are its East Village or Notting Hill – still fashionable, but younger, less ostentatiously moneyed and with more of a skip in their step. Streets are crammed with bars and restaurants, including one of the country's finest, **Mani** (see page 53), clambering over the steep hills and buzzing with young and arty middle-class Paulistanos.

There's also an array of boutiques featuring the city's freshest designer labels. Younger boutique brands have set up shop in Vila Madalena (see Shopping, page 60). Galleries such as **Choque Cultural** ① *R Medeiros de Albuquerque 250, Vila Madalena, T011-3061 4051, Mon-Fri 1000-1700, Sat 1100-1700, www.choquecultural.com.br*, sell work by the newest wave of the city's increasingly famous street artists (as well as prints available online) and the **Beco do Batman** (Rua Gonçalo Afonso) – an alley daubed with the latest brightly coloured art from the city's streets – has become a must-see both for impoverished graffiti artists and well-to-do gallery browsers.

With music on every corner in both neighbourhoods – from spit-and-sawdust samba bars to mock-Bahian *forró* clubs and well-established live music venues – the districts attract rich and famous boho residents. Seu Jorge lives and drinks in Vila Madalena, as does leading avant garde musician, Max de Castro.

There are a few art galleries worth a browse. They include the **Instituto Tomie Ohtake** ① *R dos Coropés 88, T011-2245 1900, www.institutotomieohtake.org.br, Tue-Fri 1100-1800, free, although there's a fee for some exhibitions, Metrô Faria Lima*, a monolithic, rather ungainly red and purple tower by Unique Hotel architect Ruy Ohtake. It has galleries inside devoted to the work of his Japanese-Brazilian artist mother, Tomie, and a series of other exhibition halls with work by up-and-coming artists.

As well as **Choque Cultural** (see above), commercial galleries in the area include **Fortes Vilaça** ① *R Fradique Coutinho 1500, Vila Madalena, T011-3032 7066, and R James Holland 71, Barra Funda, T011-3392 3942, www.fortesvilaca.com.br, Tue-Fri 1000-1700, Sat 1000-1800,* which exhibits leading Brazilian contemporary artists including Os Gêmeos, Ernesto Neto and Nuno Ramos as well as a handful of international (mostly British) names such as Cerith Wyn Evans.

On Sundays there's an open-air market in the Praça Benedito Calixto in Pinheiros selling antiques, curios, clothing and general bric-a-brac. It's very hippy chic, attracting the city's middle and upper-middle classes, many of whom gather to dance samba or listen to live *chorinho* (from 1430). There are dozens of cafés, snack bars on and around the *praça*, as well as simple restaurants serving feijoada, escondidinho and other hearty fare.

Parque do Ibirapuera

Entrance on Av Pedro Álvares Cabral, T011-5573 4180, www.parquedoibirapuera.com, daily 0500-2400, free, unsafe after dark. Metrô Ana Rosa is a 15-min walk east of the park: turn right out of the station and walk due west along Av Conselheiro Rodrigo Alves, continue onto Av Dante Pazzanese which comes to the Av 23 de Maio urban freeway, the park sits in front of you on the other side of the road and can be reached via a footbridge 200 m to the right in front of the new MAC gallery (still known as the Detran building); alternatively bus 5164-21 (marked Cidade Leonor, direção Parque do Ibirapuera) leaves every 30 mins from Metrô Santa Cruz for Ibirapuera; any bus to DETRAN (labelled in huge letters) stops opposite Ibirapuera. Lines include 175T-10, 477U-10 and 675N-10. Metrô Ibirapuera, which will stop outside the Ibirapuera shopping mall, is under construction. It will be a 20-min walk from the park.

The park was designed by architect Oscar Niemeyer and landscape artist Roberto Burle Marx for the city's fourth centenary in 1954. It is the largest of the very few green spaces in central São Paulo and its shady woodlands, lawns and lakes offer a breath of fresher air in a city that has only 4.6 sq m of vegetation per inhabitant.

The park is also home to a number of museums and monuments and some striking Oscar Niemeyer buildings that were designed in the 1950s but which have only been constructed in the last five years. These include the **Pavilhão Lucas Nogueira Garcez**, most commonly referred to as the **Oca** ⓘ *Portão 3, open for exhibitions*, a brilliant white, polished concrete dome, built in homage to an indigenous Brazilian roundhouse. It stages major international art exhibitions (see the Ibirapuera website for what's on). Next to it is the **Auditório Ibirapuera** ⓘ *Portão 3, www.auditorioibirapuera.com.br*, a concert hall shaped like a giant wedge. The **Fundação Bienal** ⓘ *Portão 3, T011-5576 7600, www.bienal.org.br, open for exhibitions*, are also by Niemeyer and house the city's flagship fashion and art events: the twice yearly **São Paulo fashion week** and the **Art Biennial**, the most important events of their kind in the southern hemisphere.

A **sculpture garden** separates the Bienal from the Oca; this garden is watched over by the **Museu de Arte Moderna** (**MAM**) ⓘ *Portão 3, T011-5085 1300, www.mam.org.br, Tue-Sun 1000-1800 (ticket office closes at 1700), US$1.50, free on Sun*. This small museum, with a giant mural outside by Os Gêmeos, showcases the best Brazilian contemporary art in temporary exhibitions. There is always something worth seeing and the gallery has an excellent buffet restaurant and gift shop.

MAM is linked by a covered walkway to the **Museu Afro-Brasil** ⓘ *Portão 10, T011-3320 8900, www.museuafrobrasil.com.br, Tue-Sun 1000-1700, US$1.50, free on Sat*, which lies inside Niemeyer's spectacular stilted **Pavilhão Manoel da Nobrega** building and devotes more than 12,000 sq m to a celebration of black Brazilian culture. Events include regular films, music, dance, and theatrical events and there is an archive of over 5000 photographs, paintings, ritual objects and artefacts which include the bisected hull of a slaving ship showing the conditions under which Africans were brought to Brazil.

A few hundred metres to the west of here, on the shores of the artificial lake, the **Planetário e Museu de Astronomia Professor Aristóteles Orsini** (**Planetarium**) ⓘ *Portão 10, T011-5575 5206, www.prefeitura.sp.gov.br/astronomia, Sat and Sun 1200-1800, US$3*, has state-of-the-art Star Master projection equipment by Carl Zeiss, and is now one of the most impressive in Latin America. Shows are in Portuguese.

Less than 100 m to the south, is the **Pavilhão Japonês** ⓘ *Portão 10, T011-5081 7296, www.bunkyo.org.br/pt-BR/pavilhao-japones, Wed, Sat, Sun and holidays 1000-1200 and 1300-1700, US$2*. The building is inspired by the historic Kyoto summer residence

ON THE ROAD

Oscar Niemeyer in São Paulo

Brazil's most famous modern architect Oscar Niemeyer died in 2012 at the age of 105. He was working until the year of his death and left behind an extensive legacy in sinuous concrete. São Paulo is home to many of his most impressive buildings, a number of which have only opened to the public in the last few years. Others are still being built.

- **Auditório Ibirapuera** (Parque Ibirapuera), a stunning door-wedge shape with a sinuous portal entrance.
- **Bienal buildings** (Parque Ibirapuera), home of Fashion Week and the Art Bienal; the serpentine walkways are fabulous.
- **Edifício Copan** (Centro/Consolação), a tower built as a swirling wave.
- **Ibirapuera museums and walkways** (Parque Ibirapuera), minimalist blocks with vast interior spaces linked by classic Niemeyer curving walkways.
- **Memorial da América Latina** (Barra Funda), a gargantuan concrete wave between towering rectilinear monoliths.
- **The Oca** (Parque Ibirapuera), a bright white concrete half-dome, in homage to indigenous communal houses.
- **Sambódromo do Anhembi** (Anhembi), the stadium venue for São Paulo carnival built right after Rio's.

of Japanese emperors, the Palácio Katsura, which was built 1620-1624 under the Tokugawa shogunate. The pavilion itself was built in Japan under the supervision of Sutemi Horiguchi – one of 20th-century Japan's foremost modern architects, responsible for buildings including the Machinery Hall, which he designed for the Tokyo Peace Exhibition of 1922. The pavilion is built in strict adherence to Japanese aesthetic principles and re-assembled next to the park's largest lake (which has illuminated fountain displays on weekday evenings). The pavilion on the lower floor has an exhibition space devoted to Japanese-Brazilian culture and has a traditional Japanese tearoom upstairs.

The park also has a running track, **Pista de Cooper** (with pit stops for exercise with pull-up bars, weight machines and chunky wooden dumbells), football pitches and hosts regular open-air concerts on Sundays. Those seeking something quieter on a Sunday can borrow a book from the portable library and read it in the shade of the **Bosque da Leitura** or 'reading wood'. Bicycles can be hired in the park (US$2 per hour) and there are dozens of small snack vendors and café-restaurants.

Ibirapuera also has a few monuments of note. **O Monumento as Bandeiras**, which sits on the northern edge of the park, is a brutalist tribute to the marauding and bloodthirsty slave traders, or *bandeirantes*, who opened up the interior of Brazil. It was created by Brazil's foremost 20th-century sculptor, Victor Brecheret. The **Obelisco aos Héroes de 32**, on the eastern edge of the park, is a monumental Cleopatra's needle built in honour of the Paulistano rebels who died in 1932 when the dictator Getúlio Vargas crushed resistance to his Estado Novo regime. Above the rushing Sena Madureira urban highway – where it thunders into the tunnel which passes beneath the park – is **Velocidade, Alma e Emoção** (Speed, Soul and Emotion), a bronze tribute to one of São Paulo's favourite sons, the Formula One driver **Ayrton Senna**, by local artist Melinda Garcia.

A bridge leads across the 16-lane Avenida 23 de Maio urban highway in the southeast of the park near Portao 4 to the former DETRAN building, which is a giant oblong on stilts by Oscar Niemeyer. Until 2007 it was home to the state transit authority. In 2012 after a US$28-million refurbishment, it reopened as the new central São Paulo wing of the **Museu de Arte Contemporanea de São Paulo** (**MAC**) ① *Av Pedro Álvares Cabral 1301, T011-5573 9932, www.mac.usp.br, Tue-Sun 1000-1800, free.* The gallery currently shows only temporary exhibitions, drawn from the museum's extensive archive of pictures. For details of what's on see the MAC website.

Listings São Paulo city *maps p28, p32 and p40*

Tourist information

There are tourist information booths with English-speaking staff in international and domestic arrivals (on the ground floor near the exit) at Cumbica Airport (Guarulhos) (www.aeroportoguarulhos.net).

There are also tourist information booths in the bus station and in the following locations throughout the city: **Praça da Luz** (in front of the Pinacoteca café, daily 0900-1800), **Av São João** (Av São João 473, Mon-Fri 0900-1800), **Av Paulista** (Parque Trianon, T011-3251 0970, Sun-Fri 0900-1800), and **Av Brig Faria Lima** (opposite the Iguatemi shopping centre, T011-3211 1277, Mon-Fri 0900-1800). An excellent map is available free at these offices.

The websites **www.guiasp.com.br** and **www.vejasp.abril.com.br** (both in Portuguese only) have comprehensive entertainment listings.

Where to stay

São Paulo has the best hotels in Latin America and by far the best city hotels in Brazil. There are designer hotels that Ian Shrager would be proud of, including business towers that combine all the requisite facilities with an almost personal touch. However, rooms are expensive and while there are some reasonable budget options they are not in the best locations. Sampa (as São Paulo is affectionately known) is a place where you have to spend money to enjoy yourself. The best places to stay are Jardins (the most affluent area) and

on and around Av Paulista (close to one of the business centres).

Backpackers should consider **Vila Madalena** which is a lively nightlife centre. Some of the better hostels are in seemingly random locations and there are cheap options in the seedy centre, which is an undesirable place to be at night.

Business travellers will find good hotels on **Faria Lima** and **Av Luís Carlos Berrini** (in the new centre in the south of the city).

Centro Histórico *map p32*
Metrô República and Anhangabaú
The city centre is very busy during the day but decidedly sketchy after dark. Consider taking a cab from your hotel door and be extra careful if you resolve to walk around. Be sure to book rooms on upper floors of hotels, preferably not facing the street, for a quiet night in the city centre.

$$$ Marabá
Av Ipiranga 757, T011-2137 9500,
www.hotelmaraba.com.br.
By far the best small hotel in the city centre, this refurbished building has colourful, well-appointed modern rooms with concessions to boutique hotel design.

$$$ Novotel Jaraguá Convention
R Martins Fontes 71, T011-2802 7000,
www.novotel.com.
This chain hotel with Wi-Fi in all rooms is the only business hotel of quality in the old centre.

$$ Formule 1
Av São João 1140, Centre, just off Praça da República, T011-2878 6400, www.accor.com. br. 5 mins' walk from Metrô República.
You'll feel like you're part of a process rather than a guest at this tall chain hotel tower. However, the modern, functional and anonymous little a/c boxes are spick and span and come with en suites, TVs, work places and space for up to 3 people.

$$ Itamarati
Av Dr Vieira de Carvalho 150, T011-3474 4133, www.hotelitamarati.com.br.
This long-standing cheapie is popular with budget travellers and represents the best value for money of any hotel in the city centre.

Avenida Paulista and Jardins *map p40*
Metrô Brigadeiro, Trianon MASP and Consolação
These plush neighbourhoods are among the safest in the city and offer easy walking access to São Paulo's finest restaurants, cafés, and shops. Those close to Av Paulista are a stroll from one of a string of *metrô* stations.

$$$$ Emiliano
R Oscar Freire 384, T011-3069 4369, www.emiliano.com.br.
Together with the **Fasano** and the **Tivoli**, these are best suites in the city: bright, light and beautifully designed with attention to every detail. No pool but a relaxing small spa. Excellent Italian restaurant, location and service.

$$$$ Fasano
R Vittorio Fasano 88, T011-3896 4077, www.fasano.com.br.
One of the world's great hotels. There's a fabulous pool, a spa and the best formal haute cuisine restaurant in Brazil, which was awarded a Michelin star in 2015. The lobby bar is a wonderful place to arrange a meeting. It's in an excellent position in Jardins.

$$$$ George V
R Jose Maria Lisboa 1000, T011-3088 9822, www.george-v.com.br.
This tower block in the heart of Jardins offers some of the largest apartments in central São Paulo covering 60-180 sq m. Living areas and bedrooms have flatscreen TVs, fully equipped kitchens (with dishwashers and washing machines), huge marble bathrooms, closets and comprehensive business services.

$$$$ L'Hotel
Av Campinas 266, T011-2183 0500, www.lhotel.com.br.
Part of the **Leading Hotels of the World** group, with a series of suites decorated with mock-European paintings and patterned wallpaper, in emulation of the classic hotel look of New York's Upper East Side. The St Regis this is not, but it's comfortable, intimate, offers good, discreet service and a respectable French restaurant. A convenient base for Paulista.

$$$$ Renaissance
Alameda Santos 2233 (at Haddock Lobo), T011-3069 2233, www.marriott.com.
This tall tower designed by Ruy Ohtake one of the better business hotel around Av Paulista, with spacious and well-appointed rooms (the best with wonderful city views), a good spa, gym, pool and 2 squash courts.

$$$$ Tivoli Mofarrej
R Alameda Santos 1437, Jardins, T011-3146 5900, www.tivolihotels.com.
Vies with the **Emiliano** and **Fasano** as the best hotel in the city with a selection of plush, modern carpeted suites and smaller rooms, the best of which are on the upper storeys and have superb city views. The hotel has the best spa in the city – run by the **Banyan Tree** group and a superb top-storey Spanish restaurant, the **Torres**.

$$$$ Unique
Av Brigadeiro Luís Antônio 4700, Jardim Paulista, T011-3055 4700, www.hotelunique.com.

The most ostentatiously designed hotel in the country: an enormous half moon on concrete uprights with curving floors, circular windows with a beautiful use of space and light. The bar on the top floor is São Paulo's answer to the LA Sky Bar and is filled with the beautiful and famous. Come for sunset views and expensive cocktails.

$$$ Golden Tulip Park Plaza
Alameda Lorena 360, T011-2627 6000, www.goldentulipparkplaza.com.
Modern tower hotel with a pool, spa, business centre, gym, also has freshly re-vamped apartments of some 30 sq m. All have a clean, modern look with wood-panel floors, fitted wardrobes, good-sized workplaces and firm beds.

$$$ Transamérica Ópera
Alameda Lorena 1748, T011-3062 2666, www.transamericagroup.com.br.
Elegant and well-maintained modern flats of 42 sq m in a tower between the heart of Jardins and Av Paulista. Choose a room above floor 15 for quietness and views.

$$$-$$ Pousada Dona Zilah
Alameda Franca 1621, Jardim Paulista, T011-3062 1444, www.zilah.com.
Little *pousada* in a renovated colonial house with plain but well-maintained rooms and common areas decorated with thought and a personal touch.

$$ Estan Plaza
Alameda Jau 497, Jardins, T011-3016 0000, www.estanplaza.com.br.
Well-kept, simple and pocket-sized rooms in a well-situated tower block close to both the restaurants of Jardins and Av Paulista. Rooms are at a similar price to hostel doubles making this excellent value.

$$ Ibis São Paulo Paulista
Av Paulista 2355, T011-3523 3000, www.accorhotels.com.br.
Great value. Modern, business-standard rooms with a/c in a tower right on Av Paulista. Cheaper at weekends. Online reservations.

$$ Paulista Garden
Alameda Lorena 21, T011-3885 8498, hotelpaulistagarden.com.br.
Very simple, uninspiring hotel, but the location is excellent.

Vila Madalena and Pinheiros
maps p28 and p40
Metrô Vila Madalena and Fradique Coutinho
These are great neighbourhoods to stay in, with a wealth of little shops, café-restaurants, bars and nightclubs. The *metrô* station is 10 mins' walk from most of the action but there are fast subway trains from here to the city centre and connections to Paulista and the *rodoviária*.

$$$ Guest Urban
R Lisboa 493, www.guesturbansp.com.br.
A converted townhouse in a quiet back street in the fashionable Pinheiros neighbourhood. Bright, airy rooms have boutique hotel touches like colourful scatter cushions, heavy cotton, art photography prints, and there's a sun deck lounge and free bikes for guests.

$$ Guest 607
R João Moura 607, Pinheiros, T011-2619 6007, www.guest607.com.br.
This very simple but colourfully painted little guesthouse, a stroll from the Benedito Calixto weekend market, offers a bright and cosy stay, albeit it in tiny rooms. There's a decent food in the little café-restaurant, free Wi-Fi and the rooms are about as cheap as it gets in São Paulo outside a hostel dorm.

$$ Lime Time
R Mourato Coelho 973, T011-3798 0051, www.limetimehostels.com.
There are only 4 rooms in this tiny hostel and whilst they're all dorms they can be booked as private rooms. One is for women only. The hostel began life as a bar and the after-hours party atmosphere remains to this day,

so it's not an option for those craving peace or privacy. Free Wi-Fi and a restaurant.

$$ Sampa Hostel
R Girassol 519, T011-3031 6779, www.hostelsampa.com.br.

This small hostel is in the heart of Vila Madalena, close to shops, cafés and bars. The 4 private rooms (single, double, triple and quadruple) fill up quickly so book ahead, the rest of the accommodation is in dorms. All are fan cooled. Prices include breakfast. Wi-Fi is available.

South of the centre *map p28*
Metrô Anhangabaú, Liberdade, Paraíso and Vergueiro

This is the best area for quality budget accommodation and is well situated for the metro.

$$$-$$ Paradiso Hostel
R Chuí 195, T011-9981 18633.

Rooms in 2 modest townhouses in a quiet street just behind the Orthodox cathedral, 200 m from Metrô Sumaré. All are spacious, clean and quiet and come with free Wi-Fi. While there is no breakfast there's a very good *padaria* round the corner. Service can be a lackadaisical. The hostel can also organize stays in other locations around the city, including in private flats in Niemeyer's iconic Edifício Copan and in converted VW campervans.

$$ 3 Dogs Hostel
R Cel Artur Godoi 51, Vila Mariana, T011-2359 8222, www.3dogshostel.com.br.

Double rooms and dorms, breakfast and bed linen included, with garden and free Wi-Fi.

$$ Formule 1
R Vergueiro 1571, T011-5085 5699, www.accorhotels.com.br.

Another great-value business-style hotel, with a/c apartments big enough for 3 (making this a $ option for those in a group). Right next to Metrô Paraíso, in a safe area.

$$ Pousada dos Franceses
R dos Franceses 100, Bela Vista, T011-3288 1592, www.pousadadosfranceses.com.br. Price per person.

A plain little *pousada* with an attractive garden, a barbecue area, laundry facilities, dorms, doubles and singles. 10 mins' walk from Metrô Brigadeiro. Free internet, TV room and breakfast included.

$$ Praça da Árvore
R Pageú 266, Saúde, T011-5071 5148, www.spalbergue.com.br.

This pleasant little hostel with friendly, helpful and English-speaking staff, lies 2 mins from the Metrô Praça do Arvore, some 20 mins' ride from the city centre. It is situated in a large residential house in a quiet back street. Facilities include a kitchen, laundry and internet service.

$$ Vergueiro Hostel
R Vergueiro 434, Liberdade, T011-2649 1323, www.hostelvergueiro.com.

Simple eggshell blue or burnt ochre rooms and dorms with parquet wood or square-tile floors, some of which have balconies. It's only 4 mins' walk from Metrô Vergueiro.

Restaurants

Those on a budget can eat to their stomach's content in per kilo places or, if looking for cheaper still, in *padarias* (bakeries). There is one of these on almost every corner; they all serve sandwiches such as *Misto Quentes*, *Beirutes* and *Americanos* – delicious Brazilian burgers made from decent meat and served with ham, egg, cheese or salad. They always have good coffee, juices, cakes and *almoços* (set lunches) for a very economical price. Most have a designated seating area, either at the *padaria* bar or in an adjacent room; you aren't expected to eat on your feet as you are in Rio. Restaurants in São Paulo are safe on the stomach. Juices are made with mineral or filtered water.

Centro Histórico *map p32*

Metrô Luz, República, São Bento, Anhangabaú, Sé

You are never far from a café or restaurant in the city centre and Luz. The Pinacoteca galleries, the Centro Culutral Banco do Brasil and the Pátio de Colégio all have decent cafés, and there are dozens in the streets around the Mosteiro São Bento and the Teatro Municipal. Most tend to be open during lunchtime only and there are many per kilo options and *padarias*.

$$$ Terraço Itália
Av Ipiranga 344, T011-3257 6566, www.terracoitalia.com.br.

An overpriced average Italian restaurant, with stodgy pasta, although it's worth a visit for the best views in the city of any dining room in São Paulo, located on the top floor of Edifício Itália (see page 36). Be warned, there is a minimum charge of US$12.50 to eat even bread and olives.

$$-$ Ponto Chic
Largo do Paiçandu 27, T011-3222 6528, www.pontochic.com.br.

Paulistanos rave about this rather unprepossessing little corner café in the heart of the city. A slice of Brazilian culinary history, the Bauru sandwich was born here in 1922. A bronze bust of Casemiro Pinto Neto (who apparently first conceived the groundbreaking idea of combining cheese, salad and roast beef in a French bread roll) adorns the back wall. The sandwich itself has a page of the menu devoted to its history, but arrives with little ceremony on a plain white plate, overflowing with gooey cheese and thick with finely cut beef.

Luz *map p28*

$$-$ Café da Pinacoteca
Pinacoteca Museum, Praça da Luz 2, Luz, T011-3326 0350, www.pinacoteca.org.br.

This Portuguese-style café with marble floors and mahogany balconies overlooks the Parque da Luz on the basement floor of the Pinacoteca gallery. It serves great coffee, sandwiches, snacks and cakes. There is also a café of similar quality in the Estação Pinacoteca gallery.

Barra Funda and Higienópolis *map p28*

$$$ Carlota
R Sergipe 753, Higienópolis, T011-3661 8670, www.carlota.com.br.

Chef Carla Pernambuco was a pioneer of fine dining in Brazil when she first opened her restaurant in the mid-1990s. Her recipe of unpretentious, homey surrounds, warm service and Brazilian and Mediterranean fusion cooking has been copied by numerous others in São Paulo. Dishes include fillet of grouper with plantain banana purée and fresh asparagus.

$$$ Corrientes 348
R Bahia, 364, Higienópolis, T011-3849 0348, www.corrientes348.com.br.

One of several branches of the superb **Vila Olimpia** Argentinian meat restaurant (see page 55), which has long held the reputation for having the best steaks in the city. There's an excellent wine list.

Avenida Paulista and Consolação
map p40

Metrô Consolação, Trianon-MASP, Brigadeiro

Restaurants in this area lie along the course of Av Paulista or in the up-and-coming nightlife area of Consolação to the north. Jardins lies within easy access to the south.

$$$ Spot
Av Ministro Rocha Azevedo 72, T011-3284 6131, www.restaurantespot.com.br.

This chic São Paulo take on an American diner has been a favourite before-and-after club spot for fashionable Paulistanos for more than a decade.

$$$-$$ Tordesilhas
R Bela Cintra 465, Consolação, T011-3107 7444, www.tordesilhas.com.

This homey restaurant with shady plants, polished floor tiles and plenty of natural light feels as informal as a barbecue in the back yard. Cooking, likewise, is Brazilian home comfort fare, albeit with a contemporary creative touch – delicious *tutu à mineira* (pork with puréed beans and farofa), *moquecas* (including a plantain banana option for vegetarians), and for dessert dishes like *cupuaçu* crème brûlée.

$$ Restaurante do MASP
Av Paulista 1578, T011-3253 2829
(see page 41).
This bright, hospital-clean buffet restaurant in the basement of the museum serves good-value comfort food such as lasagne and stroganoff, accompanied by salad from the buffet bar.

$$-$ America
Av Paulista 2295, Consolação, T011-3067 4424, www.americaburger.com.br.
This immensely popular a/c tribute to the New York diner and the North American burger is a great choice for families, with branches all over the city.

$$-$ Fran's Café
Av Paulista 358, and all over the city. Open 24 hrs.
Coffee chain serving aromatic, strong, richly flavoured coffee at a civilized temperature and in European-sized china cups, together with a menu of light eats.

Jardins *map p40*
Metrô Consolação or Trianon-MASP 10 mins' walk
Most of the city's fine dining restaurants lie in this upmarket grid of streets to the south of Av Paulista.

$$$ Dalva e Dito
R Padre Joao Manoel 1115, T011-3064 6183, www.dalvaedito.com.br.
Brazil's most internationally vaunted chef, Alex Atala, received a Michelin star in 2015 for this restaurant, which serves Brazilian home cooking with a gourmet twist. Dishes include roast pork with puréed potato and catfish with aromatic capim-santo grass from the plains of the Brazilian interior.

$$$ DOM
R Barão de Capanema 549, T011-3088 0761, www.domrestaurante.com.br.
This has been Jardins' evening 'restaurant of the moment' for almost a decade. The kitchen is run by double-Michelin-starred chef Alex Atala, who currently stands at number 9 on the San Pellegrino 'World's 50 Best Restaurants' list. Contemporary food fuses Brazilian ingredients with French and Italian styles and is served in a large, open, modernist dining room to the sharply dressed.

$$$ Fasano
Fasano Hotel (see Where to stay, page 48), R Fasano, T011-3062 4000, www.fasano. com.br.
The flagship restaurant of the Fasano group has long been regarded as the best restaurant for gourmets in São Paulo and in 2015 it was awarded a Michelin star. It has some stiff competition nowadays, but the menu still offers a delectable choice of modern Italian cooking, from chef Luca Gozzani (of the **Fasano al Mare** in Rio) and served in a magnificent room where diners have their own low-lit booths and are served by flocks of black-tie waiters. The wine list is exemplary and the dress code formal.

$$$ Figueira Rubaiyat
R Haddock Lobo 1738, T011-3063 1399, www.rubaiyat.com.br.
The most interesting of the Rubaiyat restaurant group, with steaks prepared by Brazilian chef, Francisco Gameleira. Very lively for lunch on a Sun. It's remarkable principally for the space: open walled, light and airy and shaded by a huge tropical fig tree.

$$$ Gero
R Haddock Lobo 1629, T011-3064 0005, www.fasano.com.br.
Fasano's version of a French bistro serves pasta and light Italian food in carefully designed, casually chic surrounds.

$$$ La Tambouille
Av 9 de Julho 5925, Jardim Europa, T011-3079 6277, www.tambouille.com.br.

The favourite fusion restaurant of the city's old-money society. Chef Giancarlo Bolla, a native of San Remo in northern Italy, learnt his trade on the Italian Riviera and prepares dishes like fillet of sole with passion fruit sauce served with banana and shrimp *farofa*.

$$$-$$ Marakuthai
Alameda Itu 1618, T011-3896 5874, www.marakuthai.com.br.
A Paulistano take on Indian and Southeast Asian food, with a flavour-filled but very lightly spiced menu from 20-something chef Renata Vanzetto.

$$ A Mineira
Alameda Joaquim Eugenio de Lima 697, T011-3283 2349, www.grupoamineira.com.br.
This self-service restaurant offers Minas food by the kilo from a buffet which sizzles in earthenware pots over a wood-fired stove.

$$ Santo Grão
R Oscar Freire 413, T011-3082 9969, www.santograo.com.br.
This smart café with tables spilling out onto the street is a favourite coffee and cakes or light lunch stop for wealthy society shoppers. The coffee is superb, freshly roasted and comes in a number of varieties.

$$ Sattva
Alameda Itu 1564, T011-3083 6237, www.sattvanatural.com.br.
Light vegetarian curries, stir fries, salads, pizzas and pastas all made with organic ingredients. There is a great-value dish of the day lunchtime menu on weekdays and live music most nights.

$$ Tavares
R da Consolação 3212, T011-3062 6026, www.facebook.com/CasaTavares.
Good-value breakfasts and *prato feito* lunches (beef/chicken/fish with rice, beans, chips and salad) and a broad à la carte menu ranging from pasta and pizzas to steaks and bacalhau.

$ Cheiro Verde
R Peixoto Gomide 1078, Jardins, T011-3262 2640, www.cheiroverderestaurante.com.br. Open for lunch only.
Hearty vegetarian food, such as vegetable crumble in gorgonzola sauce and wholewheat pasta with buffalo mozzarella and sundried tomato.

Vila Madalena and Pinheiros
maps p28 and p40
The streets of Vila Madalena are lined with restaurants and cafés, particularly Aspicuelta and Girassol. Most of the bars and clubs serve food too, and some (such as **Grazie o Dio!**) have designated restaurants. Pinheiros has some of the best fine dining restaurants in the city.

$$$ Jun Sakamoto
R Lisboa 55, Pinheiros, T011-3088 6019, www.facebook.com/pages/Jun-Sakamoto.
This Michelin-starred restaurant serves Japanese cuisine with a French twist. They use superb fresh ingredients, some of them flown in especially from Asia and the USA. The dishes of choice are the degustation menu and the duck breast teppanyaki.

$$$ Mani
R Joaquim Antunes 210, Pinheiros, T011 3085 4148, www.manimanioca.com.br.
A superior light Mediterranean menu, which utilizes Brazilian ingredients and perfectly complements the waistlines of the celebrity crowd, features in this restaurant, which was awarded a Michelin star in 2015. Daniel Redondo and partner Helena Rizzo have worked in Michelin-starred restaurants in Europe and are one of just 2 restaurants in Brazil to appear on the coveted San Pellegrino 'World's 50 Best' list.

$$ Goshala
R dos Pinheiros 267, Pinheiros, T011-3063 0367, www.goshala.com.br.
Brazilian with and Indian face – cheese samosas with *pupunha* taste more like a *pastel* than the real thing, the curries are

moquecas by another name. But there's plenty of choice and variety and the menu is 100% veggie.

$$ Peixeria
R Inacio Pereira da Rocha 112, T011-2859 3963.
This rustic-chic fish restaurant with raw brick walls, wood tables, colanders for lampshades and a giant model tarpon suspended from the ceiling draws a fashionable crowd sick of the inflated prices of gourmet São Paulo and seduced by the ultra-fresh fish, seafood *petiscos* and modest bills.

$$-$ Deli Paris
R Harmonia 484, Vila Madalena, T011-3816 5911, www.deliparis.com.br.
This Paulistano homage to a French café serves light and flavourful sweet and savoury crêpes, sickly sweet petit gateaux au chocolat, cheese-heavy quiches, salads and crunchy sandwiches to a busy lunchtime and evening crowd.

$$-$ Genial
R Girassol 374, T011-3812 7442, www.bargenial.com.br.
This bar, with a black-and-white mosaic floor and black-tie waiters, is decorated with album covers by famous traditional musicians such as João do Vale and Luiz Gonzaga. The *chope* is creamy and best accompanied by a *petisco* bar snack, like *caldinho de feijão* (bean broth) or *bolinhos de bacalhau* (codfish balls), both of which are among the best in Vila Madalena. There's a hearty and very popular *feijoada* on Sat and Sun lunch.

South of the centre *maps p28 and p32*
Liberdade is dotted with Japanese restaurants and has a lively market on Sun with plenty of food stalls. Bela Vista is replete with Italian restaurants, most of them rather poor, with stodgy pasta and gooey risotto. Ibirapuera Park has lots of mobile snack bars selling ice cream, sugar cane juice, hot dogs and snacks, and there is a good-value buffet restaurant close to the Museu Afro Brasileiro.

$$$-$$ Famiglia Mancini
R Anhandava, T011-3255 6599, www.famigliamancini.com.br.
This pretty little pedestrianized street 10 mins' walk from Terraço Itália is lined with Italian restaurants and delicatessens, almost all of them in the locally owned Famiglia Mancini group. Here, the big dining room with formal waiters and an enormous menu of meats, pastas, risottos, fish and (inevitably for São Paulo) pizzas, is the family's flagship restaurant. Walls are lined with the faces of famous Brazilians who have dined here.

$$ Aska Lámen
R Galvão Buemno 466, Liberdade, T011-3277 9682, www.facebook.com/pages/Aska-Restaurante. Tue-Sun lunch and dinner.
One of Liberdade's more traditional Japanese restaurants with a bar overlooking an open kitchen where chefs serve piping ramen noodle dishes to lunchtime diners who are 90% *issei* (Japanese immigrants and their descendants).

$$ Prêt
Museu de Arte Moderna (MAM), Parque Ibirapuera, T011-5574 1250, www.mam.org.br. Closed evenings.
The best food in the park: ultra-fresh pre-prepared soups, salads, chicken, fish, meat and vegetarian dishes.

$$ Sushi Yassu
R Tomas Gonzaga 98, T011-3288 2966, www.sushiyassu.com.br.
The best of Liberdade's traditional Japanese restaurants with a large menu of sushi/sashimi combinations, *teishoku* (complete set meals with cooked and raw dishes) and very sweet Brazilianized desserts.

Itaím, Vila Olímpia, Moema and Vila Nova Conceição
These areas, south of the centre, have dozens of ultra-trendy restaurants with beautiful people posing in beautiful surroundings. We include only a handful of the best.

$$$ Attimo
R Diogo Jacome, 341, Vila Nova Conceição, T011-5054 9999, www.attimorestaurante. com.br.
Star São Paulo chef Jefferson Rueda (formerly of **Pomodori**) heads the kitchen in this high society restaurant, which was awarded a Michelin star in 2015, and crafted his menu after months touring the Michelin-starred restaurants of Europe, including **El Celler de Can Roca**.

$$$ Corrientes 348
R Comendador Miguel Calfat, 348 Vila Olímpia, T011-3849 0348, http://www.corrientes348.com.br.
An Argentinian restaurant with the best steak in the country and the choicest cuts available on export from Buenos Aires. The *ojo del bife* cuts like brie and collapses in the mouth like wafered chocolate. The accompanying wines are equally superb, especially the 2002 Cheval dos Andes. One of 4 **Corrientes 348** restaurants in the city. Great, unpretentious atmosphere.

$$$ Kinoshita
R Jacques Félix 405, Vila Nova Conceição, T011-3849 6940, www.restaurantekinoshita.com.br.
Tsuyoshi Murakami offers the best menu of traditional cooked or Kappo cuisine in Brazil, dotted with creative fusion dishes in a **Nobu** vein at this Michelin-starred restaurant. His cooking utilizes only the freshest ingredients and includes a sumptuous degustation menu with delights such as tuna marinated in soya, ginger and garlic, served with ponzo sauce and garnished with kaiware (sprouted daikon radish seeds). Murakami trained in the ultra-traditional 100-year-old **Uzushl** restaurant in Tokyo, **Shubu Shubu** in New York and **Kyokata** in Barcelona.

$$$ La Mar
R Tabapuã 1410, Itaim, T011-3073 1213, lamarcebicheria.com.br.
La Mar brings Peruvian seafood flavours to São Paulo. Most of the tangy ceviches have been spiced-down for the more sensitive Brazilian palate (though there's a *caliente* option for those used to chilli and a choice degustation for beginners).

$$$ Parigi
R Amauri 275, Itaim, T011-3167 1575, www.fasano.com.br.
One of the premier places to be seen; celebrity couples come here for intimate, public-view Franco-Italian dining. The menu also has classical French dishes such as coq au vin. Attractive dining room, beautifully lit, and decked out in lush dark wood.

Bars, clubs and live music

With no beach, Paulistanos meet for drinks and dancing and the city is prides itself on having great nightlife. There is live music on most nights of the week. Large concert venues, such as the Pacaembu Stadium, host the likes of U2 or Ivete Sangalo. Medium-sized venues, such as Credicard Hall, are played by acts like Caetano Veloso, Gilberto Gil and Chico Buarque.

Smaller venues include SESCs (cultural centres with excellent concert halls), and are found in Vila Mariana and Pompéia. They host smaller, classy artists such as Otto, Naná Vasconcelos, João Bosco and Seu Jorge. It is also worth checking out the established smaller live venues in and around Vila Madalena and Itaim, such as Bourbon St, A Marcenaria and Grazie a Dio for samba-funk acts such as Tutti Baê and Funk como le Gusta, designated samba bars like Ó do Borogodó (also in Vila Madalena) and venues on the burgeoning alternative music scence, such as the CB Bar in Barra Funda.

DJs like Marky, and the sadly deceased Suba, made the São Paulo club scene world famous, but gone are the days when Marky was resident DJ at the **Lov.E Club** and the city danced to home-grown sounds in clubs like **Prime**. São Paulo's sound systems and clubs are slicker and swankier than they have ever been, but the music is painfully derivative of New York and Europe.

The city has a bar at every turn – from spit-and-sawdust corner bars serving cold lager beer to an unpretentious blue-collar cord, to smarter botecos where penguin-suited waiters whirl around the tables brandishing frothy glasses of draught lager or *chope* (pronounced 'chopee') and self-consciously chic cocktail bars where Paulistano high society flashes its Vartanian jewels and flexes its gym-toned pecs beneath its Osklen. Almost all serve food and many have live music. Beer and snacks are also available at the bar in any *padaria* (bakery).

Barra Funda *map p28*

This dark and edgy neighbourhood northwest of Luz is dotted with dance clubs and venues playing host to a bewildering variety of acts which have little to nothing in common beyond existing beyond the mainstream. It's not safe to walk around here after dark. Take the *metrô* and a cab.

Bar do Alemão
Av Antártica 554, Água Branca, T011-3879 0070, http://bardoalemao.zip.net.
This cosy little brick-walled bar and restaurant, on an ugly main road in a semi-residential quarter of Barra Funda, is famous for its live samba. There are samba shows most nights with an especially lively crowd at the weekends. Clara Nunes used to play here and famous samba musicians often appear, including Paulo Cesar Pinheiro and Eduardo Gudin.

Clash Club
R Barra Funda 969, T011-3661 1500, www.clashclub.com.br.
Funky and intimate modern club with space for just a few hundred 20-somethings, decorated with raw brick and lit with cellular lights and 3D projections. Music varies hard core techno and hip hop and rare groove. Few Brazilian sounds.

D-Edge
Alameda Olga 170, T011-3667 8334, www.d-edge.com.br.

São Paulo's leading temple to electronica is one of the few clubs of this kind to play Brazilian as well as international sounds. However, those searching for something new will be disappointed by the homages to Ibiza and New York which dominate on most nights. The sound-systems, however, are superb.

SESC Pompeia
R Clélia, 93, Pompéia, T011-3871 7700, www.sescsp.org.br.
There's always a great show at this arts and cultural centre in the neighbouring bairro to Barra Funda. Some of Brazil's best small acts play at weekends.

The Week
R Guaicurus 324, Barra Funda, T011-3872 9966, www.theweek.com.br.
One of the city's biggest gay- and lesbian-dominated dance clubs.

Avenida Paulista and Consolação
map p40
Until a few years ago the dark streets of Consolação were home to little more than rats, sleazy strip bars, street-walkers and curb-crawlers, but now it harbours a thriving alternative weekend scene with a new club opening virtually every other month.

Astronete
R Augusta 335, Consolação, T011-3151 4568, www.astronete.tumblr.com.
One of the area's longest-established clubs drawing a mixed crowd from mock Brit popsters to emo 20-somethings and resolute rockers. The bands and DJs are equally varied, from Mickey Leigh (Joey Ramone's bother) to Pernambuco rap rocker China.

Beco 203
R Augusta 609, Consolação, T011-2339 0351, www.beco203.com.br.
Cutting edge alternative rockers from Brazil and the world over play here. Past acts have included the reformed Television, British indie Shoegazers Foals, Pata de Elefante and alternative scene DJs like Gabriel Machuca.

Caos
R Augusta 584, Consolação, T011-2365 1260, https://en-gb.facebook.com/caosaugusta.
One of the area's most popular bars with an astonishing variety of music spun by local DJs from Speed Caravan and Serbian gypsy rock to Algerian Rai disco and vintage soul.

Clube Royal
R Consolação 222, T011-3129 9804, www.royalclub.com.br.
One of the most fashionable funk and rare groove clubs on the young, wealthy and need-to-be-seen São Paulo circuit is decorated like a New York dive bar in Brazilian tropical colours. Don't expect to hear any Brazilian music.

Inferno
R Augusta 501, Consolação, T011-3120 4140, www.infernoclub.com.br.
Pounding rock, thrashing metal and the occasional svelte samba-funk act play to a packed crowd at this leopard-skin lined sweaty club.

Kabul
R Pedro Taques 124, Consolação, T011-2503 2810, www.kabul.com.br.
Live music ranging from Brazilian jazz to samba rock, and alternative acts. DJs play between and after shows. Lively and eclectic crowd.

Mono
R Augusta 480, T011-2371 0067, www.clubmono.com.br.
A good looking 20- and 30-something crowd gather here to dance to international drum'n'bass and soul (Thu), house (Fri) and rock and disco (Sat). The decor is very typical of Consolação: low-lighting, off-the-wall retro movie projections, quirky stills from Scarface, pick-up trucks, huge 1950s fridges, etc.

Outs Club
R Augusta 486, T011-3237 4940, www.clubeouts.com.
One of the bastions of the alternative, rock and hard rock scene with a mix of DJs playing everything from UK indie to heavy Brazilian metal bands.

Vegas Club
R Augusta 765, T011-3231 3705, www.vegasclub.com.br. Tue-Sat.
International and local DJs spin a predictable menu of techno, psi-trance and house to a mixed gay and straight crowd dancing on 2 sweaty floors.

Jardins *map p40*

Bar Balcão
R Doutor Melo Alves 150, T011-3063 6091.
After-work meeting place, very popular with young professionals and media types who gather on either side of the long low wooden bar, which winds its way around the room like a giant snake.

Barretto
Fasano Hotel, see Where to stay, page 48.
A rather conservative atmosphere with heavy dark wood, mirrors and cool live bossa jazz. The crowd is mostly the Cuban cigar type with a sprinkling of the tanned and toned, in figure-enhancing designer labels.

Casa de Francisca
R José Maria Lisboa 190 at Brigadeiro Luís Antônio, T011-3493 5717, www.casadefrancisca.art.br.
This intimate, live music restaurant-bar plays host to the refined end of the musical spectrum with acts such Chico Saraiva, Arthur de Faria or Paulo Braga. The best tables to book are those on the upper deck.

Finnegan's Pub
R Cristiano Viana 358, Pinheiros, T011-3062 3232, www.finnegan.com.br.
One of São Paulo's Irish bars. This one is actually run and owned by an Irishman and is very popular with expats.

Skye
The rooftop bar at Unique Hotel (see Where to stay, page 48).

Another fashionable spot with a definite door policy. Come for sunset and city views – some of Sao Paulo's best.

Vila Madalena and Pinheiros *map p28*

Vila Madalena and adjacent Pinheiros lie just northeast of Jardins. A taxi from Jardins is about US$5.50; there is also a *metrô* station, but this closes by the time the bars get going. These suburbs are the favourite haunts of São Paulo 20-somethings, more hippy chic than Itaim, less stuffy than Jardins. This is the best part of town for live Brazilian music and uniquely Brazilian close dances such as *forró*, as opposed to international club sounds. It can feel grungy and informal but is buzzing. The liveliest streets are Aspicuelta and Girassol.

Bambu

R Purpurina 272, Vila Madalena, T011-3031 2331, www.bambubrasilbar.com.br.
A kind of backland desert jig called *forró* has everyone up and dancing in this slice of mock-Bahia, with live northeastern accordion and *zabumba* drum bands in the front room and a hippy middle-class student crowd downing industrial strength caipirinhas out the back.

Canto da Ema

Av Brigadeiro Faria Lima 364, T011-3813 4708, www.cantodaema.com.br.
Very popular *forró* club with great live bands from the northeast.

Grazie a Dio

R Girassol 67, T011-3031 6568, www.grazieadio.com.br.
The best bar in Vila Madalena to hear live music. There's a different (but always quality) band every night with acts ranging from Banda Gloria, Clube do Balanco and Japanese-Brazilian samba-funk band Sambasonics. Great for dancing. Always packed.

Ó do Borogodó

R Horácio Lane 21, Vila Madalena, T011-3814 4087, www.facebook.com/odoborogodobar.
It can be hard to track down this intimate

club opposite the cemetery. It's in an unmarked house next to a hairdressers on the edge of Vila Madalena. The tiny dance hall is always packed with people between Wed and Sat. On Wed there's classic samba *canção* from retired cleaner Dona Inah who sings material from the likes of Cartola and Ataulfo Alves; and on other nights there's a varied programme of *choro*, and MPB from some of the best samba players in São Paulo.

Posto 6

R Aspicuelta 644, Vila Madalena, T011-3812 7831, www.barposto6.com.br.
An imitation Rio de Janeiro *boteco* with attractive crowds and backdrop of bossa nova and MPB. Busy from 2100.

Sub Astor

R Delfina 163, Vila Madalena, T011-3815 1364, www.subastor.com.br.
This velvety mood-lit lounge bar looks like a film set from a David Lynch movie and is filled with mols, vamps and playboys from the upper echelons of São Paulo society. The cocktails are superb.

Itaím, Vila Olímpia and Moema

This area, just south of Ibirapuera and north of the new centre, is about US$10.50 by taxi from Jardins and US$15 from the centre, but well worth the expense of getting here. It is packed with street-corner bars, which are great for a browse. The bars here, although informal, have a style of their own, with lively and varied crowds and decent service. The busiest streets for a bar wander are: R Atilio Inocenti, near the junction of Av Juscelino Kubitschek and Av Brigadeiro Faria Lima; Av Hélio Pellegrino; and R Araguari, which runs behind it.

Bourbon Street Music Club

R dos Chanés 127, Moema, T011-5095 6100, bourbonstreet.com.br.
Great little club with acts like funkster Tutti Bae, Funk Como Le Gusta, Max de Castro and Wilson Simoninha and international acts like BB King.

Disco
R Professor Atílio Inocennti 160, Itaim, T011-3078 0404, www.clubdisco.com.br.
One of the city's plushest high-society discos and a favourite with leading socialites and models, especially during Fashion Week. The decor is by Isay Weinfeld who designed the **Fasano**, and the music standard Eurotrash and US club sounds.

Na Mata Café
R da Mata 70, Itaim, T011-3079 0300, www.namata.com.br.
Popular flirting and pick-up spot for 20- and 30-somethings who gyrate in the dark dance room to a variety of Brazilian and European dance tunes and select live bands. Decent comfort food and snacks.

Provocateur
R Jerônimo Da Veiga 163, Itaim Bibi, T011-2339 2597, www.provocateurclubsp.com.br.
São Paulo's love affair with New York nightlife continues with the opening of the Latin American branch of the modish Manhattan nightclub.

Entertainment

For listings of concerts, theatre, museums, galleries and cinemas visit www.guiasp.com.br, or check out the *Guia da Folha* section of *Folha de São Paulo*, and the *Veja São Paulo* section of the weekly news magazine *Veja*.

Cinema
Entrance is usually half price on Wed; normal seat price is US$7. Most shopping centres have multiplexes showing the latest blockbuster releases. These are usually in their original language with Portuguese subtitles (*legendas*). Where they are not, they are marked 'DUB' (*dublado*).

There are arts cinemas at the **SESC**s (notably at the **Cine Sesco**, R Augusta 2075, Jardins, T011-3087 0500, www.cinesescsp.org.br, and at **Pompeia** and **Vila Mariana**, www.sescsp.org.br); and at the **Centro Cultural Banco do Brasil** (see page 33).

Other arts cinemas are at **Belas Artes** (R da Consolação 2423, T011-3258 4092, www.confrariadecinema.com.br); **Espaço Unibanco** (R Augusta 1470/1475, www.unibancocinemas.com.br); **Museu da Imagem e do Som** (Av Europa 258, T011-2117 4777, www.mis-sp.org.br); **Itaú Cultural** (www.itaucultural.org.br); and **Centro Cultural São Paulo** (www.centrocultural.sp.gov.br), see below.

Classical music, ballet and theatre
In addition to those listed below, there are several other first-class theatres: **Aliança Francesa**, R Gen Jardim 182, Vila Buarque, T011-3259 0086, www.aliancafrancesa.com.br; Teatro **Itália**, Av Ipiranga 344, T011-3120 6945, www.teatroitalia.com.br; Teatro **Paiol Cultural**, R Amaral Gurgel 164, Santa Cecília, T011-3337 4517, www.teatropaiolcultural.com; free concerts at **Teatro do Sesi**, Av Paulista 1313, T011-3284 9787, Mon-Sat 1200, under MASP.
Centro Cultural São Paulo, *R Vergueiro 1000, T011-3397 4002, www.centrocultural.sp.gov.br.* A 50,000-sq-m arts centre with concert halls, where there are regular classical music and ballet recitals, a library with work desks, theatres and exhibition spaces. See the website for details of events.
Sala São Paulo, *see page 38*. This magnificent neo-Gothic hall with near perfect acoustics is the city's premier classical music venue and is home to Brazil's best orchestra, the **Orquestra Sinfônica do Estado de São Paulo** (www.osesp.art.br). The OSESP has been cited as one of 3 up-and-coming ensembles in the ranks of the world's greatest orchestras by the English magazine *Gramophone*. They have a busy schedule of performances (details available on their website) with concerts usually on Thu, Fri and Sat.
Teatro Municipal Opera House, *see page 37*. Used by visiting theatrical and operatic groups, as well as the City Ballet Company and the Municipal Symphony Orchestra, who give regular performances.

Festivals

Throughout the year there are countless anniversaries, religious feasts, fairs and exhibitions. To see what's on, check the local press or the monthly tourist magazines. Fashion Week is held in the **Bienal Centre** (Bienal do Ibirapuera) in Ibirapuera Park, T011-5576 7600, www.bienal.org.br.

25 Jan Foundation of the city.
Feb Carnaval. Escolas de samba parade in the Anhembi Sambódromo. During Carnaval most museums and attractions are closed.
Jun Festas Juninas and the **Festa de São Vito**, the patron saint of the Italian immigrants.
Sep Festa da Primavera.
Dec Christmas and **New Year** festivities.

Shopping

São Paulo isn't the best place to shop for souvenirs, but it remains Latin America's fashion and accessory capital and the best location in the southern hemisphere for quality fashion and jewellery.

Books and music

Livrarias Saraiva and **Laselva** are found in various shopping malls and at airports, they sell books in English. **FNAC**, Av Paulista 901 (at Metrô Paraíso) and Praça Omaguás 34, Pinheiros (Metrô Pinheiros), www.fnac. com.br, has a huge choice of DVDs, CDs, books in Portuguese (and English), magazines and newspapers.

Fashion boutiques

São Paulo is one of the newest hot spots on the global fashion circuit and is by far the most influential and diverse fashion city in South America. The designers based here have collections as chic as any in Europe or North America. Best buys include smart casual day wear, bikinis, shoes, jeans and leather jackets. Havaiana flip-flops, made famous by Gisele Bundchen and Fernanda Tavares, are around 60% of the price of Europe. The best areas for fashion shopping are Jardins (around R Oscar Freire) and the **Iguatemi Shopping Centre** (Av Faria Lima), while the city's most exclusive shopping emporium is **Shopping JK** (see page 63). The 1st **Issa** boutique in Brazil was opened in the city by designer Daniella Helayel who made her name in London, becoming a favourite designer for Catherine Duchess of Cambridge.

Adriana Barra, *Alameda Franca 1243, T011-2925 2300, www.adrianabarra.com.br.* Her showroom is in a converted residential house whose façade is entirely covered with vines, bromeliads and ferns. Adriana is best known for her long dresses and bell-sleeved tunics, made of silk and jersey and printed with designs which take classic belle époque French floral and abstract motifs and reinterpret them in 1970s tropicalia-laced colours and patterns. She now sells homeware, with everything from sofas and scatter cushions to bedspreads, amphorae and notebooks.

Adriana Degreas, *R Dr Melo Alves 734, Jardins, T011-3064 4300, www.adrianadegreas. com.br.* Adriana opened her flagship store in Jardins with a zesty collection premiered at Claro Rio Summer Fashion Show. She now sells at Barneys and Bloomingdales in New York and in Selfridges in London.

Alexandre Herchcovitz, *R Melo Alves 561, T011-4306 6457, http://herchcovitch.uol. com.br.* Perhaps the most famous young Brazilian designer, using brightly coloured materials to create avant garde designs influenced by European trends but with their own decidedly tropical bent.

Amir Slama, *R Oscar Freire 977, Jardins, T011-3061 0450, www.amirslama.com.br.* As the creator of the Rosa Chá brand which was worn by supermodels and celebrities from LA to Mumbai, Amir Slama is one of the world's top swim and beach wear designers. This is his new flagship shop, launched under his own name.

Carina Duek, *R Oscar Freire 736, T011-2359 5972, www.carinaduek.com.br*. Another rising young star with a boutique designed by **Fasano** architect Isay Weinfeld. Her simple, figure-hugging light summer dresses and miniskirts are favourites with 20-something Paulistana socialites.

Carlos Miele, *R Bela Cintra 2231 and Shopping Cidade Jardim, Consolação, T011-3062 6144, www.carlosmiele.com.br*. Modern Brazil's biggest international brand with collections sold in more than 30 countries and his own brand-name shops in New York and Paris. His bright, slick and sexy prêt-à-porter designs have been used in TV shows from Ugly Betty to Gossip Girl. In Brazil, Carlos Miele is best known for **M.Officer** (branches in major malls), a brand celebrated for jeans and casual wear.

Fause Haten, *Alameda Lorena 1731, Jardins, T011-3081 8685, www.fausehaten.com.br*. One of Brazil's most internationally renowned designers who works in plastic, lace, leather, mohair and denim with laminate appliqués, selling through, amongst others, **Giorgio Beverly Hills**.

Forum, *R Oscar Freire 916, Jardins T011-3085 6269, www.forum.com.br*. A huge white space attended by beautiful shop assistants helping impossibly thin 20-something Brazilians squeeze into tight, but beautifully cut, jeans and other fashion items.

Iodice, *R Oscar Freire 940, T011-3085 9310, and Shopping Iguatemi, T011-3813 2622, www.iodice.com.br*. Sophisticated and innovative knitwear designs sold abroad in boutiques like **Barney's NYC**.

Lenny, *Shopping Iguatemi, T011-3032 2663, R Sarandi 98, T011-3798 2044, and R Escobar Ortiz 480, Vila Nova Conceicao, T011-3846 6594, www.lenny.com.br*. Rio de Janeiro's premier swimwear designer and Brazil's current favourite.

Mario Queiroz, *R Alameda Franca 1166, T011-3062 3982, www.marioqueiroz.com.br*. Casual and elegant clothes with a strong gay element, for 20-something men.

Osklen, *R Oscar Freire, 645, T011-3083 7977, www.osklen.com*. Brazil's answer to Ralph Lauren, with stylish but casual beach and boardwalk wear for men.

Ricardo Almeida, *Bela Cintra 2093, T011-3887 4114, and Shopping JK*. One of the few Brazilian designers who styles for men. His clothes are a range of dark suits, slick leather jackets and finely cut and tailored jeans.

Ronaldo Fraga, *R Aspicuelta 259, Vila Madalena, T011-3816 2181, www.ronaldo fraga.com*. Fraga's adventurous collection combines discipline with daring, retaining a unified style across the sexes yet always surprising and delighting with its off-the-wall creativity.

UMA, *R Girassol 273, T011-3813 5559, www.uma.com.br*. Raquel Davidowicz offers rails of sleek contemporary cuts set against low-lit, cool white walls with a Japanese-inspired monochrome minimalism mixed with colourful Brazilian vibrancy.

Victor Hugo, *R Oscar Freire 816, T011-3082 1303, www.victorhugo.com.br*. Brazil's most fashionable handbag designer.

Zoomp, *R Oscar Freire 995, T011-3064 1556, Shopping Iguatemi, T011-3032 5372, www.zoomp.com.br*. Zoomp has been famous for its figure-hugging jeans for nearly 3 decades and has grown to become a nationwide and now international brand.

Bargain fashion If the upper crust shop and sip coffee in Jardins, the rest of the city buys its wares on the other side of the old city centre in Bom Retiro (Metrô Mal Deodoro, CPTM Julio Prestes/Luz). At first sight the neighbourhood is relentlessly urban; ugly concrete with rows of makeshift houses converted into hundreds of shops selling a bewildering array of clothing. Much of it is trash, and during the week wholesale stores may specify a minimum number of items per buyer. But a few hours of browsing will yield clothing bargains to rival those in Bangkok. Many of the outfitters manufacture for the best mid-range labels in São Paulo, including those in

Shopping Ibirapuera (see Shopping malls, below). The best shopping is on and around R José Paulino, a street with more than 350 shops. The best day to come is Sat from 0800, when most items are sold individually.

Shopping 25 de Março (R 25 de Março, www.25demarco.com.br, Metrô São Bento), in the city centre offers a similarly large range of costume jewellery, toys and small decorative items (best on Sat 0800-1430).

The neighbourhood of **Brás** stocks cheaper but lower quality items. For more information see **www. omelhordobomretiro.com.br**.

Handicrafts

São Paulo has no handicrafts tradition but some items from the rest of Brazil can be bought at Parque Tte Siqueira Campos/ Trianon on Sun 0900-1700.

Casa dos Amazonas, *Al dos Jurupis 460, Moema, www.arteindigena.com.br*. Huge variety of Brazilian indigenous arts and crafts from all over the country.

Galeria Arte Brasileira, *Av Lorena 2163, T011- 3062 9452, www.galeriaartebrasileira.com. br*. Folk art from the northeast, including the famous clay figurines from Caruaru, Ceará lace, Amazonian hammocks, carved wooden items from all over the country and indigenous Brazilian bead and wicker art.

Sutaco, *R Boa Vista 170, Edif Cidade I, 3rd floor, Centro, T011-3241 7333*. Handicrafts shop selling and promoting items from the state of São Paulo.

Jewellery

Antonio Bernardo, *R Bela Cintra 2063, Jardins, T011-3083 5622, www.antonio bernardo.com.br*. Bernardo is as understated as **Vartanian** is bling, and offers elegant, contemporary gold and platinum designs and exquisite stones. The designer has branches all over the city and in locations throughout Brazil.

H Stern, *www.hstern.com.br, with shops all over the city including: R Augusta 2340; R Oscar Freire 652; at Iguatemi,*

Ibirapuera, Morumbi, Paulista and other shopping centres; at large hotels; and at the international airport. Brazil's biggest jewellers, represented in 18 countries. In Brazil they have designs based on Brazilian themes, including Amazonian bead art and Orixa mythology.

Vartanian, *NK, R Bela Cintra 2175, Jardins, and Shopping JK, T011-3061 5738, www. jackvartanian.com*. Jack Vartanian creates fashion jewellery with huge Brazilian emeralds and diamonds set in simple gold and platinum – much beloved of Hollywood red-carpet walkers including Zoe Saldana, Cameron Diaz and Demi Moore. His low-lit Jardins shop showcases jewellery only available only in Brazil.

Markets

Ceasa Flower Market, *Av Doutor Gastão Vidigal 1946, Jaguaré. Tue and Fri 0700-1200*. Should not be missed.

MASP Antiques Market, *takes place below the museum. Sun 1000-1700*. Some 50 stalls selling everything from vintage gramophones to ceramics, ornaments and old vinyl.

Mercado Municipal, *R da Cantareira 306, Centro, T011-3326 3401, www.oportaldo mercadao.com.br. Metrô São Bento*. This renovated art deco market was built at the height of the coffee boom and is illuminated by beautiful stained-glass panels by Conrado Sorgenicht Filho showing workers tilling the soil. It's worth coming here just to browse aisles bursting with produce: *açai* from the Amazon, hunks of *bacalhau* from the North Sea, mozzarella from Minas, sides of beef from the Pantanal and 1000 other foodstuffs. The upper gallery has half a dozen restaurants offering dishes of the day and a vantage point over the frenetic buying and selling below.

Oriental Fair, *Praça de Liberdade. Sun 1000- 1900*. Good for Japanese snacks, plants and some handicrafts, very picturesque, with remedies on sale, tightrope walking, gypsy fortune tellers, etc.

Praça Benedito Calixto, *Pinheiros. Metrô Pinheiros*. The best bric-a-brac market in São Paulo takes place here Sat 0900-1900, with live *choro* and samba 1430-1830. There are many stylish shops, restaurants and cafés around the square.

Av Lorena, which is one of the upmarket shopping streets off R Augusta in Jardins, has an open-air market on Sun selling fruits and juices. There is a flea market on Sun in **Praça Don Orione** (main square of the Bixiga district).

There is also a Sunday market in the **Praça da República** in the city centre (see page 36).

Shopping malls and department stores
Shopping Cidade Jardim, *Av Magalhães de Castro 12000, T011-3552 1000, www. cidadejardimshopping.com.br.* CPTM Hebraica-Rebouças (and then 5-10 mins by taxi). Brazilian names like **Carlos Miele** and **Osklen**, whose casual beach and adventure clothes look like Ralph Lauren gone tropical and are aimed at a similar yacht-and-boardwalk crowd.
Shopping Ibirapuera, *Av Ibirapuera 3103, www.ibirapuera.com.br, Metrô Ana Rosa and bus 695V (Terminal Capelinha).* A broad selection of mid-range Brazilian labels and general shops including toy and book shops.
Shopping Iguatemi, *Av Brigadeiro Faria Lima 2232, www.iguatemi.com.br.* A top-end shopping mall just south of Jardins with a healthy representation of most of Brazil's foremost labels.
Shopping JK Iguatemi, *Av Presidente Juscelino Kubitschek 2041, Vila Olimpia, T011-3152 6800, www.jkiguatemi.com.br.* The fashion, jewellery and lifestyle shopping centre of choice for Sao Paulo's high society, wannabes and window shoppers. With many of Brazil's choicest labels from Daslu to Carlos Miele and international names like Burberry, Calvin Klein, Diesel and Chanel. Also houses one of the city's best cinemas and a huge food court.

What to do

Football
The most popular local teams are Corinthians, Palmeiras and São Paulo who generally play in the Morumbi and Pacaembu stadiums, see page 42 for details of visiting the latter. See also **Museu do Futebol**, page 42.

Language courses
The official **Universidade de São Paulo (USP)** is situated in the Cidade Universitária (buses from main bus station), beyond Pinheiros. They have courses available to foreigners, including a popular Portuguese course. Registry is through the **Comissão de Cooperação Internacional** (Rua do Lago 717, sala 130, Cidade Universitária, T011-3091 3572, http://ccint.fflch.usp.br). Other universities include the **Pontifical Catholic University (PUC)**, and the **Mackenzie University**. Both these are more central than the USP, Mackenzie in Higienopolis, just west of the centre, and PUC in Perdizes. Take a taxi to either. Both have noticeboards where you can leave a request for Portuguese teachers or language exchange, which is easy to arrange for free. Any of the gringo pubs are good places to organize similar exchanges.

Personal drivers
If you plan on taking more than a few taxi rides around the city then consider booking a personal driver instead. At around US$130 a day they work out far better value and are safer than hailing a street cab.
Francisco Fransa, *T/WhatsApp-11-97155 4705, ffranssa@yaho.com.br.* Excellent personal driver and informal guide. Airport transfers, pick-ups and bespoke visits to all the main sights. Safe, secure, reliable and on time. Book ahead through email or WhatsApp.

Personal shoppers
Ale Ribeiro, *T011 96621 7294, alessandraribeiro@me.com*. Ale has spent over 20 years working for the cream of Brazil's fashion houses, including **Cris Barros**, **Carlos Miele**, **Rosa Cha** and **Osklen**. She has unique access to the latest lines, can secure discounts of as much as 30% and has impeccable taste.

Tour operators
São Paulo has several large agencies offering tours around the country.
Ambiental Viagens e Expedições, *www.ambiental.tur.br*. Good for trips to less well-known places throughout the country, such as Jalapão. English and Spanish spoken, helpful.
Edson Endrigo, *www.avesfoto.com.br*. Edson is one of Latin America's best birding guides and photographers. Trips run throughout São Paulo state and southeast Brazil.
Matueté, *R Tapinás 22, Itaim, T011-3071 4515, www.matuete.com*. Luxury breaks throughout Brazil and city tours, including personal shopping. Ask for Camilla. English spoken.
SPin Brazil Tours, *T011-5904 2269, T011-9185 2623 (mob), www.spintours.com.br*. Tailor-made services and private tours of São Paulo city and state with options on destinations further afield. These include bilingual 3- to 4-hr tours of the city of São Paulo (including key sights like the Museu do Futebol and MASP), tailor-made bilingual tours, and visits to football matches and the Brazilian Grand Prix. Expect to pay from US$30 per hr for a simple city tour and around US$75 per hr for special interest tours. SPin can arrange accommodation for a surcharge and offer a driver/guide service for business trips. Comfortable cars and excellent organization.

Transport

Air   *See also box, Arriving late at night, opposite.*
Guarulhos Airport   São Paulo is Brazil's main international entry point and its domestic transport hub. Nearly all international flights and many of the cheapest internal flights arrive at Guarulhos Airport (Guarulhos, 25 km northeast of the city, T011-2445 2945, www.aeroportoguarulhos.net), officially known as **Cumbica**. Be sure to allow plenty of time for transit and to arrive with plenty of time for checking in as long queues form for immigration and customs: passenger numbers have doubled at the airport over the past decade, airport upgrade works are late and insufficient and the airport is often overcrowded.

There are plenty of banks and money changers in the international and domestic arrivals hall (which are in different terminals), open daily 0800-2200, and cafés, restaurants and gift shops on the 2nd floor and arrivals lobby. There is a post office on the 3rd floor of Asa A. Tourist information, including city and regional city maps and copies of the entertainment section from the *Folha de São Paulo* newspaper with current listings, is available from **Secretaria de Esportes e Turismo** (**SET**) (ground floor of both terminals, Mon-Fri 0730-2200, Sat, Sun and holidays 0900-2100).

Rush-hour traffic can easily turn the 40-min journey between the airport and the centre into an hour or even two. Rush hours are 0700-0900 and 1700-1830. A new fast road (with exclusive bus lanes) linking the airport and the city centre in Tucuruvi (on the Linha 1-Azul *metrô* line) is due to open this year.

Designated airport taxis charge around US$30-45 to the centre, depending on traffic and time of day (they charge more at night), and operate on a ticket system: go to the 2nd booth on leaving the terminal and book a co-op taxi at the **Taxi Comum** counter;

ON THE ROAD

Arriving late at night

São Paulo's international airport, **Cumbica** in Guarulhos, has 24-hour facilities in case you arrive late at night or in the early hours of the morning. It is a long drive from the airport to the city. The air-conditioned **Airport Bus Service** operates night buses on most of its routes, except the service to Avenida Paulista which doesn't run from 2315 to 0610. **Emtu** buses don't operate between 2240 and 0540 to destinations such as Praça da República, although they do run to Congonhas all night. A late night taxi to the centre of the city will cost around US$35.

Congonhas Airport, which is connected to most of Brazil's major cities, is in the city centre. Although there are no 24-hour services there are hotels across the road from the terminal (via the footbridge) and most areas in and around the centre are a maximum of US$20 taxi ride away.

There are a number of hotels close to both airports which have late night/early morning check-in with prior notice.

Within 6 km of Guarulhos are Slaviero Fast Sleep Guarulhos (www.fastsleep. com.br), Ibis Guarulhos (www.ibis.com) and the Pullman (www.pullmanhotels.com).

Within 1 km of Congonhas are Ibis Sao Paulo Congonhas (www.ibis.com), **Transamerica Executive Congonhas** (www.transamericagroup.com.br) and **Blue Tree Premium** (www.bluetree.com.br).

these are the best value. **Guarucoop** (T011-6440 7070, 24 hrs, www.guarucoop.com. br) is a leading, safe radio taxi company operating from the airport. Prices are around 15% higher than **Taxi Comum** co-op taxis.

The quickest and most comfortable way (short of taking a taxi) to reach the city/airport is on the fast, a/c **Airport Bus Service** (T0800-285 3047, www.airportbusservice. com.br) leaving from outside international Arrivals (look for their distinctive red and blue logo outside the main exit or ask at the tourist information desk if you can't find the lounge), where it has a ticket office. Buses make no stops before they reach central São Paulo. It has routes as follows: to the Tietê bus terminal (40 mins); Praça da República (1 hr); Av Paulista (1 hr 15 mins, but may take longer as it calls at hotels); Itaim Bibi (1 hr 20 mins); Brooklin Novo – World Trade Centeri (1 hr 10 mins), Barra Funda Rodoviária (1 hr 20 mins); Av Luís Carlos Berrini (1 hr 30 mins); Aeroporto Congonhas (1 hr 10 mins), all US$11, under 5s are free.

Most buses leave at least once an hour 0530-2400 and every 90 mins thereafter, though there are no services after 2215 to Barra Funda and 2315 to Av Paulista and Brooklin Novo. A free newspaper and a bottle of water are provided for the journey. They also run a service directly from the airport to Ubatuba and São Sebastião (for Ilhabela). Full details of this and other services are listed on their website.

The following **Emtu buses** (www.emtu. sp.gov.br/aeroporto), run every 30-45 mins (depending on the bus line) from Guarulhos between 0545 and 2215, to the following locations: **Nos 257** and **299** for Guarulhos to Metrô Tatuape (for the red metro line and connections to the centre), US$1.50; **No 258** for Congonhas airport via Av 23 de Maio and Av Rubem Berta, US$11; **No 259** for the Praça da República via Luz and Av Tiradentes, US$11; **No 316** for the principal hotels around Paulista and Jardins via Av Paulista, R Haddock Lobo and R Augusta, US$11; **No 437** for Itaím and Av Brigadeiro Faria

Lima in the new business district, via Av Nove de Julho and Av Presidente Juscelino Kubitschek; and **No 472** for the Barra Funda Rodoviária and *metrô* station via Rodoviária Tiete. A full timetable for each line with precise leaving times is listed on the website.

If you have a flight connection to **Congonhas**, your airline will provide a courtesy bus.

Congonhas Airport The domestic airport, Congonhas (Av Washington Luiz, 7 km south of the centre, 5 km from Jardins, T011-5090 9000, www.aeroporto congonhas.net), is used for the Rio–São Paulo shuttle (US$60-120 single, depending on availability). The shuttle services operate every 30 mins 0630-2230. Sit on the left-hand side for views to Rio de Janeiro, the other side coming back; book flights in advance. To get to Congonhas Airport, take a bus or *metrô*/bus (see www.sptrans.com.br) or a taxi (roughly US$15-25, depending on traffic, from the centre, Vila Madalena or Jardins). A new metro line – the Jade line – is expected to connect to the aiport by 2017.

Viracopos Airport A number of flights with **Azul** (www.voeazul. com.br) run from Viracopos Airport in the city of Campinas around 95 km from São Paulo, which the company cheekily calls São Paulo Campinas airport. Fares are very competitive and the company runs a bus connection between Campinas and São Paulo which connects with the flights. Azul buses leave from Congonhas airport, Terminal Barra Funda and Shopping Eldorado (Estação CPTM Hebraica Rebouças) around every 30 mins; details are on the website. To reach these from Guarulhos you will need to take a cab. Viracopos is an efficient airport with a helpful information desk, a Campinas tourist office (not always manned), food outlets, shops, ATMs and a bank upstairs, car hire and 2 taxi offices. **VB** and **Lira** have frequent buses to **Tietê** for US$3.50 and **VB** to **Campinas** US$2.60; their joint office is in

the car hire section. The nearest hotels are about 7 km away: **Golden Park Viracopos** (T19-3725 1600, www.goldenparkviracopos. com.br) and **Ibis Indaiatuba** (T19-3801 2400, www.ibis.com). Campinas is a provincial university town with little to see.

Bus

Local City buses in São Paulo are operated by **SP Trans** (www.sptrans.com.br), who have an excellent bus route planner on their website. The system is fairly self-explanatory even for non-Portuguese speakers, with boxes allowing you to select a point of departure (*de*) and destination (*para*). It also enables you to plan using a combination of bus, *metrô* and urban light railway (*trem*). Google maps mark São Paulo bus stops and numbers. Right clicking on the number shows the bus route and time and there is a search facility for planning routes.

There is a flat fee of US$1.20 for any bus ride, payable to a conductor sitting behind a turnstile in the bus. The conductors are helpful in indicating where to hop on and off. Buses are marked with street names indicating their routes, but these routes can be confusing for visitors and services.

Maps of the bus and *metrô* system are available at depots, eg Anhangabaú. See also Getting around, page 26.

Long-distance See www.buscaonibus. com.br or www.passagem-em-domicilio. com.br (in Portuguese only) for information on the latest services and prices. Both sites give times and routes and redirect to the bus company website, through which it is possible to buy tickets. There are 4 bus terminals: **Tietê**, **Barra Funda**, **Bresser** and **Jabaquara**. All are connected to the *metrô* system.

Rodoviária Tietê This is the main bus station and has a convenient *metrô* station. Unfortunately the only way to the platforms is by stairs which makes it very difficult for people with heavy luggage and almost impossible for those in a wheelchair. Tietê

O Bilhete Único

This electronic ticket is similar to a London Oyster card – integrating bus, *metrô* and light railway in a single, rechargeable plastic swipe card. US$0.90 serves for one *metrô* or CPTM journey and three bus journeys within the space of three hours and cards must be validated before travel, either in the turnstile on the *metro* or at a machine at the bus stop before boarding a bus. Swipe cards can be bought at *metrô* stations.

handles buses to the interior of São Paulo state, to all state capitals and international destinations. To **Rio**, 6 hrs, every 30 mins, US$25, special section for this route in the *rodoviária*, request the coastal route via Santos (*via litoral*) unless you wish to go the direct route. To **Florianópolis**, 11 hrs, US$110 (*leito* US$95). To **Porto Alegre**, 18 hrs, US$60. To **Curitiba**, 6 hrs, US$25. To **Salvador**, 30 hrs, US$100. To **Recife**, 40 hrs, US$120. To **Campo Grande**, 14 hrs, US$180. To **Cuiabá**, 24 hrs, US$65. To **Porto Velho**, 60 hrs (or more), US$100. To **Brasília**, 16 hrs, US$60 (*executivo* US$60). To **Foz do Iguaçu**, 16 hrs, US$30, To **Paraty**, 6 hrs, US$15. To **São Sebastião**, 4 hrs, US$15 (ask for 'via Bertioga' if you want to go by the coast road, a beautiful journey but few buses take this route as it is longer).

International connections Buses to Uruguay, Argentina and Paraguay.
    Barra Funda (Metrô Barra Funda), to cities in southern **São Paulo state** and many destinations in Paraná, including **Foz do Iguaçu** (check for special prices on buses to **Ciudad del Este**, which can be cheaper than buses to Foz). Buses to **Cananéia** daily at 0900 and 1430, 4 hrs. Alternatively, go via **Registro** (buses hourly), from where there are 7 buses daily to Cananéia and regular connections to **Curitiba**.
    Bresser (Metrô Bresser), for **Cometa** (T011-6967 7255) or **Transul** (T011-6693 8061) serving destinations in Minas Gerais. **Belo Horizonte**, 8 hrs, US$35.
    Jabaquara (at the southern end of the *metrô* line), is used by buses to **Santos**, US$7,

every 15 mins, taking about 50 mins, last bus at 0100. Also serves destinations on the southern coast of São Paulo state.

Car hire
The major names all serve São Paulo and have offices at the airports.

CPTM (urban light railway)
The **CPTM** (**Companhia Paulista de Trens Metropolitanos**) (www.cptm.sp.gov.br) is an urban light railway which serves to extend the *metrô* along the margins of the Tietê and Pinheiros rivers and to the outer city suburbs. There are 6 lines, which are colour-coded like the *metrô*. Ticket prices on the CPTM are the same as the *metrô* (see below and box, above).
Linha 7 Rubi (ruby) runs from Jundiaí, a satellite commuter town, to the Estação da Luz via Barra Funda and the Palmeiras football stadium.
Linha 8 Diamante (diamond) runs from Amador Bueno to the Estação Júlio Prestes railway station in Luz, near the Pinacoteca and next to the Estação da Luz via Osasco.
Linha 9 Esmeralda (emerald) runs between the suburb of Osasco and the suburb of Grajaú in the far south. This is the a useful line for tourists as it runs along the Pinheiros river, stopping at Pinheiros (where there is an interchange for the Metrô Linha Amarela), the Cidade Universitária (for Butantã), Hebraica-Rebouças (for Shopping Eldorado and the Azul bus to Campinas airport, see page 66), Cidade Jardim (for Shopping Cidade Jardim, see page 63), Vila Olímpia (close to one of

the nightlife centres) and Berrini (in the new business district).

Linha 10 Turquesa (turquoise) runs from Rio Grande da Serra in the Serra do Mar mountains (from where there are onward trains to Paranapiacaba) to the Estação da Luz.

Linha 11 Coral (coral) runs from the Estudantes suburb in the far east to the Estação Julio Prestes via Mogi das Cruzes, and the Corinthians stadium at Itaquera, where there is an interchange for the Metrô Linha 3 Vermelha. Expect this train service to be very busy.

Linha 12 Safira (sapphire) runs from Calmon Viana suburb in the east to Brás where there is an interchange for the Metrô Linha 3 Vermelha.

Metrô

The best way to get around the city is on the efficient and safe **metrô system** (daily 0500-2400, www.metro.sp.gov.br, with a clear journey planner and information in Portuguese and English). It is integrated with the overground CPTM light railway. São Paulo's was the first *metrô* in Brazil, beginning operations in 1975. It now has 5 main lines with a new line connecting to the airport due to open in 2017.

Directions are indicated by the name of the terminus station. Network maps are displayed only in the upper concourses of the *metrô* stations; there are none on the platforms. Many of the maps on the internet are confusing as they incorporate the CPTM overground train routes, also with colour codes.

Journeys can get extremely crowded at peak times (0700-1000, 1630-1900). Services are also plagued by unannounced and unexplained stops and cancellations.

Fares are at a flat rate of US$.90. See also box, page 67.

Linha 1 Azul (blue) runs from Tucuruvi in the north to the Rodoviária Jabaraquara in the south and passing through Luz, the centre and Liberdade.

Linha 2 Verde (green) runs from Vila Madalena to Vila Prudente, via Consolação, Av Paulista and the MASP art gallery.

Linha 3 Vermelha (red) runs from the Palmeiras football stadium in Barra Funda to the Corinthians football stadium in Itaquera, via the city centre

Linha 4 Amarela (yellow) will run between between Morumbi football stadium and Luz, via USP University at Butantã, Faria Lima and Av Paulista. At present not all the stations are open and the line only extends west as far as Butantã but the line is expected to be completed by 2017.

Linha 5 Lilás (lilac) running in São Paulo's far southwest, between Capão Redondo favela and Adolfo Pinheiro. An extension to Chacara Klabin on the 2 Verde line via Estação Eucaliptus (for Moema and Shopping Ibirapuera) is expected to open by 2017.

Taxi

Taxis in São Paulo are white with a green light on the roof. They display their tariffs in the window (starting at US$1.20) and have meters. Ordinary taxis are hailed on the street or more safely at taxi stations (*postos*), such as Praça da República, which are never more than 5 mins' walk away anywhere in the city. Hotels, restaurants and some venues will call a taxi on request, either from a *posto* or a taxi driver.

For Radio Taxis, which are more expensive but involve fewer hassles, try: **Central Radio Táxi**, T011-6914 6630; **São Paulo Rádio Táxi**, T011-5583 2000; **Fácil**, T011-6258 5947; or **Aero Táxi**, T011-6461 4090. Alternatively, look in the phone book; calls are not accepted from public phones.

Train

From **Estação da Luz** and **Estação Júlio Prestes** (Metrô Luz).

Iguaçu Falls
& the Pantanal

Essential Iguaçu Falls

Access

From Brazil Buses leave Foz do Iguaçu town from the **Rodoviária Terminal Urbana** (Avenida Juscelino Kubitschek, one block from the infantry barracks). The *Transbalan No 120* service runs to the falls every half an hour 0530-2330, past the airport and **Hotel Tropical das Cataratas** (40 minutes, US$0.75 one way, payable in reais only). Return buses run 0800-1900. The bus terminates at the visitor centre, where you must pay the entrance fee and transfer to the free park shuttle bus, which leaves every five minutes 0900-1830. If driving, cars must be left in the visitor centre car park. Taxis from Foz do Iguaçu charge US$15 one way. You can negotiate in advance the return trip, including waiting, or pay separately for each journey. Many hotels organize tours to the falls, which have been recommended in preference to taxi rides. Be wary of transfer offers from Iguaçu's travel agencies – they are often even more expensive than taking your own taxi.

From Argentina Transportes El Práctico buses run every half hour from the Puerto Iguazú bus terminal, stopping at the park entrance to buy entry tickets. Fares cost US$6 return to the visitor centre. The first bus leaves at 0700, and the last return is at 1900, journey time 30 minutes. Buses are erratic, especially when wet, even though the times are clearly indicated. There are fixed rates for taxis, US$30 one-way for up to five people. A tour from the bus terminal, taking in both sides of the falls, costs US$10.

For more information on the border crossing, see box, page 181.

Entry fee

Tickets costs about US$15 (Brazil) or US$19 (Argentina) (with a discount for Mercosur members). If you buy your ticket on the Argentine side only Argentine pesos are accepted (there are ATMs at the entrance, and a currency exchange; poor rates); if you buy on the Brazilian side you can pay in dollars, euro or reais.

Getting around

There are national parks protecting extensive rainforest on both sides. Transport between the two parks is via the Ponte Tancredo Neves, as there is no crossing at the falls themselves.

Money

Whether you stay on the Argentine or Brazilian side, most establishments will accept reais, pesos or dollars. Cross-border transport usually accepts Paraguayan guaraníes as well.

When to go

The busiest times are holiday periods and on Sunday, when helicopter tours are particularly popular.

Time required

Both the Argentine and Brazilian parks can, if necessary, be visited in a day, starting at about 0700. However, in the heat, the brisk pace needed for a rapid tour is exhausting. To fully appreciate the falls, the forest, with its wildlife and butterflies, you need to spend a leisurely two days and get well away from the visitor areas.

What to take

In the rainy season when water levels are high, waterproof coats or swimming costumes are advisable for some of the lower catwalks and for boat trips. Cameras should be carried in a plastic bag (a completely water-tight one if you plan on taking a boat trip on the river). Wear shoes with good soles, as the rocks can be very slippery in places.

Paraná

Paraná is most famous for the Iguaçu Falls, the largest and most magnificent waterfalls in the Americas. No guidebook can do justice to the spectacle and they are a must on any itinerary to Brazil.

Iguaçu Falls

the most spectacular waterfalls on Earth, in a vast rainforest

Foz do Iguaçu, or Las Cataratas del Iguazú as they are known in Spanish, are arguably the most remarkable waterfalls in the world. Situated on the Rio Iguaçu (meaning 'big water' in Guaraní), which forms the border between Argentina and Brazil, they are made up of no less than 275 separate waterfalls. The Iguaçu area is heavily forested, largely protected as national parks (with healthy populations of indicator species like jaguar and puma) and with wilds extending from Brazil into Argentina and Paraguay along a triple frontier (Paraguay does not own territory at the falls themselves but the Paraguayan city of Ciudad del Este lies just a few kilometres away).

The most spectacular portion of the falls is the **Garganta do Diabo** (Devil's Throat), a thundering curtain of water which sits at the heart of a 28-km-long cliff-face stretching downstream to the Alto Río Paraná. The Garganta lies right next to the **Belmond Hotel** (see page 78), the only accommodation at the falls themselves. It is spectacular; the water tumbles and roars over the craggy brown cliffs, framed by verdant rainforest encrusted with bromeliads, orchids, begonias and dripping ferns. A seemingly perpetual rainbow hovers over the scene and toco toucans, flocks of parakeets, caciques and great dusky swifts dodge in and out of the vapour whilst a vast number of butterflies dance over the forest walkways and lookouts nearby.

A visit to the Argentinian side enables you to stand right over the Garganta itself, on a platform reached via a long winding walkway which extends out over the river. See Essential Iguaçu Falls, opposite.

Weather Iguaçu Falls

January	February	March	April	May	June
33°C	33°C	31°C	28°C	25°C	23°C
20°C	20°C	18°C	15°C	12°C	10°C
182mm	104mm	173mm	126mm	155mm	151mm

July	August	September	October	November	December
24°C	25°C	27°C	29°C	31°C	33°C
10°C	11°C	14°C	15°C	17°C	19°C
84mm	96mm	148mm	171mm	112mm	185mm

The town nearest the falls is also, confusingly, called Iguaçu – or to give it its full name – Foz de Iguaçu. There are many advantages to staying in Foz do Iguaçu town and commuting to the Argentine side; it has, for example, the best infrastructure, such as a much bigger choice of hotels and restaurants. Around 80% of the falls lie in Argentina, which offers the most spectacular views. The Brazilian park offers a superb panoramic view of the whole falls and is best visited in the morning (four hours is enough for the highlights) when the light is better for photography. The Argentine park (which requires at least half a day) includes a railway trip in the entrance fee as well as offering closer views of the individual falls. Sunset is best from the Brazilian side.

Parque Nacional Foz do Iguaçu (Brazil)
The Brazilian national park was founded in 1939 and designated a World Heritage Site by UNESCO in 1986. The park covers 185,262 ha on the Brazilian side and 67,000 ha on the Argentinian side, extending along the north bank of the Rio Iguaçu, then sweeping northwards to Santa Tereza do Oeste on the BR-277. The subtropical rainforest benefits from the added humidity in the proximity of the falls, creating an environment rich in flora and fauna. Given the massive popularity of the falls, the national parks on either side of the frontier are surprisingly little visited.

1 Iguaçu Falls orientation

Where to stay 🛏
Hostel Natura 1

HI Paudimar
Campestre 2

Fauna The parks on both sides of the falls are replete with wildlife and are a haven for birders. The most common mammals seen are coatis, which look like long-nosed racoons and squeakily demand food from visitors; do not be tempted as these small

Tip...
Be sure to visit both the Brazilian and Argentinian sides. They offer quite different experiences.

animals can be aggressive. There are other mammals here too, including jaguar, puma, ocelot and margay, which can occasionally be seen along the park roads just before and after dawn. They are wary of humans, although in 2003 a jaguar broke into the Parque das Aves (see page 79) and ate the zoo's prize caiman. Most frequently encountered are little red brocket deer, white-eared opossum, paca (which look like large dappled guinea pigs) and a subspecies of the brown capuchin monkey. Other mammals include white-lipped peccary, bush dog and southern river otter. The endangered tegu lizard is common. Over 100 species of butterfly have been identified, among them the electric blue morpho, the poisonous red and black heliconius and species of papilionidae and pieridae.

The birdlife is especially rewarding. Five members of the toucan family can be seen: toco and red-breasted toucans, chestnut-eared araçari, saffron and spot-billed toucanets. From the bamboo stands you may see spotted bamboo wren, grey-bellied spinetail, several antshrikes and short-tailed ant-thrush. In the forest you might see rufous-thighed kite, black-and-white hawk-eagle, black-fronted piping-guan, blue ground dove, dark-billed cuckoo, black-capped screech-owl, surucua trogon, rufous-winged antwren, black-crowned tityra, red-ruffed fruitcrow, white-winged swallow, plush-crested jay, cream-bellied gnatcatcher, black-goggled and magpie tanagers, green-chinned euphonia, black-throated and ultra-marine grosbeaks, yellow-billed cardinal and red-crested finch.

➡ **Iguaçu Falls maps**
1 Iguaçu Falls orientation, page 74
2 Iguaçu Falls, page 76
3 Foz do Iguaçu, page 80

The falls All cars and public buses stop at the **visitor centre**, where there are souvenir shops, a **Banco do Brasil** with ATM and *câmbio*, a small café and car park. If possible, visit on a weekday when the walks are less crowded. The centre is open daily 0900-1700. There is a US$4 car-parking fee, payable only in reais. This includes a transfer to the free park shuttle bus.

The first stop on the shuttle bus is the **Macuco Safari** ① *www.macucosafari. com.br, 0900-1730, leaving every 10-15 mins, 2-hr tour with optional boat trip on the river, US$50, under-12s half-price (bookable through most agencies, which may charge a premium for transfers).* The safari visits the forest near the falls on an electric jeep to a beach on the Garganta do Diabo. From here there are great views of the falls from below and the option to take a boat to the falls themselves; trips dunk visitors under one of the smaller cascades. Be sure to bring a fully waterproof, sealable plastic or rubber bag. Despite what guides say to the contrary, you and all your belongings will get completely soaked on this boat trip, which is the only part of the safari that can't be done solo. Visitors to Iguaçu will see as much wildlife and forest walking their own trails and boardwalks as they will with Macuco.

Iguazú Explorer ⓘ *Sheraton Hotel, www.iguazujungle.com, daily 0845-1530, 80 mins, US$60, no under 12s*, offers a 'Gran Aventura', or Great Adventure, a similar though shorter trip to **Macuco's** from the Argentinian side. It involves bombing through the jungle in a truck followed by a short walk and a boat trip up the Garganto do Diabo to the falls. A better deal is the 12-minute solo boat trip up the Garganta for US$13, without the truck and trail walk.

The second stop is the **Cataratas Trail** (starting from the hotel of the same name; non-residents can eat at the hotel, midday and evening buffets). This 1.5-km paved walk runs part of the way down the cliff near the rim of the falls, giving a stupendous view of the whole Argentine side of the falls. It ends up almost under the powerful Floriano Falls; from here there is a lift to the top of the Floriano Falls; a path adjacent to the lift leads to Porto Canoa. A catwalk at the foot of the Floriano Falls gives a good view of the Garganta do Diabo.

The **Porto Canoas** complex, with its snack bar, toilets, souvenir shops and terraces with views of the falls, was completed in 2000 after some controversy. Its restaurant serves a hearty US$15 buffet.

2 Iguaçu Falls

Parque Nacional Iguazú (Argentina)

Created in 1934, the park extends over an area of 67,620 ha, most of which is covered by the same subtropical rainforest as on the Brazilian side. It is crossed by Route 101, a dirt road that runs southeast to Bernardo de Yrigoyen on the Brazilian frontier. Buses operate along this route in dry weather, offering a view of the park.

Fauna You would have to be very lucky to see jaguars, tapirs, brown capuchin monkeys, collared anteaters and coatimundi. As in Brazil, very little of the fauna in the park can be seen around the falls; even on the nature trails described below you need to go in the early morning and have luck on your side. Of the 400 species of bird, you are most likely to spot the black-crowned night heron, plumed kite, white-eyed parakeet,

⇒ **Iguaçu Falls maps**
1 Iguaçu Falls orientation, page 74
2 **Iguaçu Falls, page 76**
3 Foz do Iguaçu, page 80

Where to stay 🛏
Belmond Hotel
das Cataratas **1**

Sheraton Internacional
Iguazú Resort **2**

BACKGROUND

Iguaçu Falls

The Caiagangue people originally inhabited the region, but the first European visitor to the falls was the Spaniard Alvaro Núñez Cabeza de Vaca in 1541. He nearly fell off one of the waterfalls on his search for a connection between the Brazilian coast and the Río de la Plata, and named them the Saltos de Santa María (Santa Maria waterfalls). Though the falls were well known to the Jesuit missionaries, they were largely forgotten until the area was explored by a Brazilian expedition sent out by the Paraguayan president, Solano López, in 1863.

blue-winged parrolet, great dusky swift, scale-throated hermit, suruca trogon, Amazon kingfisher, toco toucan, tropical kingbird, boat-billed flycatcher, red-rumped cacique, and the colourful purple-throated euphonia.

The falls The park is open daily 0800-1800 in summer and 0800-1700 in winter. Tickets must be paid for in Argentine pesos only (US$22); there are two cash machines by the entrance. Guests at the **Hotel Sheraton** should pay and get tickets stamped at the hotel to avoid paying again. The visitor centre includes a museum of local fauna and an auditorium for slide shows (available on request, minimum of eight people). It also sells a good guide book on Argentine birds. Food and drinks are available in the park but are expensive, so it is best to take your own. There is a Telecom kiosk at the bus stop.

A free train service leaves every 30 minutes from the visitor centre, departing for the start of two sets of walkways, both taking about an hour. The '**Circuito Inferior**' or Lower Trail, leads down very steep steps to the lower falls and the start of the boat trip to Isla San Martin (see below). The easy '**Circuito Superior**', Upper Trail, follows the top of the falls, giving panoramic views. The **Sendero Verde** path, taking about 20 minutes from near the visitor centre, leads to the start of the Upper and Lower trails. A second train route takes visitors to the start of an easy walkway that leads just over 1 km to the Garganta del Diablo (Devil's Throat), last train at 1610. A visit here is particularly recommended in the evening when the light is best and the swifts are returning to roost on the cliffs, some behind the water.

Below the falls, a free ferry leaves regularly, subject to demand, and connects the Lower Trail with **Isla San Martín**. A steep path on the island leads to the top of the hill, where there are trails to some of the less-visited falls and rocky pools (take bathing gear in summer).

Listings Iguaçu Falls *maps p74 and p76*

Tourist information

Both parks have visitor centres, though the information provided by the Argentine centre is far superior to that in the Brazilian centre. Tourist facilities on both sides are constantly being improved.

A useful guidebook is *Iguazú, The Laws of the Jungle* by Santiago G de la Vega, Contacto Silvestre Ediciones (1999), available from the visitor centre, US$6.50 along with glossy picture books and souvenirs.

See also www.fozdoiguaçu.pr.gov.br.

Where to stay

Brazil

The best hotels with the most modern facilities and the easiest access to Iguaçu are all near the falls. There is little here for budget travellers. Sleeping in your car inside the park is prohibited. You can camp at the **HI Paudimar**, but it's pretty cold and damp in winter.

$$$$ Belmond Hotel das Cataratas
Directly overlooking the falls, 28 km from Foz, T021-2545 8878, www.hoteldascataratas. com.br.
This grand hotel in the **Orient Express** group is the only establishment within the park on the Brazilian side. It is housed in a mock belle époque building with generous rooms, grand public areas and a poolside garden visited by numerous birds, butterflies and, at dawn, small mammals. The hotel is right next to the falls offering by far the easiest access and the best chance to beat the crowds.

$$-$ HI Paudimar Campestre
Rodovia das Cataratas Km 12.5, Remanso Grande, near the airport, T045-3529 6061, www.paudimar.com.br.
Youth hostel with spotless single-sex dorms, pool, communal kitchen, football pitch, camping. The gardens are visited by birds and small mammals. Full details of how to reach the hostel on the website.

$$-$ Hostel Natura
Rodovia das Cataratas Km 12.5, Remanso Grande, T045-3529 6949, www.hostelnatura. com (near the Paudimar).
Rustic hostel with a small pool set in fields pocked with large ponds and on the road to the park. Public areas include a pool table, TV lounge and a small kitchen. Their website has detailed instructions for how to reach them.

Argentina
Camping is possible at **Camping Puerto Canoas**, 600 m from Puerto Canoas, with tables, but no other facilities; the nearest drinking water is at the park entrance.

$$$$ La Aldea de la Selva
Puerto Iguazú, T+54 3757-493010, www.laaldeadelaselva.com.
Attractive hard wood and brick cabins set in rainforest on the edge of a protected area near the falls. These are linked by low-lit boardwalks, which also connect to a swimming pool, and which give a real sense of immersion in the forest. Decent restaurant and free Wi-Fi throughout.

$$$$ Sheraton Internacional Iguazú Resort
Parque Nacional Iguazú, www.sheratoniguazu.com.
A wedge of 1970s concrete built on the opposite side of the falls from the Belomond **Hotel das Cataratas**. Views are spectacular, especially from rooms with balconies on the upper storey.

Restaurants

Brazil

$$$ Belmond Hotel das Cataratas
See Where to stay, above.
The nearest dining to the falls themselves, and open to non-guests eager for the moonlight view.

What to do

A number of activities are offered, both from the visitor centre and through agencies in Puerto Iguazú (Argentina); see page 83. On clear nights the moon casts a blue halo over the falls. During the full moon, there are sometimes night-time walking tours between the **Hotel Sheraton** and the falls.

Birdwatching
Iguazú Birdwatching, *Perito Moreno 217, T+54 3757 422 554, www.iguazubirdwatching. com.ar.* The forests and national park around Iguaçu have a broad range of Atlantic coastal rainforest species, especially off the beaten

tracks or at the beginning and end of the day. Argentinian birder, Daniel Somay, speaks good English and knows his birds, where to find them and can organize equipment given a little notice.

Tour operators

Most of the mid-range and smart hotels have in-house tour agency. Packages and prices vary little.

Explorador, *Perito Moreno 217 (and the Sheraton Hotel, see above), T03757-421632, http://rainforest.iguazuargentina.com*.

A range of rainforest safaris and the standard excursions to the falls.

Iguazú Explorer, *visitor centre, Argentine side of the falls, T+54-0375 742 1696, www. iguazujungle.com*. The Argentine counterpart to **Macuco Safari** (see under Foz do Iguaçu, page 83), with combinations of trail walks, boat rides and 4WD safaris. Trips are shorter and noisier than with **Macuco** (as they use petrol rather than electric engines), but the tours are a little cheaper (US$45 for boat, trail and boat excursions) and it's possible to do just the boat trip (US$20).

Foz do Iguaçu and around

the closest town to the falls

The proximity of the falls has made Foz (260,000) the third most visited town in Brazil. It has no attractions of its own but is only 28 km from the falls and although there are some upmarket hotel options, the town has a greater range of cheap accommodation and restaurants.

From the town it is possible to visit a number of beaches on the shores of **Lake Itaipu** (see Itaipu Dam, below); the closest are at Bairro de Três Lagoas (Km 723 on BR-277), and in the municipality of Santa Terezinha do Itaipu (US$1.25), 34 km from Foz. The leisure parks have grassy areas with kiosks, barbecue sites and offer fishing as well as bathing. It is also possible to take boat trips on the lake.

The bird park, **Parque das Aves** ① *Rodovia das Cataratas Km 16, www.parquedasaves. com.br, US$8*, is well worth visiting. It contains rare South American (and foreign) birds including various currasows, guans, parrots, macaws and toucans. These are housed in large aviaries through which you can walk, with the birds flying and hopping around you.

Essential Foz do Iguaçu

Finding your feet

Foz do Iguaçu's **Aeroporto Internacional de Cataratas** is 12 km from the town centre. Taxis cost US$15 to the town centre and vice versa. **Transbalan** (Aeroporto/Parque Nacional) buses run to town, US$0.75, but don't permit large amounts of luggage; backpacks are fine. They run every 20 minutes 0545-2400. The buses go to the local bus station, the Terminal de Transporte Urbano, in the centre.

There are two terminals in Iguaçu so sometimes you have to change buses, but

you only pay once so the system acts a bit like a metro – it's an integrated transport system. Many hotels run minibus services for a small charge. From the airport, buses run to cities throughout southeastern Brazil and to Asunción in Paraguay. The rest of Argentina can easily be reached from Puerto Iguazú just across the border.

The **Foz do Iguaçu Rodoviária** is 4 km from the centre on road to Curitiba and receives long-distance buses. Buses to the centre cost US$0.75, taxis US$5.

There is also a butterfly house. The bird park is within walking distance of the **Hotel San Martín**. The **HI Paudimar Falls Hostel** (see Where to stay, below) offers a discount for its guests.The national park bus stops here, 100 m before the entrance to the falls.

Itaipu Dam
Visitor centre, T045-3520 6676, www.itaipu.gov.br. There are 3 tours of the dam: Special Tour (6 stops; US$16), Company Tour (for companies, institutions, research centres, universities, etc) and Panoramic Tour (panoramic views of the power plant and dam; US$7). Tours embark every hours or so, with most starting at 0800 and the last leaving at 1600. Buses marked 'Itaipu' run from Foz do Iguaçu's Terminal Urbana, US$1.

The Itaipu Dam, on the Río Paraná, is the site of the largest single power hydroelectric power station in the world built jointly by Brazil and Paraguay and supplying some 20%

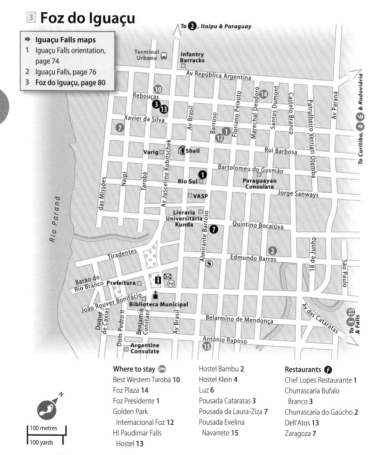

③ **Foz do Iguaçu**

➡ **Iguaçu Falls maps**
1 Iguaçu Falls orientation, page 74
2 Iguaçu Falls, page 76
3 Foz do Iguaçu, page 80

Where to stay 🛏	Hostel Bambu **2**	Restaurants 🍴
Best Western Tarobá **10**	Hostel Klein **4**	Chef Lopes Restaurante **1**
Foz Plaza **14**	Luz **6**	Churrascaria Bufalo
Foz Presidente **1**	Pousada Cataratas **3**	Branco **3**
Golden Park	Pousada da Laura-Ziza **7**	Churrascaria do Gaúcho **2**
Internacional Foz **12**	Pousada Evelina	Dell'Atos **13**
HI Paudimar Falls	Navarrete **15**	Zaragoza **7**
Hostel **13**		

100 metres
100 yards

of all Brazil's electricity. Construction of this massive scheme began in 1975 and it came into operation in 1984. The main dam is 8 km long, creating a lake that covers 1400 sq km. The height of the main dam is equivalent to a 65-storey building, the amount of concrete used in its construction is 15 times more than that used for the Channel Tunnel between England and France. The Paraguayan side may be visited from Ciudad del Este. Both governments are proud to trumpet the accolade, 'one of the seven wonders of the modern world' (the only one in South America), which was given to it by the American Society of Civil Engineering in Popular Mechanics in 1995.

The **Ecomuseu de Itaipu** ① *T0800-645 4645, Tue-Sun 0800-1630, closed on Mon, US$2.50*, and **Tatí Yupí Sanctuary Centre**, are geared to inform about the preservation of the local culture and environment, or that part of it which isn't underwater.

If it's sunny, go in the morning as the sun is behind the dam in the afternoon and you will get poor photographs.

To get to Itaipu, the 'executive' bus and agency tours are an unnecessary expense. Take bus lines '**Conjunto C Norte**' or '**Conjunto C Sul**' from Foz do Iguaçu's **Terminal de Transporte Urbano (TTU)**, tickets US$1.20.

Listings Foz do Iguaçu and around *map p80*

Tourist information

TeleTur operates a toll-free number, T0800-45 1516, which travellers can call from anywhere in Brazil to get information about Foz do Iguaçu. Operators speak English.

Secretaria Municipal de Turismo
Av das Cataratas 2330, Vila Yolanda (near the Argentine border), T045-2105 8115, www.pmfi.pr.gov.br/turismo. Daily 0800-1400.

Tourist booth
At the rodoviária, *T045-3901 3575. Daily 0630-1800. There's another one at the airport (T045-3522 1022, 0700-2100) with a free map and bus information, and at the Terminal de Transporte Urbano (T045-3523 7901, daily 0700-1830).*

Where to stay

Many hotels offer trips to the falls. In a bid to get their commission, touts may tell you the hotel of your choice no longer exists, or offer you room rates below what is actually charged. In high season (eg Christmas-New Year) you will not find a room under US$15, but in low season there are many good deals.

$$$$ Golden Park Internacional Foz
R Alm Barroso 2006, T045-3521 4100, www.goldenparkinternacionalfoz.com.br.
A faded 5-star hotel (the only one in Foz town), with decent business and conference facilities. Spacious but very standard upmarket hotel rooms and services.

$$ Best Western Tarobá
R Tarobá 1048, near Terminal Urbana, T045-2102 7700, www.hoteltarobafoz.com.br.
Good value. Clean with modern, smart rooms, a tiny indoor pool and helpful staff. There is a travel agency in the hotel.

$$ Foz Plaza
R Marechal Deodoro 1819, T045-3521 3505, www.fozplaza.com.br.
Serene and well-refurbished 1980s hotel with a restaurant and a bar, pool, souvenir shop, sauna and a games room. Request a room in the recently built modern annex.

$$ Foz Presidente
R Xavier da Silva 1000, T045-3572 4450, www.fozpresidentehoteis.com.br.
Restaurant, pool, with breakfast, convenient for buses. Brighter and more modern than most of Foz's offerings.

$$ Luz
Av Costa e Silva Km 5, near the rodoviária, T045-4053 9434, www.luzhotel.com.br.
Well-kept but bog standard small 1980s hotel with a buffet restaurant. Rooms have a/c and Brazilian TV.

$$ Pousada Cataratas
R Parigot de Sousa, 180, 8 km from the park near Boulevard Shopping, T045-3523 7841, www.pousadacataratas.com.br.
Well-maintained modern rooms with modest catalogue furniture, tile floors and en suite bathrooms with decent hot showers.

$$ Pousada Evelina Navarrete
R Irlan Kalichewski 171, Vila Yolanda, T045-3029 9277, www.pousadaevelinafoz.com.br.
Well-maintained dorms, doubles and singles (some with a/c) and good breakfast. Details of how to reach them on the website.

$ HI Paudimar Falls Hostel
R Antônio Raposo 820, T045-3028 5503, www.paudimarfalls.com.br.
Despite its name, the companion hostel to the **Paudimar** near the falls, is in the centre of town. It has similar facilities, with doubles, cramped dorms, pool and the usual hostel services.

$ Hostel Bambu
R Edmundo de Barros 621, T045-3523 3646, www.bambuhostels.com.
Dorms sleeping 4, 6, 8 and 10 in this hostel, in a charming location. Also has doubles and triples. Nice communal area with a swimming pool.

$ Hostel Klein
R Paris 230, Jardim Alice, T045-3025-3339, www.kleinhostel.com.
Laid-back hostel near the *rodoviária*. Friendly owners offer 10-bed dorms and 2 rooms. Tours to the falls organized. Refreshing pool and laundry service. Recommended.

$ Pousada da Laura-Ziza
R Naipi 671, T045-3572 3374, pousadalauraziza.com.

Secure and run by the enthusiastic Laura who speaks some Spanish, English, Italian and French. The hostel has a kitchen, laundry facilities and en suites and is a good place to meet other travellers. Good breakfast.

Restaurants

$$$ Chef Lopes Restaurante
Al Barroso 1713, T045-3025 3334, https://pt-br.facebook.com/ChefLopesFoz.
Smart per kilo place serving good quality beef and excellent salads. Popular with well-heeled Brazilian tourists.

$$$ Churrascaria Bufalo Branco
R Rebouças 530, T045-3523 9744, http://bufalobranco.com.br.
Superb all-you-can-eat *churrasco*, includes filet mignon, salad bar and dessert. Sophisticated surroundings and attentive service.

$$$ Zaragoza
R Quintino Bocaiúva 882, T045-3574 3084, http://restaurantezaragoza.com.br.
Large and upmarket, for Spanish dishes and seafood. Respectable wine list and one of the best à la carte menus in town.

$$ Dell'Atos
Av Juscelino Kubitschek 865, T045-3572 2785. Lunch only.
Per kilo buffet with various meats, salads, sushi, pizzas and puddings.

$$-$ Churrascaria do Gaúcho
Argentina 632 (across from bus station), T045-3029 1303.
One of the best churrascarias in the city. Friendly carvers slice up succulent meats grilled to perfection until you wave the white flag of surrender. It's as authentic a barbecue experience as there is in Brazil.

What to do

Helicopter tours
Helicopter tours over the falls leave from the **Hotel das Cataratas**, US$100 per person,

10 mins. Booked through any travel agency or direct with **Helisul**, T041-3529 7474, www. helisul.com. Apart from disturbing visitors, the helicopters are also reported to present a threat to some bird species which are laying thinner shelled eggs. As a result, the altitude of the flights has been increased, making the flight less attractive.

Tour operators

Beware of touts at the bus terminal who often overcharge for tours (they have been known to charge double the bus station price) and be sure that the park entrance fees of around US$25 and all the transfer fees are included in the price. There are many travel agents on Av Brasil and in almost all the hotels and hostels. Most do not accept credit cards.

Acquatur, *Av das Cataratas 1419, T045-3523 9554, www.acquaturturismo.com.br.* Offers a full range of tours in executive cars with bilingual guides and airport transfers.

Guayi Travel, *Av Nacional 611, T045-3027 0043, www.guayitravel.com.* Some of the best tours to both sides of the falls, Ciudad del Este, Itaipu and around, including options for birders and wildlife enthusiasts. Excellent English and Spanish. Comfortable cars and knowledgeable guides.

Macuco Safari, *Rodovia das Cataratas, Km 20, Parque Nacional do Iguaçu, T045-3529 7976 www.macucosafari.com.br.* A much tourist-tramped 2-hr walk, with an electric car ride and boat trip (the whole package must be taken), from US$100. The trails cut through subtropical forest next to Iguaçu to get up close to the base of the falls themselves. The tour is only worth taking for the boat trip (there is better walking for free on the Argentine side of the falls). Be sure to bring your own, completely waterproof, sealable bag strong enough to withstand total immersion. You will get completely soaked on this excursion and the bags provided by the company are inadequate.

STTC Turismo, *Av das Morenitas 2250, Jardim das Flores, T045-3529 6161, www.sttcturismo. com.br.* Standard packages to the Brazilian and Argentine side of the falls to Punta del Este, Itaipu and with trips on the river.

Transport

Air Daily flights to **Brasília**, **Rio**, **São Paulo**, **Rio de Janeiro**, **Curitiba** and other Brazilian cities with **Gol**, **Tam**, and **Azul**. The airport, Rodovia BR-469, Km 16.5, T045-3521 4200, is 12 km from the centre. It has a tourist office, **Banco do Brasil**, a **Bradesco** and a *câmbio*, car rental offices, a tourist office and an official taxi stand.

Bus For transport to the falls and crossing into Argentina, see box, page 181, and for Paraguay, see box, page 182.

To get to the long-distance bus station, Av Costa e Silva, T045-3522 3590, a few kilometres outside of town, take any bus that says '*rodoviária*'. There is a tourist office and luggage store. Buy onward tickets on arrival if possible as seats get booked up well in advance.

To **Curitiba**, **Pluma**, **Sulamericana**, 3 daily, paved road, US$15, 9-10 hrs; to **Guaíra** via Cascavel only, US$10, 5 hrs; to **Florianópolis**, **Catarinense** and **Reunidas**, US$28, 14 hrs; **Reunidas** to **Porto Alegre**, US$30; to **São Paulo**, 16 hrs, **Pluma** US$30, *executivo* 6 a day, plus 1 *leito*; to **Rio** several daily, US$45, 22 hrs. To **Asunción**, **Pluma**, **RYSA** (direct at 1430), US$25.

To **Buenos Aires** (Argentina), there is a bus direct from Foz (**Pluma** daily 1200, US$55). It is cheaper to go to **Posadas** via Paraguay. To **Asunción** (Paraguay), **Pluma** (0700), **RYSA** (direct at 1430, 1830), from the *rodoviária*, US$16.50 (cheaper if bought in Ciudad del Este).

Car hire Avis, at airport, T045-3523 1510. **Localiza** at airport, T045-3529 6300, and Av Juscelino Kubitschek 2878, T045-3522 1608. **Unidas**, Av Santos Dumont, 1515, near airport, T045-3339 0880.

Mato Grosso do Sul
& the
southern Pantanal

Mato Grosso do Sul is dominated by the Pantanal wetlands in the north and by the low Serra da Bodoquena mountains in the south, which surround the family-orientated ecotourism town of Bonito. The mountains are honeycombed by caves and cut by numerous glassy clear streams. Beyond the capital Campo Grande there are only a few towns of any size (with just four with populations over 55,000), and the state is a centre of soya plantations and cattle ranching. Budget tours of the Pantanal leave from the state capital, Campo Grande, which is a prosperous, modern city with lively nightlife. However, they take half a day to reach the Pantanal itself, which begins in earnest east of Campo Grande, near the cattle-ranching town of Miranda. The best *fazenda* ranch houses and tour operators are in and around Miranda itself and visitors should head directly here.

Corumbá, on the banks of the Rio Paraguai, was once a popular departure point for the Pantanal, though it is now a frontier town of dubious repute. It lies close to the Estrada Parque dirt road (which runs through the wetlands) and to Nhecolândia, a wilderness area visited by most of the Campo Grande backpacker tours.

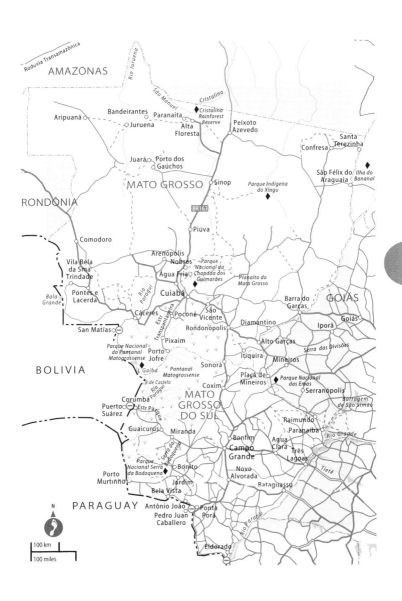

Campo Grande (population 800,000) is a pleasant, modern city laid out on a grid system, with wide avenues. It was founded in 1899 and became the state capital in 1979. Because of the *terra roxa* (red earth), it is known as the 'Cidade Morena'.

It's a prosperous, attractive rural city, but it offers few draws for travellers, who generally pass through on their way to or from the Pantanal. Tour operators based in the Pantanal, such as **Meia Lua** and **Explore Pantanal**, organize pick-ups at the bus station and airport.

Some distance from the centre is the large Parque dos Poderes, which contains the Palácio do Governo and other secretariats, paths and lovely trees. Even larger, and closer to the centre, is the 119-ha **Parque das Nações Indígenas**. It is largely covered with grassy areas and ornamental trees and is a pleasant place for a stroll or quiet read and has good birdlife. In the park is the **Museu de Arte Contemporânea (MARCO)** ⓘ *R Antônio Maria Coelho 6000, T067-3326 7449, https:// marcovirtual.wordpress.com, Tue-Fri 1200- 1800, Sat-Sun 1400-1800, free*. This preserves the largest collection of modern art in the state; permanent and temporary exhibitions. **Museu Dom Bosco (Indian Museum)** ⓘ *Av Afonso Pena 7000, Parque das Nações Indígenas, T067-3326 9788, www.mcdb.org.br, Tue-Sun 0800-1630, US$2.65*, contains relics from the various tribes who were the recipients of the Salesians aggressive missionary tactics in the early and mid-20th century. The largest collections are from the Tukano and Bororo people from the Upper Rio Negro and Mato Grosso respectively, both of whose cultures the Salesians were responsible for almost completely wiping out. It also holds temporary exhibitions. Under construction in the park is the Centro de Pesquisa e Reabilitação da Ictiofauna, commonly known as the Aquário do Pantanal, which will be the largest fresh-water aquarium in the world. In 2015 the rugby-ball shaped building and its six levels of displays and laboratories was some way from completion.

Essential Campo Grande

Finding your feet

The **airport** is 7 km from the city centre. Bus Nos 414 and 409 stop outside the airport terminal and run to the bus station, Avenida Ernesto Geisel, Avenida João Rosa Pires, Rua 26 de Agosto and Rua Rui Barbosa in the centre every 10 minutes. Buses are cash free, so buy your ticket in advance at the **Espaço VIP** shop inside the airport. Tickets are US$1. A taxi costs US$4 and takes about 10 minutes. It's safe to spend the night at the airport if you arrive late.

The new *rodoviária* is 15 km south of the city centre. Most Pantanal tour operators will meet clients off the bus and organize transfers to destinations further afield.

When to go

The Pantanal is hot and wet October to March, hot and drier from the end of March to April, and dry June to August. December to February is very wet, the Pantanal is flooded and there are many mosquitos.

Tourist information

Fundtur
*Parque das Nações Indígenas, Av Afonso
Pena 7000, Portal Guarani, T067-3318 7600,
www.turismo.ms.gov.br.*
This state tourist office is to move in 2016.

Sedesc
*Av Afonso Pena 3297, T067-3314 3580,
www.pmcg.ms.gov.br.*
The municipal tourist secretariat has
Centros de Atendimento ao Turista (**CAT**)
throughout the city, including the **airport**
(T067-3363 3116, daily 0700-2300); the
rodoviária (T067-3314 4448, Mon-Fri 0600-
2200, Sat-Sun 0630-2130); in the historic
building and exhibition centre **Morada dos
Baís** (Av Noroeste 5140, T067-3314 9968, Tue-
Sat 0800-1800, Sun 0900-1200); at the **Feira
Central market** (R 14 de Julho 3351, Wed-Sun
1800-2200, see Restaurants); and others.

Where to stay

$$$$ Jandaia
*R Barão do Rio Branco 1271, T067-
3316 7700, www.jandaia.com.br.*
The city's best hotel, aimed at a business
market. Modern well-appointed rooms (with
Wi-Fi) in a tower. The best are above the
10th floor. Pool, gym and some English spoken.

$$ Concord
*Av Calógeras 1624, T067-3384 3081,
www.hotelconcord.com.br.*
A standard town hotel with a small pool and
renovated a/c rooms with modern fittings.

$$-$ Hostel Santa Clara
*R Vitor Meirelles 125, 5 mins from
the new rodoviária, T067-3384 0583,
www.pantanalsantaclara.com.br.*
A/c doubles and dorms in a pleasant hostel
in a converted townhouse with a large
garden. Free airport pick-up, Wi-Fi, kitchen
and tour agency.

$$-$ Oka Brasil Hostel
*R Jeribá 454, not far from Campo
Grande Shopping, T067-3026 7070,
www.okabrasilhostel.com.br.*
Hostel with private rooms and dorms in a
nice old house with good kitchen and public
spaces, good beds, lockers without sockets,
towels for rent, toiletries on sale, and a safe
area. Cheaper for HI members.

What to do

Brazil Nature Tours, *R Terenos 117, sala 15,
T067-3042 4659, www.brazilnaturetours.com.*
Booking agent for nature-based tours
throughout Brazil, domestic flights and the
lodges in the Pantanal, north and south.
City Tour, *T067-3321 0800, or book through
the Campo Grande Convention & Visitors
Bureau and most larger hotels.* Half-day tours
of the city's sights including the Museu Dom
Bosco and the Parque das Nações Indígenas.
Ecological Expeditions, *R Joaquim Nabuco 185,
T067-3321 0505, www.ecologicalexpeditions.
com.br.* Offers budget camping and lodge-
based trips in Nhecolândia (sleeping bag
needed for the former) for 3, 4 or 5 days ending
in Corumbá. The first day, which involves
travel to the Buraco das Piranhas, is free.

Transport

Air The **airport**, Av Duque de Caxias,
Serradinho, T067-3368 6000, www.infraero.
gov.br, is 7 km from the city centre. For
transport from the airport to the centre, see
box, opposite. **Banco do Brasil** in the terminal
exchanges dollars; the **Bradesco** just outside
has a Visa ATM. The airport also has a tourist
information booth (little English spoken,
many pamphlets), a post office, as well as car
rental and airline offices.
Flights to **Brasília, Cuiabá, Manaus, Porto
Alegre, Rio, São Paulo, Curitiba, Campinas**
and other destinations with **Avianca, Gol,
Tam** and **Azul**.

BACKGROUND
The Pantanal

To the indigenous groups who arrived in the area tens of thousands of years before the Europeans, the Pantanal was a sea, which they called 'Xaraes'. Myths about this sea quickly reached the ears of the Spanish and Portuguese *conquistadores*, who set out to explore it. As if to presage the future, the first to arrive, in 1543, was a Spaniard called Cabeza de Vaca (Cow Head) who complained about the swarms of mosquitoes and vampire bats and promptly turned westward into the Paraguayan *chaco*.

The fate of the Pantanal and its myriad indigenous residents was left to the ruthless Portuguese and their *bandeirantes*. Apart from a few skirmishes they left the Pantanal alone for 200 years, but then gold was discovered glittering in a stream they called the River of Stars (or 'Cuiabá' by the local people), resulting in a fresh wave of migration. A settlement was established and soon the Portuguese were scouring the area for native slave labour for their mines. The indigenous people were understandably aggrieved by this and two of the fiercest tribes, the Guaicurú and the Paiaguá, combined forces to attack the Portuguese. Their tactics were highly effective: they worked in small guerrilla bands, laying ambushes when the Europeans least expected it.

The Guiacurú were horsemen, charging into battle naked but for jaguar skins, clubs, lances and machetes; crouched low on their stolen Andalusian horses, or riding on the horse's sides rather than their backs and thus invisible to the Portuguese. They used no saddles or stirrups and had just two chords for reins. The Paiaguá attacked by water and were excellent swimmers, advancing in their canoes and then leaping into the water

Bus Bus No 592 (US$1) runs every 20 mins from Praça Ary Coelho, in the centre, to the *rodoviária*, T067-3313 8703, www.transportal. com.br/rodoviaria-campo-grande. A taxi from the centre costs US$10. There's also a shuttle bus to the airport, US$5.

The new *rodoviária* is at Av Gury Marques 1215, about 15 km south of the city on the road to São Paulo (BR-163), T067-3026 6789. The terminal has a tourist office opposite platforms 5/6, cafés, internet, a handful of shops and left luggage. Campo Grande is well connected by bus to cities in the southern Pantanal and onwards to Bolivia and Paraguay, and to São Paulo, Cuiabá and Brasília/Goiânia.

To **Miranda**, 8 a day, 4 hrs, **Andorinha**, T067-3382 3710, www.andorinha.com. To **Bonito**, US$15.25-19.75, 6 hrs, 4 daily with **Cruzeiro do Sul**. São Paulo, frequent buses 0710-2340, US$56-65, 13-19 hrs. **Cuiabá**, frequent services, US$25-38, 13-14 hrs. To **Goiânia**, with **São Luiz**, 5 a day, US$30-65, 13-21 hrs, fastest at night; change here for Brasília. **Corumbá**, with **Andorinha**, 9 daily from 0630, 6½ hrs, US$28. Campo Grande–Corumbá buses connect with those from Rio and São Paulo; similarly, those from Corumbá through to Rio and São Paulo. To **Foz do Iguaçu**, 20 hrs at 1720, US$40 with **Nova Integração**, or change at Cascavel, US$27-40. To **Ponta Porã** for Paraguay, 4 hrs, US$16.50.

Car hire Agencies on Av Afonso Pena and at the airport.

and using the sides of the boats as shields. They would then suddenly right their boats and fire several volleys of arrows during the time it took the *bandeirantes* to fire one.

They soon defeated the Europeans, regaining control of the Pantanal for almost 100 years. The Portuguese were furious and accused the Guaicurú in particular of dishonourable tactics. "They fight only to win," the Portuguese claimed, "attacking only when the enemy seemed weaker". The Guiacurú responded by exposing the hypocrisy of the Portuguese: "Since the Portuguese and Spaniards claim to go to heaven when they die, they do well to die quickly. But, since they also claim that the Guiacurú go to hell after death, in that case the Guiacurú want to die as late as possible." (John Hemming, *Red Gold*).

Through subterfuge the pact was broken and, in 1734, the Portuguese regained control by means of a devastating ambush that decimated the Paiaguá. The tribes then retreated into the depths of the Pantanal where their numbers slowly diminished as a result of punitive *bandeirantes* expeditions, intertribal conflict and European diseases.

Modern Pantaneiros boast of their proud traditions, garnered from three or four generations of occupation and millennia of indigenous civilization. Nearly 25 million of their cattle roam the Pantanal. The indigenous Pantaneiros have largely disappeared. Of the 25,000 Guiacurú present in 1500, some 200 survive in their Kadiweu and Mbayá subgroups. The Paiaguá have been reduced to a sad remnant living on an island reservation near Asunción in Paraguay. Other tribes, such as the Parecis, who were enslaved in the mines, fared even worse and, of the great indigenous groups of the Pantanal, only the Terena, and the Bororo (who allied with the Portuguese), retain any significant numbers. Even their traditions have been greatly damaged by the aggressive missionary tactics of the Salesians in the 20th century.

Ponta Porã to Paraguay

sketchy and down-at-heel Paraguayan border town

Right on the Paraguay–Brazil border, Ponta Porã (population 54,000) is separated from the town of Pedro Juan Caballero in Paraguay by only a broad avenue. The town is unsafe after dark.

Ponta Porã can be reached by bus from Campo Grande. The *rodoviária* is 3 km out on the Dourados road.

Listings Ponta Porã

Transport

Bus The *rodoviária* is 3 km out on the Dourados road (Brazilian city buses from the *ponto* in the centre to Rodoviaria, 20 mins, US$1.35; taxi US$8). To/from **Campo Grande**, 4 hrs, US$16.50. From Ponta Porã to **Bonito**, either change at Jardim (US$14, 4 hrs; Jardim-Bonito 4 a day, 1½ hrs, US$4.50), or take **Cruzeiro do Sul**'s Corumbá–Ponta Porã service (see page 103).

The designated tourist town of Bonito (population 17,000) lies just south of the Pantanal in the Serra da Bodoquena hills. It is surrounded by beautiful *cerrado* forest cut by clear-water rivers rich with fish and dotted with plunging waterfalls and deep caves. The town was 'discovered' by *Globo* television in the 1980s and has since grown to become Brazil's foremost ecotourism destination.

There are plenty of opportunities for adventure activities such as caving, rafting and snorkelling, all with proper safety measures and great even for very small children. Those looking to see animals and nature should opt for forest walks by the Sucuri River.

Despite the heavy influx of visitors, plenty of wildlife appears on and around the trails when it is quiet. **Paca** and **agouti** (large, tail-less foraging rodents), **brown capuchin** monkeys and **toco toucans** (*Ramphastos toco*) are abundant, as are endangered species like the tiny and aggressive **bush dog** and cats such as **ocelot** and **jaguarundi**. **Bare-faced currasows** (*Crax fasciolata*), magnificent turkey-sized forest floor birds, can often be seen strutting around the pathways. Rarely seen small toucans such as the **chestnut-eared aracari** (*Pteroglossus castanotis*) are relatively easy to spot here, flitting in and out of the trees.

Essential Bonito

Finding your feet

The *rodoviária* is on the edge of town.

Getting around

Bonito town is a grid layout based around one principal street, Rua Coronel Pilad Rebuá, which extends for about 2 km. The town is easily negotiated on foot.

Tours

Bonito is expensive for those on a budget. All the attractions in the area can only be visited with prior purchase of a voucher at a travel agent (of which there are over 50). There are about 40 sites and agencies have a full list with prices. These are nearly all on private land and must be visited with a guide. Owners also enforce limits on the number of daily visitors. Wetsuits are provided for snorkelling and diving and you are not allowed to use sunscreen or insect repellent when in the water. Some of the sites are in Bodoquena, others in Jardim, but all are sold as tours from Bonito. As taxis are exorbitant, it is best to book with one of the agencies that offers tours and transport, or check with **Terra Transportes** and **Vanzella**. See What to do, page 95.

When to go

The wettest months are November to January; November to March are the hottest months; May to July the coolest. The number of visitors to Bonito is limited so prebooking is essential during December and January, Carnaval, Easter and July; prices during these times are also very high.

Sights

Of the 40 or so different sights in Bonito, those sketched out below are a mere representative selection. The website www.turismo.bonito.ms.gov.br has a full list, with pictures and links to each individual attraction's website. Most of the sights have their own restaurants. Meals are seldom included in the price.

Gruta Lago Azul ① *Rodovia para Três Moros 22 km, daily 0700-1700, US$16, no entry for under 5s*, is a cave 75 m below ground level with a lake 50 m long and 110 m wide. The water's temperature is 20°C, and it is a jewel-like blue, as light from the opening is refracted through limestone and magnesium. Prehistoric animal bones have been found in the lake. The light is at its best in January and February, from 0700 to 0900, but is fine at other times. A 25-ha park surrounds the cave. The cave is filled with stalactites and stalagmites. It is reached via a very steep 294-step staircase which can be slippery in the rain and is completely unilluminated.

The **Abismo Anhumas** ① *Fazenda Anhumas, Estrada para Campo dos Indios s/n, T067-3225 3313, www.abismoanhumas.com.br, US$170 (for rapelling and snorkelling) or US$250 (for rapelling and scuba diving)*, is another of Bonito's spectacular caves, filled with a glassy pool. The ticket allows visitors an abseil (of around 70 m) into the cave, followed by three to four hours snorkelling or scuba diving in glassy-clear water. Only 20 or so people are allowed into the cave per day so it is essential to book.

Other caves include the **Grutas de São Miguel** ① *Estrada para Campo dos Indios, 16 km (12 km from the centre), US$12*, a dry cave with numerous bats, albino owls and impressive cave formations entered along a vertiginous hanging bridge

On the banks of the Rio Formoso, the **Balneário Municipal** ① *7 km on road to Jardim, US$8*, has changing rooms, toilets, camping, swimming in clear water and plenty of colourful fish to see. Strenuous efforts are made to keep the water and shore clean.

The **Aquário Natural** ① *Estrada para Jardim 8 km and then 5.5 km of dirt road, daily 0900-1800, US$50 (snorkelling only), US$65 (with trail)*, is a 600-m-long clear-water river lagoon filled with *dourado* and other fish, and is formed by one of the springs of the Rio Formoso. This is the most child-friendly snorkelling in Bonito: easy and with almost no current.

One of the better value and more peaceful tours involves birdwatching and swimming or snorkelling in crystal-clear water from the springs of the **Rio Sucuri** ① *Rodovia Bonito, Fazenda São Geraldo, Km 18, T067-3255 1030, daily 0900-1800, US$40 with lunch*, to its meeting with the Formoso, followed by horse riding or trail walking.

The **Rio Formoso** ① *Estrada para Ilha do Padre 12 km, daily 0800-1700, US$30*, is a faster-flowing river where it is possible either to snorkel or float on dinghies over gentle rapids.

The little reserve of **Bonito Aventura** ① *Estrada para Jardim 8 km, T067-9986 3977, www.bonitoaventura.com.br, daily 0900-1800, US$40*, comprises a stand of pretty *cerrado* forest containing many rodents, such as paca and agouti, as well as capuchin monkeys and toco toucans in the trees. Trails cut through it to a clear-water river filled with fish.

Jardim and around

Jardim, reached by paved road (60 km from Bonito) is also surrounded by clear-water rivers and caves. There is far less infrastructure but a number of attractions are increasingly being visited by agencies from Bonito. The town itself has a wide, tree-lined main street, a handful of hotels and basic café-restaurants.

From Jardim a road leads to **Porto Murtinho**, where a boat crosses to **Isla Margarita** in Paraguay (entry stamp available on the island).

Attractions in Jardim include the **Rio da Prata** ① *BR-267, Km 512, www.riodaprata. com.br, US$70*, a long clear-water river set in *cerrado* forest and filled with fish in

BACKGROUND

Wildlife

The Brazilian Pantanal comprises a plain of around 21,000 sq km. The plain slopes 1 cm every kilometre towards the basin of the Rio Paraguai and is rimmed by low mountains which drain some 175 rivers. After heavy summer rains, these rivers burst their banks to create vast shallow lakes broken by patches of high ground and stands of *cerrado*. Plankton then swarm to form a biological soup which feeds spawning fish and amphibians. These in turn are preyed upon by waterbirds and reptiles. Herbivorous mammals graze on the stands of water hyacinth, sedge and savannah grass and are preyed upon by South America's great predators, the jaguar, ocelot, maned wolf and yellow anaconda.

In June, at the end of the wet season, when the sheets of water have reduced, wildlife concentrates around the small lakes or canals.

Mammals

Outside Africa there is nowhere better for seeing wild mammals than the Pantanal, especially between July and late September. During this time, there are groups of **capybara** – the world's largest rodent – at just about every turn. Critically endangered **marsh deer** (*Blastocerus dichotomus*), who have webbed feet to help them run through the swamp, or their more timid cousins, the **red brocket** (*Mazama americana*), and the **pampas deer** (*Ozotoceros bezoarticus*) wander in every other stretch of savannah alongside **giant anteaters**. Few visitors leave without having seen both species of peccary (which resemble pigs but are in a different family): the solitary **collared peccary** (*Pecari tajacu*) and the herd-living **white-lipped peccary** (*Tayassu pecari*), not to mention **giant otters** (*Pteronura brasiliensis*) and at least one species of cat. Lucky visitors may even see a **jaguar** (*Panthera onca*) or **tapir** (*Tapirus terrestris*). There are at least 102 mammal species here and, although most of them are bats (including vampires), the list includes eight of South America's 10 wild cats, four dog species and numerous primates ranging from the tiny palm-sized **pygmy marmoset** (*Cebuella pygmaea*) to South America's second largest primate, the **black howler monkey** (*Alouatta caraya*).

The cats are usually top of everyone's 'most wanted' list. The largest is the **jaguar** (most easily seen near Porto Jofre on the Transpantaneira), followed by the more elusive **puma** (*Puma concolor*), which has the widest distribution of any feline in the world. Even more common is the retriever-sized **ocelot** (*Leopardus pardalis*) and the tawny or black **jaguarundi** (*Puma yagouaroundi*), twice the size of a domestic cat, though more slender. The most elusive creature is the **pampas cat** (*Leopardus pajeros*), with a fawn body and striped legs, but scientists are yet to agree on its species. The other cats are all spotted and are, in size order, the **margay** (*Leopardus wiedii*), **geoffroy's cat** (*Leopardus geoffroyi*) – the most hunted in the Americas – and, the most beautiful of all, the tiger cat or **oncilla** (*Leopardus tigrinus*).

greater numbers and species variety than in the more visited rivers of Bonito. Guiding and conservation are well-managed. The reserve also manages the spectacular **Lagoa Misteriosa** ⓘ *BR-267, Km 515, www.lagoamisteriosa.com.br, US$125*, a deep, fish-filled *cenote* with glass-clear water set in verdant forest. Nearby is the

Other carnivores include **crab-eating foxes** (*Cerdocyon thous*), **coatis** and **racoons** (who often hang around the *fazendas* at night), the **maned wolf** (*Nasua nasua*), **short-eared dog** (*Atelocynus microtis*), and **bush dog** (*Speothos venaticus*), also known as *cachorro vinagre* meaning 'vinegar dog', found in the drier semi-deciduous forests. Monkeys are not as varied here as they are in the Amazon, but visitors will hear or see **black howler monkey**, the smaller **brown capuchin** (*Sapajus apella*), and possibly the **pygmy marmoset**. Other species present include various **titi monkeys** (*Callicebus sp*) and **night monkeys** (*Macaco da noite, Aotus spp*), which are most easily seen around the Estrada Parque in the south. **Woolly monkeys** (*Lagothrix spp*) can be found in the dry forests near Bonito.

Reptiles
After birds, the most easily spotted animals are caimans, of which the dominant species is the **jacaré caiman** (*Caiman yacare*), which reach a maximum length of about 1.5 m. **Yellow anaconda** (*Eunectes notaeus*), the world's heaviest snake, are abundant but difficult to see; your best chance is on the Estrada Parque in the south, which they frequently cross during the day. Other snakes, the majority of which are not venomous, are also abundant but hard to spot. The venomous species, which include **pit vipers** (*Crotalinae spp*), such as the jararaca or **fer de lance** (*Bothrops jararaca*), are nocturnal.

Birds
There are more than 700 resident and migratory bird species in the Pantanal. Birding on the Transpantaneira road in the north or at one of the *fazendas* in the south can yield as many as 100 species a day. From late June to early October there are vast numbers of birds. Try to visit as many habitat types as possible and, as well as trail-walking, jeep rides and horse riding, include river trips in your itinerary. The most emblematic bird and a symbol of the Pantanal is the giant 1.2m-tall stork jabiru or tuiuiu (*Jabiru mycteria*), which is commonly seen in marshy areas. Night safaris will maximize sightings of more unusual **heron**, such as the **boat-billed** (*Cochlearius cochlearius*), **agami** (*Agamia agami*) and **zigzag** (*Zebrilus undulatus*), and the numerous **nightjars** (*Caprimulgidae spp*) and **potoos** (*Nyctibius spp*). Specialities in the Pantanal include the 1-m-long **hyacinth macaw** (*Anodorhynchus hyacinthinus*), the world's largest parrot; the **golden-collared macaw** (*Primolius auricollis*); **blue-fronted parrot** (*Amazona aestiva*); as well as numerous parakeets including **blue-crowned** (*Aratinga acuticaudata*), **nanday** (*Nandayus nenday*), **blaze-winged** (*Pyrrhura devillei*) and **green-cheeked** (*Pyrrhura molinae*); the giant flightless **rhea** (*Rhea americana*); **chestnut-bellied** (*Penelope ochrogaster*) and **spix's guan** (*Penelope jacquacu*); **crowned eagle** (*Stephanoaetus coronatus*); **bare faced currasow** (*Crax fasciolata*); and **helmeted manakin** (*Antilophia galeata*).

Bring good binoculars and a field guide. *Pantanal, Guia de Aves* by Paulo de Tarso Zuquim Antas, published by SESC can give far greater detail than this book has space for.

Buraco das Araras ① *BR-267, Km 510, www.buracodasararas.tur.br, US$16*, is an enormous sink hole cave set in pristine forest and nested by red and green macaws (*Ara chloropterus*). Chestnut-eared aracaris and black and white hawk eagles (*Spizaetus melanoleucus*) are frequent visitors.

Tourist information

Bonito

Comtur/Sectur
*R Cel Pilad Rebuá 1780, T067-3255 1850 or
3255 2160, www.turismo.bonito.ms.gov.br.
Mon-Fri 0730-1130 and 1330-1700.*
No English spoken. See also www.
portalbonito.com.br and www.guia-
bonito.com (both in Portuguese only).

Where to stay

Bonito

$$$ Gira Sol
*R Pérsio Schamann, 710, T067-3255 2677,
www.pousadagirasol.com.br.*
An attractive *pousada* with a small pool set in
a flower-filled garden 5 mins' walk from the
town centre. Bright, spacious rooms
with balconies. Decent breakfast.

$$$ Pira Miúna
*R Luís da Costa Leite 1792, T067-3255 1058,
www.piramiunahotel.com.br.*
Ungainly brick building with the most
comfortable a/c rooms in the town centre
(the best have balconies) and a large pool
area with jacuzzis and a bar.

$$$ Pousada Olho d'Água
*Rod Três Morros, Km 1, T067-3255 1430,
www.pousadaolhodagua.com.br.*
Comfortable accommodation in fan-cooled
cabins set in an orchard next to a small lake.
Horse riding, bike rental, solar-powered hot
water and great food from the vegetable
garden. Recommended.

$$$ Tapera
*Rod Guia Lopes, Km 1, on the hill above the
Shell station on the road to Jardim, T067-
3255 1700, www.taperahotel.com.br.*
Peaceful location with fine views and cool
breezes. Very comfortable, but having your
own transport is an advantage.

$$-$ Albergue do Bonito
*R Dr Pires 850, Bairro Formosa, T067-
8180 7231, www.bonitohostel.com.br.*
A well-run HI youth hostel with a travel
agency, pool, bikes, kitchen and laundry
facilities. English spoken, very friendly.
Price per person for dorms.

$ Pousada Muito Bonito
*R Col Pilad Rebuá 1444, T067-3255 3077,
www.pousadamuitobonito.com.br.*
Well-appointed, bright white rooms, a/c, nice
patio, excellent, helpful owners, also tour
company, staff speak English and Spanish.

Camping

Camping Rio Formoso
*Rodovia Bonito/Guia Lopes da Laguna Km 06,
T067-9284 5994, www.campingrioformoso.
com.br.*
Shady campsite by the river with space for
60 tents, 6 km from Bonito.

Restaurants

Bonito

$$$-$$ Santa Esmeralda
R Col Pilad Rebuá 1831.
Respectable Italian food in one of the few a/c
dining rooms.

$$ Casa do João
*R Nelson Felício dos Santos, 664-A,
T067-3255 1212.*
Recently refurbished, this traditional family-
owned restaurant serves typical Pantanal
dishes, with fresh fish options such as the
deep-fried traíra without bones.

$$ Tapera
*R Col Pilad Rebuá 480, T067-3255 1110.
Opens 1900 for the evening meal.*
Good, home-grown vegetables, breakfast,
lunch, pizzas, meat and fish dishes.

$ Da Vovó
R Sen F Muller 570, T067-3255 2723.
A great per kilo restaurant serving Minas and local food all cooked in a traditional wood-burning aga. Plenty of vegetables and salads.

$ Mercado da Praça
R 15 Novembro 376, T067-3255 2317.
Open 0600-2400.
The cheapest in town. A snack bar housed in the local supermarket, offering sandwiches and juices.

$ Zapi Zen
R Sen Filinto Muller 573, T067-32552455.
New pizza place, with several vegetarian and organic options, plus fresh fruit juices.

Bars and clubs

Bonito

O Taboa
R Col Pilad Rebuá 1837, T067-3255 3598, www.taboa.com.br.
The liveliest in town with occasional bands and good caipirinhas and *chopp*.

What to do

Bonito
There is very little to choose between agencies in Bonito. English speakers are hard to come by. We list only those who also offer transport or a specialist service such as cave diving.
Sucuri, *R Cel Pilad Rebuá 1890, T067-3255 3994, www.agenciasucuri.com.br.* As well as selling tours, also has car hire from US$32 per day, not including insurance, with extra for car wash afterwards; you can leave the car elsewhere if required.

Ygarapé, *R Cel Pilad Rebuá 1853, T067-3255 1733, www.ygarape.com.br.* English-speaking staff, offers transport to the sights. Also PDSE accredited cave diving.

Transport

Bonito
Air The **airport** is 12 km away from the city centre by taxi. There are flights with **Azul** to **São Paulo** (Viracopos, Campinas) every Wed at 1600 and Sun at 1215.

Bus The *rodoviária* is on the edge of town, a short walk from R Cel Pilad Rebuá. To **Campo Grande**, US$15.25-19.75, 6 hrs, 4 daily with **Cruzeiro do Sul**, T067-3312 9710, www.cruzeirodosulms.com.br. Buses go via Jardim, Nioaque and Sidrolândia. See under Corumbá, page 103, for Cruzeiro do Sul's Corumbá–Ponta Porã service. **Terratransportes**, R Olívio Flores 600, T067-3255 1601, www.terratransportes.com.br, and **Vanzella**, T067-3255 3005, www.vanzellatransportes.com.br, run door-to-door services to **Campo Grande** and its airport daily (3 and 4 times respectively) and go to different local sites every day. There are other similar companies.

Jardim
Bus To **Campo Grande**, 0200, 0700, 1030, 1300, 1530 and 1900, US$15, 3½ hrs. To **Bonito** 4 buses daily, US$5. To **Miranda** and **Corumbá** at 1030. To **Dourados**, 0600. To **Bela Vista** (Paraguayan border) at 0300, 1100, 1500, 190, US$ 6.0. To **Porto Murtinho**, at 0001, 0300 and 1500 (bus from Bonito connects), US$ 12. To **Ponta Porã**, at 1500.

The little farming town of Miranda (population 23,000) built around a now disused mill and a railway station lies some 200 km west of Campo Grande at the turn-off to Bonito. It has long been overlooked as a gateway to the Pantanal and Bonito, but is actually far closer to both than Campo Grande and is the ideal starting point of a tour. Miranda is also a real town, preoccupied more with its own local economy and culture than with tourism. The town extends for less than 2 km north–south and only has a few streets.

Miranda lies in the heart of indigenous Terena land and the communities have a large **Cultural and Arts Centre** ① *on the roundabout at the entrance to town, Mon-Fri 0700-2200, Sat and Sun 0800-2200, free*, with panels on Terena history and arts and crafts for sale. The Salobra, Miranda and the crystal-clear Salobrinho rivers – all just outside town – have great birdlife and resident giant otters. There is a wonderful British girder bridge 16 km west of town given as a gift to Brazil by King George V. Underneath it is **Hotel Pesqueira da Cida**, where boats can be taken to see the meeting of the Miranda and Salobra rivers (one clear and dark water, the other silty).

Tours to all local attractions can be arranged with **Explore Pantanal** (see What to do, page 98).

Fazendas in the southern Pantanal

Where to stay 🛏
Fazenda 23 de Março **1**
Fazenda Baia Grande **2**
Fazenda Barra Mansa **3**
Fazenda Barranco Alto **9**
Fazenda San Francisco **6**
Fazenda Santa Clara **10**
Fazenda Xaraés **12**
Núcleo Salvar a Vida **4**
Pantanal Jungle Lodge **5**
Passo do Lontra Parque **11**
Rancho Meia Lua **7**
Refúgio Ecológico Caiman **8**

Fazendas around Miranda

Many *fazendas* sit in a transition zone between the Pantanal proper and the *cerrado* woodlands and pasture land around Miranda. Prices of packages include accommodation, all food and at least two guided trips per day. Standard packages include jeep trips, trail walks, horse riding, boat trips (where the *fazenda* has a river) and night safaris. They do not

Tip...

The best tour operator is **Explore Pantanal** (see What to do, page 98), who can provide information in English. Be wary of the lower-end operators for the Pantanal because many cut corners to save money and services are not always reliable.

always include transfer from Miranda or the Buraco das Piranhas and this should be checked when booking. Unless otherwise indicated the standard of wildlife guiding will be poor, with only common familial or generic names known for animals and little awareness of species diversity or numbers. Keen birdwatchers should request a specialist birding guide through their tour operator or *fazenda*. Also take a good pair of binoculars and some field guides.

Listings Miranda *map p96*

Where to stay

$$$ Nativos
R Manoel R da Costa 59, T067-3242 1427, pousadanativos@outlook.com.
Contemporary cabins with bedroom upstairs, some with kitchenette, away from centre but not far from the *rodoviária*, parking. Backpacker rooms to be opened in 2016.

$$$ Pantanal
Av Barão do Rio Branco 609, T067-3242 1068.
Well-maintained, large a/c rooms with en suites, a/c, swimming pools, regarded as the best in town.

$$$-$$ Águas do Pantanal
Av Afonso Pena 367, T067-3242 1242, www.aguasdopantanal.com.br.
In the town itself, with comfortable a/c rooms and shared rooms for up to 6, good breakfast, laundry service, tour agency (see What to do, below) and an attractive pool surrounded by tropical flowers. Usually have a rep waiting at the *rodoviária*.

$$ Chalé
Av Barão do Rio Branco 685, T067-3242 1216, www.hotelchalems.com.br.
Plain a/c, motel-like rooms with tiled floors, some with balcony, pool.

Fazendas around Miranda

The following *fazendas* can be booked through **Explore Pantanal** in Miranda, see below. Tours are the same price even if you are on your own, but there are almost always other guests. See also page 102.

$$$$ Refúgio Ecológico Caiman
36 km from Miranda, T011-3706 1800, www.caiman.com.br. Open sporadically; check the website.
The most comfortable, stylish accommodation in the Pantanal in a hotel reminiscent of a Mexican hacienda. Tours and guiding are excellent. Part of the **Roteiros de Charme** group (see page 19).

$$$ Fazenda 23 de Março
Aquidauna, turn off BR 262 at Km 541, 15 km before Miranda, T067-3321 4737, www.fazenda23demarco.com.br.
Charming *fazenda* with only 4 rooms, great food and a swimming pool. There's a **Centrapan** centre for the preservation of Pantanal culture, where visitors can learn to lasso, ride a bronco and turn their hand to other Pantanal cowboy activities. The wilderness around is pristine and filled with wildlife.

$$$ Fazenda Baia Grande
Estrada La Lima, Km 19, T067-3303 0162, www.fazendabaiagrande.com.br.
Very comfortable a/c rooms set around a pool in a bougainvillea and *ipê*-filled garden. The *fazenda* is surrounded by savannah and stands of *cerrado* broken by large lakes. The owner, Alex, is very friendly, eager to please and enthusiastic.

$$$ Fazenda San Francisco
Turn off BR-262 30 km west of Miranda, T067-3242 3333, www.fazendasanfrancisco.tur.br.
One of the most popular and heavily visited ranches in the Pantanal with large day groups, especially at weekends, and simple rustic a/c cabins gathered around a pool in a garden filled with rheas. Food and guides are excellent.

$$$ Núcleo Salvar a Vida
BR-262 Km 554, 3 km from Miranda, T067-99223714, nucleoserviravida@gmail.com, contact Miriam and Wagner.
A project based on sustainable principles with recycling of all water, organic vegetables and fruit, composting toilets, etc. Work with the rehabilitation of former addicts. Guests can volunteer to work and can pay what they feel is appropriate. Bicycles to borrow to ride to town on a back road. Open 2016.

$$$ Rancho Meia Lua
BR-262 Km 547, east of Miranda, T067-9686 9064.
Being completely refurbished in late 2015, 8 rooms set in gardens, with pool, lunch and dinner extra, trips include riding, free bikes, night walks and fishing in lake.

Restaurants

$ Zero Hora
Av Barão do Rio Branco at the rodoviária, T067-3242 1330.
24-hr snack bar, provision shop and, at the back, there's an average but good-value per kilo restaurant, with its own private waterfall.

What to do

Águas do Pantanal, *Av Afonso Pena 367, T067-3242 1242, www.aguasdopantanal.com.br.* Based at the hotel of the same name; see Where to stay, above. Tours to the Pantanal and Serra do Bodoquena, associated with many hotels, very helpful.
Explore Pantanal Brasil Turismo, *R São Benedito 780, Miranda, T067-3242 1403, T9831 3038, www.explorepantanal.com.* Run by a Kadiweu Amerindian, with 30 years of experience, and British expat Ekta Shah. The only company in the Pantanal working with indigenous Terena and Kadiweu guides. Great for small groups who want to get off the beaten track. Excellent English, French, Spanish and Italian spoken, and decent Hebrew. A range of trips, including

fascinating stays with indigenous people in the Pantanal. Prices are competitive. For the best rates book ahead.

Transport

Bus *Rodoviária* is on R / de Setembro. To **Campo Grande**, 8 a day with **Andorinha**, 4 hrs, US$14. **Expreso Miranda**, T067-9937 7782, runs a daily car service to Campo Grande, US$120 per car. To **Corumbá**; 11 daily, 4 hrs, US$14. From Buraca das Piranhas, **Catarino** runs a daily door-to-door service to **Bonito**, 191 km, at 1400, 5 hrs, US$18.75 pp; **Prainha**, leaves for Campo Grande also at 1400, 5 hrs. Ask **Barba** (see above) to book either in advance. See under Corumbá, page 103, for **Cruzeiro do Sul**'s Corumbá–Ponta Porã service (**Miranda** T067-3242 1060, open 0730-1030, 1330-1430).

Corumbá, the Bolivian border and the Estrada Parque

border town with beautiful views of the river, especially at sunset

Situated on the south bank by a broad bend in the Rio Paraguai, 15 minutes from the Bolivian border, Corumbá (population 95,000) is hot and humid (70%). It's cooler in June to July, but very hot from September to January. It also has millions of mosquitoes in December to February.

There is a spacious shady Praça da Independência and Avenida General Rondon between Frei Mariano and 7 de September has a pleasant palm-lined promenade which comes to life in the evenings. From General Rondon streets drop steeply to the waterfront, which has a row of colourful colonial buildings, a park and the conference centre, with cinema and cultural events. Also on the waterfront is the **Museu de História do Pantanal** ⓘ *R Manoel Cavassa 275, T67-3232 0303, www.muhpan.org.br, Mon-Sat 1300-1800, free*, which is a good place to learn about the Pantanal, especially if arriving from Bolivia.

The Forte Junqueira, the city's most historic building, was built in 1772. It may be visited accompanied by a soldier from the base in which it is situated, but you must apply in advance.

Border with Bolivia

The BR-262 is paved most of the way from Campo Grande to Corumbá and the Bolivian border. Over the border from Corumbá are Arroyo Concepción, Puerto Quijarro and Puerto Suárez. From Puerto Quijarro a 650-km-long railway and a paved road run to Santa Cruz de la Sierra. There are flights to Santa Cruz from Puerto Suárez.

For Brazilian immigration, the Brazilian Polícia Federal and immigration are at the border complex right at the frontier (open daily 0800-1730); there may be queues for entry stamps but it's much quicker for exit. If leaving Brazil merely to obtain a new visa, exit and entry must not be on the same day. Money changers (usually women sitting at tables) on the Bolivian side and in Quijarro (there is none on the Brazilian side) offer the same rates as in Corumbá. There's a **Bolivian consulate** ⓘ *R Firmo de Matos com Porto Carreiro, T067-3231 5605, consuladoboliviacorumba@ gmail.com, Mon-Fri 0800-1230, 1400-1730,* in Corumbá. A fee is charged to citizens of those countries which require a visa. A yellow fever vaccination certificate is not required to enter Brazil, but regulations

Tip...
Travel between Campo Grande and Corumbá during the day to take advantage of the marvellous scenery.

BACKGROUND
Vegetation in the Pantanal

Forest types and what lives where

Although the Pantanal is often described as an ecosystem in its own right, it is actually made up of many habitats, which have their own, often distinct, biological communities. The Pantanal is of recent geological origin and has very few endemic plant species. Botanically it is a mosaic: a mixture of elements from the Amazon region including *várzea* and gallery forests and tropical savannah, the *cerrado* of Central Brazil and the dry *chaco* region of Paraguay.

Pantanal *cerrado* forest

The *cerrado* is found both in the upland areas, which are not prone to flooding, and in some areas that may be inundated for a short period. It is dominated by the *cerrado* **pequi tree** (*Caryocar brasiliense*) whose fruits have a famous spiny interior, the beautiful flowering legume **sucupira** (*Bowdichia virgiloides*) and the **sandpaper tree** (*Curatella americana*). But the most conspicuous trees in the *cerrado* are **trumpet trees** (various *ipê*); these are characterized by their brilliant colours (indigo in *Tabebuia impetignosa* and yellow in *Tabebuia aurea*) and no leaves in the dry season. Sometimes these trees stand as the dominant species in vast areas of semi-agrarian parkland. Within the dry *cerrado* are numerous stands of **bocaiúva palm** (*Acrocomia aculeate*) characterized by its very spiny trunk and leaves; its fruit is an important food source for macaws and larger parrots. In the wetter *cerrado* are numerous islands of dense savannah forest or *cerradão*, often thick with **acuri palm** (*Attalea phalerata*), whose woody fruit is the principal food for the hyacinth macaw and, when fallen, for **peccaries** (*javali* in Portuguese) and **agouti** (rabbit-sized, tailless rodents; *cutia* in Portuguese). *cerrado* habitats are also important refuges for the larger sheltering mammals, such as jaguar and tapir, who will flee into the densest wet *cerrado* to escape predators.

change, so enquire at a consulate before arriving at the border. A tourist office on the Brazilian side is open Monday-Saturday 0730-1330.

Buraco das Piranhas and the Estrada Parque

Many tours out of Campo Grande and Miranda take a dirt road running off the BR-262 Campo Grande–Corumbá highway, called the **Estrada Parque**. It begins halfway between Miranda and Corumbá at a turn-off called **Buraco das Piranhas** (Piranha Hole). Here there is a police post and a bar and information centre run by a man called Barba. He has been helping travellers for 15 years and can find accommodation at lodges if you have no reservation, has all transport details (see below) and knows everything you need to know.

The road heads north into the Pantanal and then, after 51 km, turns west to Corumbá at a point called the **Curva do Leque** (with **Bar do Que Qué**). This is the overland access point to **Nhecolândia**, a region rich in wildlife. There is a ferry ① *daily 0700-1700 daily, US$9.50 for a car*, across the Rio Paraguaí at Porto da Manga. The Estrada rejoins the BR-262 at Lampião Aceso, south of Corumbá. There are several good *fazendas* off the Estrada Parque road.

Semi-deciduous tropical forest

This taller, denser forest occurs on higher ground such as the Serra do Bodoquena south of Miranda, and comprises a mix of species from the Paraguayan *chaco* and the Amazon. For instance **jutaí** (*Hymenaea courbaril*), from which the sacred copal resin is extracted, comes from the Amazon; while the **monkey-ear plant** (*Enterolobium contortisquam*), recognized by its curved seed pods, is a common *chaco* species. More primate species can be found here than elsewhere in the Pantanal, along with smaller toucans, such as the **chestnut eared aracari** (*Pteroglossus castanotis*), and rare mammals like bush dog and **tayra** (*Eira barbara*).

Swamp and seasonally flooded land

This varies greatly, from Amazonian habitats characterized by riverine forests such as *várzea* (seasonally flooded riverbank forest) to seasonally flooded grassland and palm savannah dominated by **carunda palms** (*Copernicia alba*). Alongside these are permanently marshy areas and open lakes and oxbows thick with floating plants. This diversity of habitats means a great diversity of species and nowhere is better than these areas for seeing large concentrations of birds and mammals. *Várzea*, which is best seen by canoe or paddle boat, is good for mammals such as tapir and giant otter, and for riverine birds like the **southern screamer** (*tachã* – Chauna torquata), the five species of Brazilian **kingfisher**, **black-collared hawks** (*Gaviao belo*) and many species of heron and stork. Apart from *várzea*, much swampland is dominated by the papyrus-like **sedge** (*Cyperus giganteus*) or **reed mace** (*Typha dominguensis*) or by floating plants like **water hyacinth** (*Eichhornia crassipes*), which caiman and capybara use as cover.

Xeric vegetation

This permanently dry scrub forest found in elevated areas is dominated by *chaco* species such as various types of **cacti** (such as *Cereus peruvianus* and *Opuntia stenartha*) together with the swollen-trunked, baobab-like pot-bellied **chorisia** (*Bombacaceae*). Many distinct species occur here, including one of the world's rarest cats, the **pampas cat**, and rare birds, such as **black-legged seriemas** (*Chunga burmeisteri*) and *chaco* **earthcreepers** (*Upucerthia certhioides*).

Listings Corumbá, the Bolivian border and the Estrada Parque

Tourist information

Corumbá

Fundação de Turismo do Pantanal
Ladeira Cunha e Cruz 37, by the port, T067-3232 7139. Mon-Fri 0730-1130 and 1330-1730. There's an additional office at the *rodoviária*, open 0700-1800. See also the informative www.corumba.travel.

Where to stay

Corumbá

There are 2 Cama e Café (Brazilian homestay) options in Corumbá: **Casa da Mamã** (R Firmo de Mattos 1400, T067-3232 4240, elmamonaco@gmail.com), with 1 double room and 1 twin, shared bath, a/c, parking, convenient location; and **Casa Marela** (R Dom Aquino 597, T067-3233 4578, iaramarela@hotmail.com), 1 room with bath, fan. In both you share facilities with the family, **$** per person.

There are hostels around the bus station; however, this is a 10-min walk from the centre of town where most of the hotels, restaurants and tour agencies are found. For a full list of hotels see www.corumba.travel.

$$$-$$ Nacional
R Dom Aquino Corrêa 1457, T067-3234 6000, www.hnacional.com.br.
The smartest in town with recently refurbished a/c rooms in a 1980s block, a pool and sauna.

$$ El Dorado
R Porto Carreiro 554 esq Tiradentes, close to the rodoviária, *T067-3231 6677, hotel_eldorado@top.com.br.*
46 rooms with electric shower. No-frills place but OK.

The Estrada Parque
See map, page 96.

$$$$ Fazenda Xaraés
www.xaraes.com.br.
One of the most luxurious *fazendas*, with a pool, tennis court, sauna, airstrip and modest but well-appointed a/c rooms in cream and terracotta. The immediate environs have been extensively cleared, but there are some wild areas of savannah and *cerrado* nearby and there are giant otters in the neighbouring Rio Abobral.

$$$$-$$$ Fazenda Barra Mansa
www.hotelbarramansa.com.br.
One of the better lodges in the region in a wild area right on the banks of the Rio Negro and between 2 large tracts of wetland. Like all the Rio Negro *fazendas* it is famous for its jaguars. Specialist guiding is available on request; be sure to stipulate this in advance. The farm also offers sport fishing, horse riding and canoe trips on the river. Accommodation for up to 16 is in rustic a/c rooms with hammocks. There is a small library of field guides at the *fazenda*.

$$$$-$$$ Fazenda Barranco Alto
Aquidauana, T067-3241 4047, www. fazendabarrancoalto.com.br.

A beautiful, remote large ranch on the banks of the Rio Negro. It is one of the oldest *fazendas* in the Pantanal with farm buildings dating from the first half of the 20th century. The surrounding area has stands of *cerrado* set in seasonally flooded savannah cut by the river. Guiding is good but stipulate your interest in wildlife in advance, especially if you are a birder.

$$$ Fazenda Santa Clara
Estrada Parque s/n, T067-3384 0583, www.pantanalsantaclara.com.br.
The most comfortable budget option for staying in a ranch house in the southern Pantanal, on the banks of the Rio Abobral (where there's a community of giant otters), and with a pool, games areas, double rooms and dorms, full transfers from Campo Grande, full board and tours included. Well organized and well run.

$$$ Pantanal Jungle Lodge
7 km from Buraca das Piranhas by the bridge over Rio Miranda, T067-3242 1488, reserve@pantanaljunglelodge.com.br.
New lodge with 12 rooms, 5 dorms and 1 room with disabled access, all a/c, fridge, all-inclusive, but meals can be paid for separately, TV room, bar, pool, laundry service, all guides speak English, 1-night packages include 5 activities, longer stays include all 9 activities (canoeing, safaris day and night, on land and on water, fishing, swimming).

$$$ Passo do Lontra Parque Hotel
1.5 km from Estrada Parque, turn off just after Rio Miranda bridge, T067-3245 2407, www.passodolontra.com.br.
Cabin blocks on stilts, also 4 dorm rooms, dining room with Wi-Fi, good food, all meals included, packages of 2 or more nights, day use also available, offers boat trips, but no walks. Walking and riding can be done at the same group's $$$ **Fazenda São João**, further along the Estrada Parque, which also has lodging and dining room.

What to do

Corumbá

Most tour operators for the southern part of the Pantanal are in Campo Grande or Miranda, but a few agencies keep offices here and there are a number of upmarket cruise companies along the waterfront. There is a list on www.corumba.travel; companies include include **Joice Pesca & Tur**, *T067-3232 4048, T9912 0265, www.joicetur.com.br*, with good boats, crew and service; and **Pérola do Pantanal**, *T067-3231 1460, www.peroladopantanal.com.br*, with its boat *Kalypso*.

Mutum Turismo, *R Frei Mariano 17, T067-3231 1818, www.mutumturismo.com.br.* Cruises and upmarket tours (mostly aimed at the Brazilian market) and airline, train and bus reservations.

Transport

Corumbá

Air **Airport**, R Santos Dumont, 3 km. **Azul** flies to **São Paulo** (Viracopos, Campinas) at 1345 every Mon, and Wed, Fri and Sun at 1320. Infrequent bus from airport to town, so take a taxi, US$5. Car hire at the airport.

Bus The local bus station is 6 blocks from the *rodoviária* at 13 de Junho e Tiradentes; there is another stand at Delamare e Antônio Maria Coelho by the Praça da República. The *rodoviária* is on R Porto Carreiro at the south end of R Tiradentes, 10 mins' walk from the centre. City bus to *rodoviária* from Praça da República, US$1.35; taxis are expensive but mototaxis charge US$1. **Andorinha**, T067-3231 2033, services to all points east. To **Campo Grande**, 7 hrs, US$28,

9 buses daily, from 0630-2359, connections from Campo Grande to all parts of Brazil. **Cruzeiro do Sul**, T067-3231 9318, www.cruzeirodosulms.com.br, office open 0600-1000, 1300-1630, has a daily service except Sun to **Ponta Porã** via Miranda, Bodoquena, Bonito, Jardim and Bela Vista, in a 20-seater bus towing a trailer for luggage, leaving at 0700, arriving **Miranda** 1000, US$14, **Bonito** 1200, US$22 (US$8 Miranda–Bonito) and **Ponta Porã** at 1930, US$35. It returns from Ponta Porã at 0630, passing Bonito at 1200 and Miranda at 1430.

Border with Bolivia: Corumbá/Arroyo Concepción

Bus Leaving Brazil, take city bus marked Fronteira from either of the stops given above to the Bolivian border (15 mins, US$1.35), walk over the bridge to Bolivian immigration, then take a colectivo to Quijarro or Puerto Suárez. Taxi from Corumbá *rodoviária* to the border US$8. Brazilian taxis are not allowed to cross into Bolivia, but it is only a short walk between the 2 frontier posts. For onward travel, always buy train or bus tickets once in Bolivia.

When travelling from Quijarro, take a taxi to the Bolivian border to go through formalities. Cross the bridge to Brazilian immigration. On the left, 50 m from the border is the stop for taxis to Corumbá and a little further on, the bus stop; don't believe taxi drivers who say there is no bus.

Train Timetables for trains from Puerto Quijarro to Santa Cruz change frequently, so check on www.fo.com.bo or on arrival in Corumbá. If you haven't booked a ticket via the website, it may be best to stay in Quijarro to get tickets.

Mato Grosso &
the northern Pantanal

Mato Grosso, immediately to the north of Mato Grosso do Sul, shares the Pantanal with that state and has equally well-developed tourism facilities. Although there are just as many opportunities for seeing wildlife, trips from the state capital, Cuiabá, tend to be more upmarket than those leaving from Campo Grande in Mato Grosso do Sul. The state also has abundant though rapidly depleting areas of Amazon forest.

Alta Floresta, in the north, has an excellent birdwatching and wildlife lodge, and one of the Amazon's most comfortable lodges, the Jardim da Amazônia, lies in the middle of vast fields of soya to the southwest.

The much-vaunted Chapada dos Guimarães hills, near Cuiabá, offer good walking and birdwatching, although the natural landscape has been damaged by farming and development.

Cuiabá

a prosperous city, the starting point for trips into the northern Pantanal

Cuiabá (population 543,000), the state capital, is an ordered and increasingly wealthy city having grown rich on soya from the vast plantations to the north. It has few sights of interest but its many leafy *praças* have resulted in it being called the 'Cidade Verde' (Green City) by Matogrossenses. Cuiabá was the smallest host city for the 2014 FIFA World Cup™, and went through a construction frenzy before the event. However, many works were left unfinished.

Cuiabá is in reality two twinned cities, separated by the sluggish Rio Cuiabá, an upper tributary of the Rio Paraguai. **Cuiabá** is on the east bank of the river, and **Várzea Grande** on the west, where the airport lies.

Essential Cuiabá

Finding your feet

Flights arrive at **Marechal Rondon Airport** 10 km from the centre. To get to the centre, take buses Nos 651 and 652 from in front of the airport to Avenida Tenente Coronel Duarte in the centre. Taxis cost US$12.50 to the centre. Bus No 7 operates from the airport to the *rodoviária*. The VLT (Veículo Leve sobre Trilhos) urban light rail system running between the airport, the city centre and the Arena Pantanal stadium is one of World Cup projects left unfinished. It is due to be completed for late 2016.

Interstate buses arrive at the *rodoviária* north of the centre at Rua Jules Rimet, Bairro Alvorada, T065-3621 3629. Town buses stop at the entrance of the *rodoviária*. See Transport, page 109.

Getting around

Many bus routes have stops in the vicinity of Praça Ipiranga. Bus No 501 or 103 ('Universidade') to the university museums and zoo (ask for 'Teatro') leave from Avenida Tenente Coronel Duarte by Praça Bispo Dom José, a triangular park just east of Praça Ipiranga.

When to go

Cuiabá vies with Teresina in Piauí and Corumbá in Matto Grosso do Sul as the hottest city in Brazil, with the highest temperatures recorded during the summer months of November to March. The coolest months are June, July and August in the dry season.

Weather Cuiabá

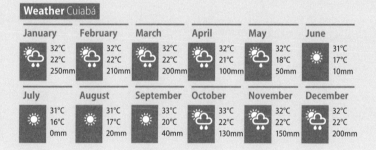

January	February	March	April	May	June
32°C 22°C 250mm	32°C 22°C 210mm	32°C 22°C 200mm	32°C 21°C 100mm	32°C 18°C 50mm	31°C 17°C 10mm

July	August	September	October	November	December
31°C 16°C 0mm	31°C 17°C 20mm	33°C 20°C 40mm	33°C 22°C 130mm	32°C 22°C 150mm	32°C 22°C 200mm

Sights

The most pleasant public space in Cuiabá is the lush **Praça da República** which is surrounded by a cluster of imposing buildings and dotted with sculptures and shady trees. Pedestrian shopping streets and further squares lead off the *praça*. The brutalist façade of the **cathedral**, flanked by two functionalist clock towers, dominates the square. Until the late 1960s a beautiful 18th-century baroque church stood here but this was demolished to make way for the current building in a sweep of modernization that saw almost all the city's colonial charm destroyed.

On **Praça Ipiranga**, at the junction of Avenidas Isaac Póvoas and Tenente Coronel Duarte, a few blocks southwest of the central squares, there are market stalls and an iron bandstand from Huddersfield in the UK, or Hamburg in Germany, depending on which story you believe. There is live acoustic music on Thursday and Friday on the **Praça da Mandioca**, a small square just east of the centre.

On a hill beyond the square is the extraordinary church of **Bom Despacho**, built in the style of Notre Dame. Recently renovated, the church is open to visitors daily (except for Monday mornings). In front of the Assembléia Legislativa, on Praça Moreira Cabral, is a point marking the **Geodesic Centre of South America** (see also under Chapada dos Guimarães, page 115).

The rather dusty **Museus de Antropologia, História Natural e Cultura Popular** ① *Fundação Cultural de Mato Grosso, Praça da República 151, Mon-Fri 0800-1730, US$0.50,* are worth a look. There are interesting historical photos, a contemporary art gallery, indigenous weapons, archaeological finds and pottery. The section displaying stuffed wildlife from the Pantanal is disturbingly compelling.

At the entrance to the Universidade de Mato Grosso, by the swimming pool, 10 minutes by bus from the centre, is the small **Museu do Índio/Museu Rondon** ① *T065-3615 8489, www.ufmt.br/ichs/museu_rondon/museu_rondon.html, Tue-Sun 0800-1100, 1330-1700, US$1,* with artefacts from tribes mostly from the state of Mato Grosso. Particularly beautiful are the Bororo and Rikbaktsa headdresses made from macaw and currasow

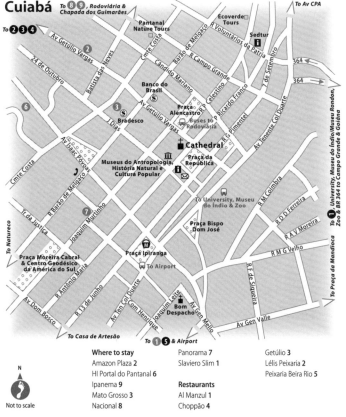

Where to stay	Panorama 7	Getúlio 3
Amazon Plaza 2	Slaviero Slim 1	Lélis Peixaria 2
HI Portal do Pantanal 6		Peixaria Beira Rio 5
Ipanema 9	Restaurants	
Mato Grosso 3	Al Manzul 1	
Nacional 8	Choppão 4	

feathers, and the Kadiwéu pottery (from Mato Grosso do Sul). Continuing along the road through the campus, signed on the left before a right turn in the road, is the **Zoológico** ⓘ *Tue-Sun 0800-1100, 1330-1700, free*. The jacaré, capybara, tortoise and tapir can be seen at any time, but are best in the early morning or late afternoon. It also has coatis, otters, rhea, various monkeys and peccaries and a few birds.

Built as an arsenal for the Portuguese crown early in the 19th century, the yellow neoclassical building now occupied by **Sesc Arsenal** ⓘ *R Treze de Junho, s/n, T65-3611 0550*, hosts performances, plays and the weekly market **Bulixo** ⓘ *Thu, 1800-2200*, which has stalls offering both typical *cuiabana* and international food and local crafts.

The **Águas Quentes** hot springs are 86 km away (9 km south of the BR-163, 77 km east of Cuiabá) and can be visited as a day trip.

Listings Cuiabá *map p106*

Tourist information

Sedtur
Inside the rodoviária, Av Jules Rimet; in the city centre, Praça Rachid Jaudy; inside Museu da Caixa d'Água Velha, R Nossa Senhora de Santana, 1-105; with a smaller office at R Ricardo Franca at Voluntarios da Pátria, 118, T065-3613 9300, www.sedtur.mt.gov.br. Mon-Fri 0800-1200, 1300-1700.
Provides maps and general information on hotels and car hire and has a website in English. Staff are friendly and speak English and Spanish. They are very helpful in settling disputes with local tour companies.

Where to stay

$$$$ Amazon Plaza
Av Getúlio Vargas 600, T065-2121 2000, www.hotelamazon.com.br.
By far the best in the centre with very smart modern rooms in a tower with good views.

$$ Mato Grosso
R Comandante Costa 643, T065-3614 7777, www.hotelmt.com.br.
The best-value mid-range option in the centre with a/c or fan-cooled rooms with tiled floors and chintzy beds, the brightest of which are on the 2nd floor or above.

$$ Nacional
Av Jules Rimet 22, T065-3054 2462.
Opposite the front of the bus station and convenient for those who are just passing through. Plain a/c en suite rooms.

$$ Panorama
Praça Moreira Cabral 286, T065-3264 2462.
A frayed 1980s tower with very simple, plain a/c or fan-cooled rooms with en suites; some have good views.

$$ Slaviero Slim Cuiabá Aeroporto
Av Gov João Ponce de Arruda, 860, T065-3026 9600.
Opened in 2015, this chain hotel is 100 m away from the airport and offers standard comfortable rooms at a reasonable price.

$$-$ HI Portal do Pantanal
Av Isaac Póvoas 655, T065-3624 8999, www.portaldopantanal.com.br.
Large, bare dorms (segregated by sex) and doubles, a TV lounge area and a small kitchen. Price per person, breakfast included, internet access, laundry and a kitchen.

$$-$ Ipanema
Av Jules Rimet 12, opposite the front of the bus station, T065-3621 3069.
Very well-kept a/c or fan-cooled rooms, some with armchairs, cable TVs and smart en suites. Internet access and a huge lobby TV for films or football. Many other options between here and the **Nacional**.

Restaurants

Many restaurants in the centre are only open weekdays for lunch. On Av CPA and Av Getúlio Vargas there are many good restaurants and small snack bars. R Jules Rimet, across from the *rodoviária*, has several cheap restaurants and *lanchonetes*.

$$$ Al Manzul
Av Jornalista Arquimedes Pereira Lima 6131, Altos do Copipó, T065-3667 3661, www.almanzul.com.
A local pride for *cuiabanos*: Al Manzul won a number of national and international prizes for its Arab food. Cuiabá has welcomed a number of Lebanese immigrants in the past century. The restaurant's closure in 2011 generated public outcry. In 2015, the restaurant reopened in a new location serving their famous banquets of 19 or 29 dishes.

$$$ Getúlio
Av Getúlio Vargas 1147 at São Sebastião, T065-3264 9992, www.getuliogrill.com.br.
An a/c haven to escape from the heat. Black-tie waiters, excellent food with meat specialities and pizza, and a good buffet lunch on Sun. Live music upstairs on Fri and Sat from significant Brazilian acts.

$$$ Lélis Peixaria
R Mal Mascarenhas de Moraes 36, T065-3322 9195, www.lelispeixaria.com.br.
Cuiabanos love their freshwater fish so much that they have fish *rodízio* just like Brazilian barbecue restaurants. This all-you-can-eat meal includes alligator sausage, deep-fried *pintado* and *pacu* ribs (the latter both Brazilian freshwater fish). Avoid going during *piracema*, mid-Oct to mid-Feb, when fishing is banned due to fish migration.

$$$-$$ Choppão
Praça 8 de Abril, T065-3623 9101, www.choppao.com.br.
Established 30 years ago, this local institution is buzzing at any time of day or night. Huge portions of delicious food or *chopp*. The house speciality chicken soup promises to give diners drinking strength in the early hours and is a meal in itself. Warmly recommended.

$$ Peixaria Beira Rio
10 km away from the airport, in the fishing village of Bomsucesso, T065-3686 8111.
This restaurant overlooking the river serves one of the best and the freshest fish *rodízio* around, at a reasonable price. There's no a/c so prepare to face high temperatures and don't miss the dessert, local milk *rapadura*, which also comes in small cubes with the bill.

Shopping

Local handicrafts in wood, straw, netting, leather, skins, Pequi liquor, crystallized caju fruit, compressed guaraná fruit and indigenous crafts are on sale at the airport, *rodoviária*, craft shops in the centre, and at the interesting daily market in the Praça da República. There's also a picturesque fish and vegetable market at the riverside.

Casa de Artesão, *Praça do Expedicionário 315, T065-3321 0603*. All types of local crafts in a restored building.

What to do

Tours to the northern Pantanal
Reef and Rainforest Tours, *A7 Dart Marine Park, Steamer Quay, Totnes, Devon TQ9 5DR, UK, T01803-866965, www.reefandrainforest. co.uk.* Specialists in tailor-made and group wildlife tours.

Cuiabá
Travel agencies in Cuiabá also offer trips to the Chapada dos Guimarães.

Expect to pay US$70-100 per person per day for tours in the northern Pantanal. Budget trips here are marginally more expensive (around US$10-15 per day more) than those in the southern Pantanal, but accommodation in the *fazendas* is more comfortable. For longer tours or special programmes, book in advance and be very wary of cut-price cowboy operators, some of whom hang around in the airport.

Ecoverde Tours, *R Pedro Celestino 391, Centro, T065-9638 1614, www.ecoverdetours.com.br.* No-frills, but well-run backpacker tours of the Pantanal with Joel Souza, who has many years guiding experience, knows his birds and beasts and speaks good English. Ask if he is available as other guides are not always of the same standard. The best option in Cuiabá for a budget trip to the Pantanal.

Natureco, *R Benedito Leite 570, Cuiabá, T065-3321 1001, www.natureco.com.br.* A range of *fazenda*-based Pantanal tours, trips to the Xingu, Cáceres, Alta Floresta and Barão de Melgaco. Specialist wildlife guides available with advance notice. Some English spoken. Professional and well run.

Pantanal Nature Tours, *R Campo Grande 487, Centro, T065-3322 0203, T065-9955 2632 (mob), www.pantanalnature.com.br.* Great trips to the northern Pantanal, both to the *fazendas* along the Transpantaneira and to Porto Jofre – from where the company runs the best jaguar safari in the Pantanal – and to Nobres, the Chapada dos Guimarães and Pousada Jardim da Amazônia. Guiding is excellent (bilingual) and service professional.

Pantanal wildlife and birding guides

All guides work freelance; companies employ extra guides for trips when busy. Most guides wait at the airport for incoming flights; compare prices and services in town if you don't want to commit yourself. The tourist office can recommends guides, however, their advice is not always impartial. Those recommended below can be booked with advance notice through **Natureco** (see above).

Ailton Lara, *T065-3322 0203, ailton@pantanalnature.com.br.* Excellent and good-value birding trips to the Chapada, Pantanal and other destinations around Mato Grosso.

Boute Expeditions, *R Getúlio Vargas 64, Várzea Grande, near the airport, T065-3686 2231, www.boute-expeditions.com.* Paulo Boute is one of the most experienced birding guides in the Pantanal and speaks good English and French. His standard tours operate in Mato Grosso (including

the Amazon and the *chapada* alongside the Pantanal). He also runs tours to the Atlantic coastal forests and other bespoke destinations on request.

Fabricio Dorileo, *fabriciodorileo18@yahoo.com.br, or contact through Eduardo Falcão, rejaguar@bol.com.br.* Excellent birding guide with good equipment, good English and many years' experience in the Pantanal and Chapada dos Guimarães. Trained in the USA. Book him through the Cuiabá operators.

Giuliano Bernardon, *T065-8115 6189, T065-9982 1294, giubernardon@gmail.com.* Young birding guide and photographer with a good depth of knowledge and experience in the *chapada*, Pantanal, Mato Grosso, Amazon and Atlantic coastal forest.

Pantanal Bird Club, *T065-3624 1930, www.pantanalbirdclub.org.* Recommended for even the most exacting clients, **PBC** are the most illustrious birders in Brazil with many years of experience. Braulio Carlos, the owner, has worked with Robert Ridgely and Guy Tudor and his chief guide, Juan Mazar Barnett, is one of the editors of *Cotinga* magazine. Tours throughout the area and to various parts of Brazil.

Transport

Air For information on transport from the **airport**, Av João Ponce de Arruda, s/n, Várzea Grande, T065-3614 2500, www.infraero.gov.br, see box, page 105. Flights can be booked in the airline offices at the airport or through **Pantanal Nature** (see What to do, above), or other tour operators in town, which also handle bus tickets. There are ATMs outside the airport, as well as a post office, car hire booths and **Sedtur** office.

Cuiabá has connections with **Alta Floresta**, **São Félix do Araguaia**, **Sinop**, **Belo Horizonte**, **Brasília**, **Campo Grande**, **Curitiba**, **Foz de Iguaçu**, **Goiânia**, **Manaus**, **Porto Alegre**, **Porto Velho**, **Ji-Paraná**, **São Paulo** and **Rio de Janeiro**. Airlines include: **Asta**, www.voeasta.com.br; **Avianca**, www.avianca.com.br; **Azul**, www.voeazul.com.br;

GOL, www.voegol.com.br; **Passaredo**, www. voepassaredo.com.br; **TAM**, www.tam.com.br.

Bus Bus No 329 runs to the *rodoviária* from R Joaquim Murtinho by the cathedral, 20 mins. A taxi costs US$5 from the centre. There is a Bradesco ATM, cafés and restaurants in the *rodoviária*.

Buses to **Alta Floresta**, 5 daily, US$54, 14 hrs; to **Brasília**, 6 daily, US$45, 19-22 hrs;

to **Campo Grande**, at least every hour, US$30; to **Foz de Iguaçu**, 1 daily, US$70, 32 hrs; to **Porto Velho**, 10 daily, US$50, 26 hrs; to **Santarem**, 3 daily, US$98, 24 hrs; to **São Paulo**, 5 daily, US$75, 28 hrs.

Car hire Localiza, Av Dom Bosco 965, T065-3624 7979, and at airport, T065-3925 9259. **Hertz**, at airport, T065-3682 2652. **Unidas**, at airport, T065-3682 4052.

Northern Pantanal

wildlife spotting ranch homestays in the heart of the Pantanal

The Mato Grosso Pantanal is only developed for tourism along the Transpantaneira dirt road, which is superb for seeing wildlife, especially jaguars. Other areas, around Barão do Melgaço and the colonial river port of Cáceres, are pioneer country where you will probably not encounter another tourist.

The Transpantaneira

The main access point to the northern Pantanal is the Transpantaneira dirt road, which runs south from Cuiabá to Cáceres, beginning in earnest at the scruffy town of Poconé. The

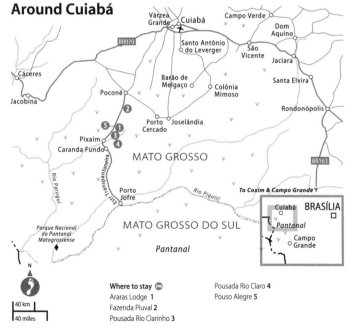

Around Cuiabá

Where to stay
Araras Lodge 1
Fazenda Piuval 2
Pousada Rio Clarinho 3
Pousada Rio Claro 4
Pouso Alegre 5

Transpantaneira cuts through the heart of the Pantanal wetland and is one of the best places for seeing wildlife in the Americas. Capybara, jaguarondi, oncilla, pacas and agoutis are common sights on the road

Tip...
The best time for a boat trip is sunset, when birds gather in huge numbers.

itself, and the wetland areas immediately to either side – which begin as ditches and stretch into wilderness – are filled with hundreds of thousands of egrets, ibises, herons and metre-tall jabiru storks. Caiman bask on the banks of the ditches and ponds and anaconda snake their way through the water hyacinth and reeds. The road is lined with a string of *fazendas* (see page 113), of various levels of comfort, which are used by tour operators from Cuiabá as bases for deeper ventures into the wetlands.

The few towns that lie along the Transpantaneira are most interesting when seen from a wing mirror, but they do sell petrol. **Poconé** is an unprepossessing dusty little place, founded in 1781 and known as the 'Cidade Rosa' (Pink City) by over-romantic locals. Until 1995 there was much *garimpo* (illicit gold mining) activity north of town and many slag heaps can be seen from the road. There are numerous cheap hotels in town but there is no real advantage in staying here.

From Poconé it is 63 km south to the one-horse town of **Pixaim**, where there is a petrol station and little else, and then a further two to three hours to **Porto Jofre**, at the end of the road on the banks of Rio Cuiabá. The town is one of the best locations in the Americas for seeing jaguar and has a few hotels and restaurants. For jaguar safari tours, see **Pantanal Nature**, page 109.

Barão de Melgaço and around
Barão de Melgaço, 130 km from Cuiabá on the banks of the Rio Cuiabá, is far less visited than the Transpantaneira; you'll see far fewer tourists here, and far fewer animals. The town sits on the edge of extensive areas of lakeland and seasonally flooded *cerrado*, and is most easily reachable via Santo Antônio do Leverger. The route via São Vicente is longer. The best way to see the Pantanal from here is by boat down the Rio Cuiabá.

Near the town, the riverbanks are lined with farms and small residences but become increasingly forested with lovely combinations of flowering trees (best seen September to October), and the environs become increasingly wild and filled with birds, rodents and reptiles. After a while, a small river to the left leads to the **Chacororé** and **Sia Mariana lakes**, which join up via an artificial canal. The canal has resulted in the larger of the two lakes draining into the smaller one, and it has begun to dry out. Boats can continue beyond the lakes to the **Rio Mutum** but a guide is essential because there are many dead ends. The area is rich in birdlife and the waterscapes are beautiful.

Boat hire costs up to US$100 for a full day and is available from restaurants along the waterfront; ask at the **Restaurant Peixe Vivo**, or enquire with travel agencies in Cuiabá, who can organize a bespoke trip. Bring a powerful torch to do some caiman spotting for the return trip in the dark.

Cáceres
Cáceres (population 86,000) is a hot, steamy but hospitable provincial town on the far western edge of the Pantanal, sitting between the stunning **Serra da Mangabeira** mountains (15 km to the east), and the broad Rio Paraguai. The city is 200 km west of Cuiabá. It has little tourist infrastructure for Pantanal visits, but makes a possible pit stop on the long road between Cuiabá and Rondônia.

It's a pleasant place, with a lovely waterfront and a number of well-preserved 19th-century buildings painted in pastel colours. It's easy to organize a short boat trip on the

BACKGROUND

Ecology, conservation and environmental concerns

Only one area of the Pantanal is officially a national park, the 135,000-ha **Parque Nacional do Pantanal Matogrossense** in the municipality of Poconé, only accessible by air or river. Permission to visit can be obtained from **Instituto Chico Mendes de Conservação da Biodiversidade** (ICMBio), www.icmbio.gov.br. Hunting is strictly forbidden throughout the Pantanal and is punishable by four years' imprisonment. However, most *fazendeiros* regularly shoot and kill jaguar, many locals are still jaguar hunters and some landowners even allow illegal private hunts.

Fishing is allowed with a licence according to strict quotas, with periods varying from year to year. For information contact local tourist offices. There are also restrictions on the size of fish that may be caught, but poaching is rife and there are plans to halt all fishing for a few years due to severe stock depletion. Illegal predatory fishing is a particular problem on the Rio Cuiabá. Application forms are available through travel agents with advance notice. Catch and release is the only kind of fishing allowed on rivers Abobral, Negro, Perdido and Vermelho. Like other wilderness areas, the Pantanal faces significant threats. Agrochemicals and *garimpo* mercury, washed down from the neighbouring *planalto*, are a hazard.

Tours to the Pantanal

Choosing a tour operator Choose an agency or *fazenda* with care. Not all operators are responsible – a number in both the north and the south have been accused of serious malpractice which extends to offering hunting safaris and illegally building on park land. We have received numerous complaints of unprofessionalism, even of tourists being stranded for hours or expected to take the local bus as part of their Pantanal safari. Be aware that cut price operators tend to cut corners and pay their staff very low wages. We list only recommended operators and consider those in Cuiabá (for the north) and Miranda (for the south) to be the best. Many operators offer an increasingly interesting range of Pantanal trips. These include hard-core camping safaris (see **Pantanal Nature**, page 109) and indigenous cultural exchanges (see **Explore Pantanal**, page 98).

Responsible travel Visitors should be aware of a few other common sense rules of thumb. Take your rubbish away with you, don't fish out of season, don't let guides kill or disturb fauna, don't buy products made from threatened or endangered species (including macaw feather jewellery), don't buy live birds or monkeys, and report any violation to the authorities. The practice of catching caiman, even though they are then released, is traumatic for the animals and has potentially disruptive long-term effects.

river from here. Until 1960, Cáceres used to have regular boat traffic downstream to the Rio de Plata. Occasional boats still run down river as far as Corumbá, and though there is no reliable service, if you're prepared to wait around for a few days you could probably hitch a ride. Travel in a pair or group if possible as the river route is a back door to Bolivia for cocaine traffickers.

The **Museu de Cáceres** ① *R Antônio Maria by Praça Major João Carlos*, is a small local history museum. Exhibits include indigenous funerary urns. The main square, **Praça Barão**

de Rio Branco, has one of the original border markers from the Treaty of Tordesillas, which divided South America between Spain and Portugal. The *praça* is pleasant and shady during the day and, in the evenings between November and March, the trees are packed with thousands of chirping swallows (*andorinhas*); beware of droppings. The square is full of bars, restaurants and ice-cream parlours and comes to life at night. Vitória regia lilies can be seen north of town, just across the bridge over the Rio Paraguai along the BR-174 and there are archaeological sites on the river's edge north of the city.

The Pantanal is wild near Cáceres, and was the site of a horrific jaguar attack in 2008 when a large female cat killed and partially ate a hunter. Trips are difficult to organize; however, there is excellent wildlife and birdwatching in the Serra da Mangabeira, a steep, jagged range covered in forest and traversed by the BR-070 federal highway running from Cuiabá to Porto Velho.

Listings Northern Pantanal *map p110*

Where to stay

Fazendas on the Transpantaneira
All prices here include tours around the *fazenda*'s grounds with a guide – either on foot and or horseback or in a jeep, and full board.

See also page 110. Distances are given in kilometres from Poconé town. For tour operators, see What to do, page 108.

$$$$ Araras Lodge
Km 32, T065-3682 2800, www.araraslodge. com.br. Book direct or through Pantanal Nature (see What to do, page 109) or any of the other operators in Cuiabá as part of a tour.
One of the most comfortable places to stay, with 14 a/c rooms. Excellent tours and food, home-made *cachaça*, a pool and a walkway over a private patch of wetland filled with capybara and caiman. Very popular with small tour groups from Europe. Book ahead.

$$$$ Fazenda Piuval
Km 10, T065-3345 1338, www.pousadapiuval.com.br.
The 1st *fazenda* on the Transpantaneira and one of the most touristy, with scores of day visitors at weekends. Rustic farmhouse accommodation, a pool, excellent horseback and walking trails as well as boat trips on the vast lake, but whilst the *fazenda* is great for kids it's not a good choice for those looking to spot wildlife and really get into the sticks.

$$$$ Pousada Rio Clarinho
Km 42, T9977 8966, www.pousadario clarinho.com.br, book through Pantanal Nature (see What to do, page 109).
Charming option on the Rio Clarinho. What it lacks in infrastructure, it makes up for in wildlife. The river has rare waterbirds such as agami heron and nesting hyacinth macaw, as well as river and giant otters and, occasionally, tapir. The boatman, Wander, has very sharp eyes – be sure to ask for him – and there is a 20-m-high birding tower in the grounds. Not to be confused with the nearby **Pousada Rio Claro** (see below).

$$$$ Pousada Rio Claro
Km 42, T065-3345 2449, www.pousada rioclaro.com.br, book through Natureco (see What to do, page 109).
Comfortable *fazenda* with a pool and simple a/c rooms on the banks of the Rio Claro, which has a resident colony of giant otters.

$$$$ Pouso Alegre
Km 36, T065-3626 1545, www.pousalegre.com.br.
Rustic *pousada* with simple a/c or fan-cooled accommodation on one of the Pantanal's largest *fazendas*. It's overflowing with wildlife and particularly good for birds. Many new species have been catalogued here. The remote oxbow lake is particularly good for waterbirds (including agami and zigzag

herons). The lodge is used by a number of birding tour operators. Proper birding guides can be provided with advance notice. Best at weekends when the very knowledgeable owner Luís Vicente is there.

Barão de Melgaço
There is a handful of cheaper options near the waterfront.

$$$$ Pousada do Rio Mutum
T065-3052 7022, www.pousadamutum.com.br, reservations through Pantanal Nature (see page 109), or through other agencies in Cuiabá.
One of the region's most comfortable lodges, with rooms housed in mock-colonial round houses or whitewash and tile-roofed cabins and set in a broad shady lawn around a lovely pool. The *pousada* organizes trips on horseback around the surrounding Pantanal, or by jeep and by boat on the adjacent river.

$$ Pousada Baguari
R Rui Barbosa 719, Goiabeiras, Barão de Melgaço, T065-3322 3585, www.pousadabaguari.com.br.
Rooms with a/c, restaurant, boat trips and excursions.

Cáceres
In Jun, accommodation is expensive and hard to find due to the city's week-long sport fishing championship for over 100,000 attendees.

$$ Hotel Porto Bello
Av São Luiz 1188, T065-3224 1437, www.hotelportobello.amawebs.com.
Basic standard rooms, with a/c, TV and private bathrooms.

$$ La Barca
R General Osório, s/n, T065-3223 5047.
Basic town hotel, single, double and triple rooms. With a/c and pool.

$$ Riviera Pantanal
R Gen Osório 540, T065-3223 1177, rivierapantanalhotel@hotmail.com.

Simple town hotel with a/c rooms, a pool and a restaurant.

$ União
R 7 de Setembro 340, T065-3223-4240.
Fan-cooled rooms, cheaper with shared bath, basic but good value.

What to do

Cáceres
Boat trips
At the waterfront you can hire a boat for a day trip, US$4 per person per hour; minimum 3 people. On public holidays and some weekends there are organized day trips on the river.

Transport

The Transpantaneira
Bus There are 6 buses a day 0600-1900 from Poconé to **Cuiabá**, US$8 with **TUT**, T065-3317 2217.

Car Poconé has a 24-hr petrol station with all types of fuel, but it's closed on Sun.

Border with Bolivia
Bus From Cáceres to **San Matías**, US$6 with **Verde Transportes**, Mon-Sat at 1400 and 1700, Sun and holidays at 1700.

Cáceres
Bus The *rodoviária*, Terminal da Japonesa, T065-3224 1261, has bus connections with Cuiabá and Porto Velho. **Verde/ Eucatur** buses to **Cuiabá**, US$15, many daily 0630-2400 from the *rodoviária* (book in advance, very crowded), 3½ hrs. To **Porto Velho**, US$45.

Boat Intermittent sailings to **Corumbá** on the *Acuri*, a luxury boat that travels between Corumbá and Cuiabá; ask at the docks when you arrive.

Car hire **Localiza**, Av São Luís 300, T065-3223 1212.

one of the most scenic areas in Mato Grosso

Although consumed by agriculture and blighted by ill-considered careless tourism development, the craggy, cave-pocked escarpments of the Chapada dos Guimarães constitute one of the oldest plateaux on earth. It is very easy to visit them on a day trip from Cuiabá. They begin to rise from the hot plains around Cuiabá some 50 km from the city, forming a series of vertiginous stone walls washed by waterfalls and cut by canyons.

A dramatic, winding road, the MT-020, ascends through one to an area of open savannah standing at around 700 m, broken by patches of *cerrado* forest and extensive areas of farmland, dotted with curiously eroded rocks, perforated by dripping caves and grottoes, and leading to whole series of viewpoints out over the dusty Mato Grosso plains. There is one small settlement, the tranquil and semi-colonial village of **Chapada dos Guimarães** (population 13,500), where life focuses on a single *praça* and people snooze through the week until the crowds rush in from Cuiabá on Fridays and Saturdays.

The *chapada* is said to be the geodesic heart of the South American continent and, about 8 km east of Chapada dos Guimarães town, at the **Mirante do Ponto Geodésico**, there is a monument officially marking this. It overlooks a great canyon with views of the surrounding plains, the Pantanal and Cuiabá's skyline on the horizon.

As the geodesic centre, the highlands are rich with **New Age folklore**. Crystals tinkle in the shops in Chapada dos Guimarães village, and peyote people in tie-dye clothing gather in cafés to murmur about apocalypse and a new human evolution, over hot chocolate and soggy cake. The *chapada*'s rocks are said to have peculiar energizing properties; a fact more solidly grounded in truth than you may suspect – a local magnetic force that reduces the speed of cars has been documented here by the police.

The *chapada* is pocked with caves. These include the **Caverna Arroe-jari** ⓘ *43 km of Chapada dos Guimarães village, daily 0800-1300, US$5, allow 3-4 hrs for the walk to and from the cave*, whose name means the 'home of souls' in a local Brazilian language. It's a haunting place: an 800-m-long cavern coursed by a little mountain stream running into a deep aqua blue lake, set in boulder-strewn grassland. It's best visited early in the day during the week, to ensure the fewest numbers of visitors possible, and to soak up the atmosphere. The walk to the cave cuts through waterfall-filled rainforest before emerging in open *cerrado*. Birdlife is rich.

The *chapada* is a popular destination for birders, who often combine it with the Pantanal and Alta Floresta to up their species count. **Birdwatching** here is fruitful, in open country and with grassland and *cerrado* species not found in Alta Floresta and the Pantanal. Guides listed under the northern Pantanal (see page 108) can organize one- or two-day trips here and many are even based in the little town of Chapada dos Guimarães. Mammals, such as puma, jaguarundi, giant river otter and black-tailed marmoset can also be seen with time and patience.

Chapada dos Guimarães village

The colourful village of Chapada dos Guimarães, 68 km northeast of Cuiabá, is the most convenient and comfortable base for trips. It's a pretty little place, with a series of simple, brightly painted buildings clustered around a small *praça* graced with the oldest church in the Mato Grosso, **Nossa Senhora de Santana** ⓘ *open intermittently*, dating from 1779 and with a simple whitewashed façade.

The *chapada* can be visited in a long day trip from Cuiabá either by self-drive (although access is via rough dirt roads that may deteriorate in the rainy season), bus or most easily through agencies such as **Pantanal Nature** or **Natureco** (see page 109).

The **Festival de Inverno** is held in the last week of July; during this time, and around **Carnaval**, the town is very busy and accommodation is scarce and expensive.

Parque Nacional da Chapada dos Guimarães

This begins just west of Chapada dos Guimarães town. The beautiful 85-m **Véu da Noiva Waterfall** (Bridal Veil), 12 km from the town, near Buriti (well signposted; take a bus to Cuiabá and ask to be dropped you off), is less blighted and can be reached by either a short route or a longer one through forest. Other sights include: the **Mutuca** beauty spot, named after a vicious horsefly that preys on tourists there and the **Cachoeirinha Falls**, where there is another small, inappropriately situated restaurant.

About 60 km from town are the archaeological sites at **Pingador** and **Bom Jardim**, which include caverns with petroglyphs dating back some 4000 years.

Nobres and Bom Jardim

Some 100 km north of the *chapada* is the little town of **Nobres**, which, like Bonito in Mato Grosso do Sul (see page 90), is surrounded by clear-water rivers full of *dourado* fish and many beautiful caves. Unlike Bonito, there are few tourists and, while still overpriced, the attractions are a good deal cheaper and far less spoilt.

Nobres is the name for the area, but the main village, with a couple of small *pousadas* and a single restaurant, is called **Bom Jardim**. The town sits 2 km from the **Lago das Araras** ⓘ *Bom Jardim, US$3*, a shallow lake surrounded by stands of buriti palm where hundreds of blue and yellow macaws roost overnight.

The restaurant **Estivado** ⓘ *Rodovia MT-241, Km 66, 500 m northeast of Bom Jardim on the Ponte Rio Estivado, US$5 for swimming (bring your own snorkel), US$7 for lunch*, offers a taste of what Nobres has to offer. It sits over the slow-flow of the Rio Esitvado, which forms a wide pool next to the restaurant and is filled with fish.

Nobres' other attractions dot the countryside around Bom Jardim and, as in Bonito, they are on private ranch land. There is good snorkelling at the **Reino Encantado** ⓘ *18 km from Bom Jardim at Alto Bela Vista, T065-9237 4471, US$20 for full day use including lunch, guide and equipment, US$45 per night for a double room in the adjacent pousada*; the **Recanto Ecológico Lagoa Azul** ⓘ *14 km from Bom Jardim at Alto Bela Vista, US$25 for entry, guide and equipment, US$8 extra for lunch*; and at the **Rio Triste** ⓘ *18 km from Bom Jardim village, US$30 for a 2-hr float with guide and equipment rental*. The former two are 500-m floats down the Rio Salobra, which is filled with piraputanga (*Brycon microlepis*), piova (*Schizodon Borelli*) and piauçu (*Leporinus macrocephalus*) fish. The Rio Triste is filled with these species as well as fierce, salmon-like dourado (*Salminus maxillosus*) and spectacular mottled fresh-water stingrays, which should be treated with caution as they will inflict a painful wound if stepped on or handled. The most spectacular cave is the **Gruta do Lagoa Azul**, which has been closed since 2014.

Taxis can be booked through the **Pousada Bom Jardim** to take visitors to the various attractions – there is no public transport. This can prove expensive (up to US$45 for a round trip to any single attraction, including waiting time). The most practical way of visiting Nobres is with a tour agency in Cuiabá, such as **Pantanal Nature** or **Trip Nobres** (see page 109). The former can include the trip in conjunction with the Chapada dos Guimarães or Jardim da Amazônia and is better for wildlife.

Tourist information

Chapada dos Guimarães
For useful information and photos, see
www.chapadadosguimaraes.com.br
(in Portuguese only).

Tourist office
*R Quinco Caldas 100, at the corner of
Av Penn Gomes with R Sete, near the
entrance to the town.*
Provides a useful map of the region and can
help organize tours.

Where to stay

Chapada dos Guimarães
See www.chapadadosguimaraes.tur.br
for further details.

$$$$ Pousada Penhasco
*2.5 km on Av Penhasco, Bom Clima, T065-
3264 1000, www.penhasco.com.br.*
A medium-sized resort complex perched on
the edge of the escarpment (for wonderful
views), with modern chalets and bungalows,
heated indoor and an outdoor pools (with
waterslides), tennis courts and organized
activities. A long way from quiet and
intimate, but good for kids.

$$$ Casa da Quineira
*R Frei Osvaldo 191, T065-3301 3301,
www.casadaquineira.com.br.*
Very close to the city centre, this homely
pousada has comfortable, modern rooms
and a swimming pool.

$$ Turismo
*R Fernando Corrêa 1065, a block from
the* rodoviária, *T065-3301 1176, www.
hotelturismo.com.br.*
A/c rooms with a fridge, cheaper with fan,
restaurant, breakfast and lunch excellent, very
popular, German-run. Ralf Goebel, the owner,
is very helpful in arranging excursions.

$$-$ Pousada Bom Jardim
*Praça Bispo Dom Wunibaldo 461, T065-
3301 2668, www.pousadabomjardim.com.br.*
A bright, sunny reception in a colonial building
on the main square leads to a corridor of
either simple fan-cooled rooms or more
comfortable a/c rooms painted light orange,
and with wicker and wood furnishings, local
art on the walls and private bathrooms.

$$-$ São José
R Vereador José de Souza 50, T065-3301 1574.
This bright yellow cottage with a terracotta
tiled roof just off the southeastern corner
of the main square, and near the church,
has an annexe of very plain fan-cooled or
a/c singles, doubles with little more than a
wardrobe and a bed (and a TV and fridge
with a/c), and windows overlooking a small
yard. The cheapest have shared bathrooms.

Camping

Oasis
*R Fernando Correa, 394, 1 block from
the main* praça, *T065-3301 2444,
www.campingoasis.com.br.*
In an excellent central location in the large
lawned garden dotted with fruit trees and
sitting behind a townhouse. Facilities include
separate bathrooms for men and women,
cooking facilities and a car park.

Nobres

$$-$ Pousada Bom Jardim and Bom Garden
*Vila Bom Jardim, T065-3102 2018,
www.pousadabomjardim.com.*
2 hotels joined as one: **Bom Garden**, out the
back, has modern, well-kept a/c rooms with
en suites and TVs; **Bom Jardim** is simpler,
with less well-appointed older and smaller
rooms. Both can organize tours (though no
English is spoken).

Restaurants

Chapada dos Guimarães
Pequi is a regional palm fruit with a deadly spiky interior used to season many foods; arroz com pequi is a popular local rice and chicken dish.

$$$ Morro dos Ventos
Rodovia MT 251, Km 1, T065-3301 1030, www.morrodosventos.com.br.
Inside a private condo, this restaurant has one of the best views of Chapada and a menu with good meat and fish dishes.

$$ Fellipe 1
R Cipriano Curvo 596, T065-3301 1793.
One of the few per kilo restaurants in the village, on the southwestern corner of the square next to the church serving mostly meaty options, beans, rice, unseasoned salads and sticky puddings. In the evenings, the menu becomes à la carte.

$$ Nivios
Praça Dom Wunibaldo 631.
A popular spot for meat and regional food.

Nobres

$ WF
T065-3102 2020. Lunch daily; dinner by reservation only.
Senhora Fatima serves a hearty meal of meat/chicken/fish with beans, rice, salad and condiments, washed down with fresh tropical fruit juice.

Shopping

Chapada dos Guimarães
Flora, *R Cipriano Curvo, Praça Dom Wunibaldo, T065-9214 8420.* Regional arts and crafts, including ceiling mobiles, wall hangings, lacework and clothing; neighbouring shops have similar offerings.

What to do

Chapada dos Guimarães
Chapada Pantanal, *Av Fernando Correa da Costa 1022, T065-3301 2757, www.chapadapantanal.tur.br.* Tours to all the principal sights in the *chapada* and trips further afield to Nobres.

Nobres
The Cuiabá agencies listed under the Pantanal, and **Chapada Pantanal** in Chapada dos Guimarães village (see above), visit Nobres.
Pantanal Nature, *see page 109.* Trips to all the attractions in Nobres. These can be combined with the Chapada dos Guimarães and Jardim da Amazônia. Excellent for wildlife.
Trip Nobres, *T065-3023 6080, www.trip nobres.com.br.* Boisterous light adventure activities in and around Nobres, including abseiling, rafting, snorkelling and diving. The owner is one of the few PADI-accredited dive instructors in the area.

Transport

Chapada dos Guimarães
Bus 7 departures daily to **Cuiabá** (Rubi, 0630-1900, last return 1800), US$5, 1½ hrs.

Nobres
There are at least 4 buses daily to **Cuiabá** (as well as services to **Sinop** and **Alta Floresta**). Regular buses to **Bom Jardim**, from where there is a single daily bus to **Cuiabá**.

Mato Grosso Amazon
soya plantations and a handful of pristine wildlife and indigenous reserves

Northern Mato Grosso is an enormous sea of soya which has washed much of the Amazon rainforest out of northern Mato Grosso under waves of agricultural expansion powered by the policies of the world's largest soya farmer: Mato Grosso's senator and former governor Blairo Maggi, who once reached number 62 on the Forbes power list. On ascending to the governership of Mato Grosso, Maggi talked of tripling the area of soya planted in the Amazon.

In an interview conducted with Larry Rohter of the *New York Times*, Maggi defended his destruction of the forest stating: "To me, a 40% increase in deforestation doesn't mean anything at all, and I don't feel the slightest guilt over what we are doing here. We're talking about an area larger than Europe that has barely been touched, so there is nothing at all to get worried about." He has been strongly supported by Lula, who declared in the same year that "The Amazon is not untouchable", and is an ally of Lula's expansionist successor, Dilma Roussef. In 2003, Maggi's first year as governor, loggers cleared 4560 sq miles of Mato Grosso forest, an area twice the size of Delaware, with annual sales raising billions of dollars. Maggi received the Golden Chainsaw Award from Greenpeace in 2005.

Since exposure in the world's press, he has since attempted to re-invent himself as a champion of the environment, buying heavily into the carbon credit market. But the damage is largely done, and only islands of forest remain in northern Mato Grosso. These are increasingly threatened by fires – usually started deliberately as a means of clearing land which would otherwise have to be protected. Fire fighters are few and far between, and mostly limited to volunteers, working for **Aliança da Terra** (www.aliancadaterra.org.br), an NGO urgently in need of funds and support.

The Xingu
The largest section of Mato Grosso forest by far is the indigenous reserves of the Xingu, which stretch into neighbouring Pará. These are home to dozens of tribal Brazilians, including the powerful Kayapó, and are protected under federal law since the indigenous cause was championed by the indefatigable Villas Boas brothers in the mid-20th century. The reserves are under threat from the Belo Monte dam – the third largest hydroelectric project in the world – which will alter the course of the Xingu River and prevent the migration of fish upriver, flood some 500 sq km of land and force some 40,000 indigenous and Caboclo people to re-locate or become dependent on government handouts for food.

São Félix do Araguaia
The main population centre in the Mato Grosso Xingu region, São Félix do Araguaia (population 14,500) has a high population of indigenous Carajás, whose handicrafts can be found between the pizzeria and **Mini Hotel** on Avenida Araguaia. There is some infrastructure for fishing. Indigenous *fazenda* owners may invite you as their guest. If you accept, remember to take a gift: pencils, radio batteries, a few sacks of beans or rice, or a live cockerel will be much appreciated. Many river trips are available for fishing or wildlife spotting.

Access to São Félix and Santa Teresinha is by bus from Cuiabá. The *rodoviária* is 3 km from the centre and waterfront, taxi US$15.

Jardim da Amazônia Reserve
300 km north of Cuiabá on the Rodovia MT-10, Km 88, São José do Rio Claro, Mato Grosso, T066-3386 1221, www.jdamazonia.com.br. Book through Pantanal Nature to ensure you have a wildlife guide as they are not available at the reserve.

Arriving at this private reserve by car is an incredible experience. The road from Cuiabá takes some five hours to drive, and is lined by soya, stretching to the horizon in every direction across the ceaseless plains. Thunderstorms flicker on the horizon and every hour or so you pass through a new agricultural town full of Stetsons and pickups.

From the main road, a turnoff leads onto a dirt track to Jardim da Amazônia and cuts immediately into thick forest, exuberant and full of life. The horizon disappears, birds flit, paca and agouti run across the dirt road and, after a mile, forest clears to reveal a beautiful house, set in tropical gardens and sitting on a lake at the bend of a healthy Amazon River. Behind are a cluster of little boutique cabins.

While it is entirely an island of forest (with no ecological corridors connecting it to the rest of the Amazon) the Jardim da Amazônia Reserve is sufficiently large to maintain healthy populations of large neotropical mammals. There are jaguar and puma here, anaconda and giant otter. Capybara graze on the garden lawns at twilight and a tapir comes to steal cashew fruits from trees near the rooms in the dead of night. The reserve is also one of the few places in the Amazon to which you can safely bring children. It offers a range of activities, including canoeing on the river, rainforest walks and wildlife watching.

Cristalino Rainforest Reserve
Alta Floresta, T066-3521 1396, www.cristalinolodge.com.br.

The road that runs due north from Cuiabá to Santarém (1777 km) is passable in all weather conditions as far as **Sinop**, and has recently been asphalted as far as **Santarém**. This will enable soya from Mato Grosso to be shipped via the Amazon to the Atlantic, out of a vast plant owned by **Cargill** but currently closed thanks to lobbying from Greenpeace Brazil. The areas around the road are among the principal victims of active deforestation, with land being cleared for cattle and soya farms. Soya is spreading beyond Mato Grosso into southern Pará.

There are, however, still extensive tracts of forest intact, especially near the Rio Cristalino, which is home to one of the Amazon's most spectacular rainforest reserves, the Cristalino Rainforest Reserve This is the best location in the Brazilian Amazon for wildlife enthusiasts, with superb guided visits to pristine rainforest, comfortable accommodation and wildlife-watching facilities as good as the best of Costa Rica or Ecuador.

Cristalino is a private reserve the size of Manhattan. It is contiguous with the 184,940-ha **Cristalino State Park**, which itself is connected to other protected Amazon areas, forming an important large conservation corridor in the southern Amazon. Ecotourism at Cristalino is a model of best practice and is streets ahead of anywhere else in Brazil. The management fulfil all four of the key conservational tourism criteria: conserving natural resources and biodiversity, conducting environmental education activities with the local community (leading to employment), practising responsible ecotourism (with recycling, water treatment, small group sizes and excellent guiding) and funding a research foundation.

Wildlife is abundant. Cristalino has so far recorded 600 bird species, with new ones

Essential Cristalino Rainforest Reserve

Finding your feet

Cristalino is reachable from Alta Floresta town, which is connected to Cuiabá by regular buses and flights. The airport, **Aeroporto Deputado Benedito Santiago**, is 4 km from the city centre.

Getting around

Alta Floresta was built in the late 1970s and laid out on a grid pattern. Finding your way around is straightforward. Cristalino Reserve representatives will meet you at the airport or bus station and transfer you to their hotels in the reserve by 4WD. Packages including transfers are available through the reserve's website.

added almost monthly. This amounts to half of the avifauna in the Amazon and a third of all species found in Brazil. All the spectacular large mammals are found here alongside very rare or endemic species, such as bush dogs, red-nosed bearded saki monkey and the recently discovered white-whiskered spider monkey. Whilst wildlife is difficult to see (as it is anywhere in the Amazon), the reserve offers some of the best facilities for viewing wildlife in the Americas – on trail walks, boat trips on the river or from the lodge's enormous birdwatching tower, which offers viewing in and above the forest canopy. There is also a hide next to a clay lick for seeing tapir, peccary and big cats, and harpy eagles nest in the grounds of the reserve's twin hotel, the **Floresta Amazônica** in Alta Floresta town. Scopes, binoculars and tape recorders are available and there is an excellent small library of field guides. The reserve also offers adventure activities including kayaking, rappelling and camping in the forest; sleeping in hammocks slung between the trees.

Listings Mato Grosso Amazon

Where to stay

São Félix do Araguaia

$$ Xavante
Av Severiano Neves 391, T066-3522 1305.
A/c, frigobar, excellent breakfast, delicious *cajá* juice, the owners are very hospitable. Recommended.

$ Pizzeria Cantinho da Peixada
Av Araguaia, next to the Texaco station, overlooking the river, T062-3522 1320.
Rooms to let by the owner of the restaurant, better than hotels. He also arranges fishing trips.

Cristalino Rainforest Reserve

$$$$ Cristalino Jungle Lodge
Reservations Av Perimetral Oeste 2001, Alta Floresta, T066-3521 1396, www.cristalino lodge.com.br. See opposite for full details.
A beautifully situated and well-run lodge on the Cristalino River in a private reserve. Facilities are the best in the Amazon and the lodge supports the local community, practices recycling and water treatment and funds a scientific research programme.

$$ Floresta Amazônica
Av Perimetral Oeste 2001, Alta Floresta, T066-3512 7100.
In the park with lovely views, pool, sports, all facilities.

$ Hotel Avenida
Av Castro Alves 47, Setor J, Alta Floresta, T066-3521 5874.
Close to the *rodoviária*, this hotel is well-run, equipped with new furniture, a/c, and serves good breakfasts.

Transport

São Félix do Araguaia
Bus To **Barra do Garças** with **Xavante** at 0830, arrive 0230; or 1930, arrive 1300 next day, US$40. Also to **São José do Xingu**, at 0800, 10 hrs, US$ 30. No buses to **Marabá**.

Jardim da Amazônia
Accessible with tour operators from Cuiabá only, or you can self drive. **Pantanal Nature Tours**, page 109, are the best option.

Cristalino Rainforest Reserve
Air Cristalino Jungle Lodge offers a free pick up and drop-off for guests. There's little reason to come if you're not going to the lodge. There are direct flights to **Cuiabá** and flights to **Brasília**, **Curitiba**, **Porto Alegre**, **Campinas**, **Cascavel**, **Ji-Paraná**, **Londrina**, **Maringá**, with **Azul**, www.voeazul.com.br.

Bus To **Cuiabá**, several daily, US$53, 12 hrs. The *leito* night bus is the best option.

The
Amazon

Amazonas &
the Amazon River

Nowhere does the Amazon feel more like the inland sea it once was than in Brazil's biggest state. The central flatlands are coursed by meandering rivers wider than the eye can see: the jet black Rio Negro swum by bubble-gum pink river dolphins, the coffee-brown Amazon or Solimões and the rushing Madeira. These are surrounded by the world's most extensive and unspoilt areas of lowland tropical forest, which rise in the north to huge boulder mountains peaking at the 2994-m Pico da Neblina.

Most tours and trips to jungle lodges begin in Manaus, a sprawling rubber-boom town. Lodge stays range from a few days on the lower Rio Negro, on the winding Urubu river or the Lago Mamori, all in easy reach of Manaus, or the wilder and remoter Mamirauá Ecological Reserve near Tefé which are better for wildlife.

There is almost nowhere in the vast forests of Amazonas state which is truly uninhabited. Civilizations have been living here from 11,000 BC and these people and their *caboclo* descendants maintain a rich cultural life. Staying with a riverine community is a fascinating experience. Although indigenous villages are very difficult to visit, their heritage can be experienced at the festivals in São Gabriel and in a popularized fashion at the Boi Bumba in Parintins, the Amazon's carnival, which takes place on an island in the middle of the river at the end of June.

Essential Manaus

Finding your feet

The modern **Eduardo Gomes Airport** is 10 km north of the city centre. Airport bus No 306 runs to the Praça da Matriz restaurant (aka Marques da Santa Cruz), next to the cathedral in the centre of town (every 30 minutes 0500-2300, US$1.00). A taxi to the centre costs around US$15 on the meter. Be warned that taxi drivers often tell arrivals that no bus to town is available.

The only usable road runs north to Boa Vista, Guyana and Venezuela. Visitors almost invariably arrive by plane or boat. The only long-distance buses arriving at the *rodoviária*, 5 km out of Manaus, are from Boa Vista, Presidente Figueiredo and Itacoatiara. To get to the centre, take a bus marked Praça Matriz or Cidade Nova, US$1, taxi US$15.

Boat passengers from Santarém, Belém, Parintins, Porto Velho, Tefé, Tabatinga (for Colombia and Peru), São Gabriel da Cachoeira and intermediate ports arrive at the **floating docks** in the centre, a couple of blocks south of Praça da Matriz, with direct access to the main artery of Avenida Eduardo Ribeiro, and 10 minutes' walk from the opera house and main hotel area. Boats from São Gabriel da Cachoeira, Novo Airão, and Caracaraí arrive at **São Raimundo**, upriver from the main port. Take bus No 101, No 112 or No 110, 40 minutes. Be careful of people who wander around boats after they've arrived at a port; they are almost certainly looking for something to steal. See also Transport, page 145.

Getting around

The Centro Histórico and dock areas are easily explored on foot. All city bus routes start on Marquês de Santa Cruz next to the Praça da Matriz and almost all then pass along the Avenida Getúlio Vargas (two blocks east of the opera house). Taxis can be found near the opera house, at the *rodoviária*, airport and in Ponta Negra. Many of the upmarket hotels are in Ponta Negra, which is 13 km from the city centre and can feel somewhat isolated.

When to go

It's good to visit any time of the year but is least comfortable in the wetter months of December to April. It's hot and humid all year.

Time required

Allow three days to explore Manaus.

Weather Manaus

January	February	March	April	May	June
30°C 23°C 249mm	30°C 23°C 231mm	30°C 23°C 262mm	30°C 23°C 221mm	30°C 23°C 170mm	30°C 23°C 84mm

July	August	September	October	November	December
30°C 23°C 58mm	31°C 23°C 38mm	32°C 23°C 46mm	32°C 24°C 107mm	32°C 24°C 142mm	30°C 23°C 203mm

Manaus (population 1.4 million), the state capital, sits at 32 m above sea level some 1600 km from the Atlantic. The city sprawls over a series of eroded and gently sloping hills divided by numerous creeks, and stands at the junction of the liquorice-black Rio Negro and the toffee-coloured Solimões, whose waters flow side by side in two distinct streams within the same river. The city is the commercial hub for a vast area including parts of Peru, Bolivia and Colombia, and ocean-going container vessels often dock here.

Manaus has been tidied up over the last 10 years and is now one of Brazil's more attractive state capitals. The **Centro Histórico** (the old rubber boom city centre), which huddles around the green and gold mock-Byzantine dome of the **Teatro Amazonas** opera house, has been tastefully refurbished and now forms an elegant pedestrian area with cafés, galleries, shops and museums. The area is a pleasant place to stroll around and sip a cool juice or a strong coffee, and many of the best hotels and guesthouses are found here. There are plenty of restaurants, bars and clubs, which support a lively, colourful nightlife.

Despite the city's size, the forest is ever present on the horizon and always feels just a short boat trip away. Beaches fringe its western extremities at Ponta Negra, whose sands are backed by towering blocks of flats, making it feel like a kind of Amazonian Ipanema.

There are plenty of sights near Manaus. The most vaunted are generally the least interesting. However, the Anavilhanas – the largest river archipelago in the world, comprising a beautiful labyrinth of forested islands, some fringed with white-sand beaches lapped by the jet-black waters of the Rio Negro – should not be missed; see page 147.

Manaus is also the main departure point for rainforest tours. There are many lodges around the city, from 20 minutes to four hours away. See boxes, pages 135 and 138. And although animals here are not as easy to see as in Mamirauá in Tefé or on the Rio Cristalino in Mato Grosso, the scenery is breathtaking.

Centro Histórico

The colonial streets that spread out from Teatro Amazonas and Praça São Sebastião are a reminder of Manaus's brief dalliance with wealth and luxury. Eduardo Ribeiro, the state governor who presided over these golden years, was determined to make 19th-century Manaus the envy of the world: a fine European city in which the nouveau riche could parade their linen and lace. He spared no expense. Trams were running in Manaus before they were in Manchester or Boston and its roads were lit by the first electric street lights in the world. The city's confidence grew with its majesty. Champagne flowed under the crystal chandeliers and prices rose to four times those of contemporaneous New York. Extravagance begot extravagance and rubber barons eager to compete in statements of affluent vulgarity fed their horses vintage wine or bought lions as guard cats.

In the 1890s, Ribeiro decided to put the icing on his cake, commissioning the Gabinete Português de Engenharia e Arquitetura to build an Italianate opera house, the **Teatro Amazonas** ⓘ *Praça São Sebastião, T096-622 1880, www.cultura. am.gov.br, Mon-Sat 0900-1700, 20-min tour US$2, students US$0.50*, and to surround it with stone-cobbled streets lined with elegant houses, plazas, and gardens replete with ornate fountains and gilded cherubs. Masks adorning the theatre walls were made in homage to great European artists, including Shakespeare, Mozart, Verdi and Molière and the driveway was paved in rubber to prevent the sound of carriage wheels spoiling performances. For the lavish interior, Ribeiro turned to the Roman painter Domenico de Angelis (who had painted the opera house in Belém in

Wildlife and people

Contrary to received wisdom the Amazon is not the best place in South America to see wildlife. Tree cover is dense, light generally low and most of the wildlife is either hidden during the day or swinging around in the canopy far above your head. If you want to see animals then you're better off visiting the Pantanal or the *cerrado* in Goiás, or Minas Gerais. However, a visit to Brazil without a visit to the Amazon is as unthinkable as a drive through Arizona without a stop at the Grand Canyon. The Amazon is simply magnificent.

Think of the Amazon not as a river or even a forest but as a huge, flowing inland sea. Water is everywhere, especially during the **wet season**, which lasts from November to May in most areas. During the floods, the water rises by 5-10 m and the forests around the main rivers form areas known as *várzea* (on brown-water rivers) and *igapós* (on black-water rivers). Trees are submerged almost to their canopies and it is possible to canoe between their trunks in search of wildlife. In the morning you can often hear the booming call of huge black caiman and the snort of dolphins. And, as the boats pass through the trees, startled hatchet fish jump into the bows. It is possible to canoe for tens of kilometres away from the main river flow, as *várzea* and *igapós* often connect one river to another, often via oxbow lakes covered in giant lilies. The lakes are formed when a meandering river changes course and leaves part of its previous flow cut off from the stream. In the **dry season** the rivers retreat into their main flow, exposing broad mudflats (on the brown-water rivers) or long beaches of fine white sand. Caiman and giant river turtles can often be seen basking on these in the evening sun, and wildlife spotting is generally a little easier at this

1883) and Giovanni Capranesi (an Italian colleague who had worked with Angelis on the Igreja de São Sebastião near the Teatro). Their grandiose decorations are magnificent both in their pomp and their execution. They include a series of trompe l'oeuil ceilings – showing the legs of the Eiffel Tower from beneath (in the auditorium) and the muse of the arts ascending to heaven surrounded by putti in the Salão Nobre reception room. Ribeiro also commissioned a Brazilian artist Crispim do Amaral to paint a stage curtain depicting *Iara*, the spirit of the river Amazon at the centre of the meeting of the waters, and a series of scenes of idealized indigenous Brazilian life based on Paulistano Carlos Gomes' opera, *O Guarany*, in the ballrooms. The steel for the building was moulded in Glasgow, the mirrors made in Venice and priceless porcelains from France, China and Japan were purchased to grace mantelpieces, stairwells and alcoves. After the theatre doors were opened in 1896, Caruso sang here and Pavlova danced.

But for all its beauty and expense the theatre was used for little more than a decade. In the early 20th century the rubber economy collapsed. Seeds smuggled by Englishman Henry Wickham to the Imperial Gardens at Kew, and thence to Malaysia, were producing a higher yield. The wild rubber economy dwindled and the doors to the opera house closed. Over the decades, the French tiles on the dome began to crack, the Italian marble darkened and the fine French furniture and English china slowly began to decay. What you see today is the product of careful restoration, which has returned the *teatro* to its time of year. Trees in the Amazon bear fruit at different times throughout the year; whenever a particular tree is in fruit it attracts large parrots, macaws and primates.

Nor is the Amazon empty. People live everywhere, and often in harmony with nature, especially in areas like the Mamirauá reserve and along the river Arapiuns near Alter do Chão. Belém and Manaus have lively urban cultural scenes, the former with great music all its own. Marajó has a unique ranch land culture built around the Asian water buffalo (the police even ride around on buffalo back) and harvesting the mangrove swamps. Parintins and Alter do Chão hold two of the liveliest and most raucous parties anywhere in Latin America. São Gabriel da Cachoeira, Tabatinga, the southern Tapajos and the Xingu, among more remote locations, are important repositories of still healthy and creative indigenous cultures.

What to take

Leave luggage with your tour operator and only take what is necessary for your trip. Long-sleeved shirts and long trousers made of modern wicking fabrics, walking boots, insect repellent and a hammock and/or mosquito net (if not provided by the local operator) are advisable for treks in the jungle – especially around the Amazon river itself where insects can be voracious. There are no mosquitoes around Alter do Chão and few on Marajó and on the Rio Negro. A hat offers protection from the sun on boat trips. Powerful binoculars are essential for spotting wildlife (at least 7x magnification is recommended, with the ability to focus at between 2.5 m and infinity). Buying bottled water at the local villages is a sure way to help the local economy, but it can be expensive in the lodges and it produces a great deal of waste plastic that is all too often thrown into the river directly or indirectly. Bring iodine, purification tablets or a modern water filter like PUR Scout or Aquapure (best with iodine for Amazon river water).

original glory. There are regular performances, which sell out very quickly, and an arts festival every April.

The Teatro Amazonas sits at the head of a handsome square, the **Praça São Sebastião** (now known as the **Espaço Cultural Largo de São Sebastião**), paved with black and white dragon's tooth stones and surrounded by attractive, freshly painted late 19th- and early 20th-century houses. Many are little cafés, galleries or souvenir shops and the area is a safe and pleasant place to while away an hour or two. There are often free concerts and street performance on weekend evenings and public holidays. In the middle of the square is another grand rubber boom construction, the bronze monument to the **Opening of the Ports**. It depicts *Iara* (the spirit of the Amazon River), embraced by Mercury, representing commerce and standing over five ships representing the continents of Europe, Africa, America, Oceania and Antarctica. In front of the monument is the modest **Igreja de São Sebastião** ⓘ *R 10 de Julho 567, T092-3232 4572*, whose interior is filled with more brilliantly coloured romantic paintings by Domenico de Angelis, Giancarlo Capranesi (who painted in the Teatro Amazonas and in Belém) and canvases by Bellerini and Francisco Campanella, both also Italian.

On the southwestern edge of the *praça* is Eduardo Ribeiro's house which, in 2010, opened as a museum. The **Museu Casa de Eduardo Ribeiro** ⓘ *R José Clemente 322, Centro, T092-3621 2938, www.cultura.am.gov.br, Tue-Sat 0900-1600, Sun 0900-1300, free guided* *tours*, showcases a little of this fascinating man's extraordinary life. The house is a tall town mansion built in a typically late-Victorian, eclectic style, with a neoclassical façade topped with balcony finished with a baroque flourish. The two floors of the three-storey interior are devoted to Ribeiro. They are sober when you consider his excesses, bringing together items known to have belonged to the ex-state governor along with photographs, letters and memorabilia, and furniture and decorations from the rubber boom period.

Ribeiro was perhaps the first black person to rise to high political office in the Americas and he did so from the simplest origins at a time when slavery had only recently been abolished. He was born in 1862 into a single parent family and rural poverty in Maranhão. Through sharp intelligence and an iron will, he obtained a scholarship to a military academy in Rio de Janeiro, graduating at the age of 25 with a degree in pure maths and natural science. He was dispatched to Manaus, which was at that time a backwater, to

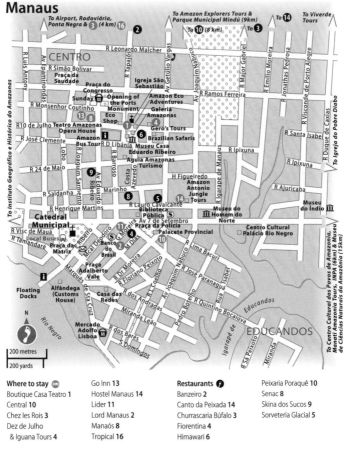

Manaus

Where to stay		**Restaurants**	
Boutique Casa Teatro **1**	Go Inn **13**	Banzeiro **2**	Peixaria Poraquê **10**
Central **10**	Hostel Manaus **14**	Canto da Peixada **14**	Senac **8**
Chez les Rois **3**	Lider **11**	Churrascaria Búfalo **3**	Skina dos Sucos **9**
Dez de Julho	Lord Manaus **2**	Fiorentina **4**	Sorveteria Glacial **5**
& Iguana Tours **4**	Manaós **8**	Himawari **6**	
	Tropical **16**		

work as an engineer for the army. It was a propitious time when a tiny outpost would begin to become one of the world's richest cities. Ribeiro had cannily positioned himself as a staunch republican during the final years of the empire and when the republic was finally proclaimed, his political postering, military pedigree and tertiary education helped him to rise through the administrative ranks of tiny Manaus. Just as the rubber boom was beginning Ribeiro ascended to power, becoming the first governor of the new Amazonas state. Despite his remarkable achievements, his fate was ultimately a sad one: he died alone, friendless and depressed, in a vast house on the outskirts of the city.

On the waterfront

The city's other sights are huddled around the waterfront. The red brick **Mercado Municipal Adolfo Lisboa** ① *R dos Barés 46*, was built in 1882 as a miniature copy of the now-demolished Parisian Les Halles. The wrought ironwork, which forms much of the structure, was imported from Europe and is said to have been designed by Eiffel. It reopened in 2014 after many years of restoration.

The remarkable harbour installations, completed in 1902, were designed and built by a Scottish engineer to cope with the Rio Negro's annual rise and fall of up to 14 m. The large **floating dock** is connected to street level by a 150-m-long floating ramp, at the end of which, on the harbour wall, can be seen the high-water mark for each year since it was built. The highest so far recorded was in 2009. When the river is high, the roadway floats on a series of large iron tanks measuring 2.5 m in diameter. The large beige **Alfândega** (**Customs House**) ① *R Marquês de Santa Cruz, Mon-Fri 0800-1300*, stands at the entrance to the city when arriving by boat. Said to be have been modelled on the one in Delhi, it was entirely prefabricated in England, and the tower once acted as a lighthouse.

Dominating the streets between the opera house and the waterfront; and right next to the local bus station, is the **Catedral Municipal**, on Praça Osvaldo Cruz, built in simple Jesuit style and very plain inside and out. Originally constructed in 1695 in wood and straw, it was burnt down in 1850. Nearby is the main shopping and business area, the tree-lined **Avenida Eduardo Ribeiro**, crossed by Avenida 7 de Setembro and bordered by ficus trees.

Some 200 m east of the cathedral is the **Biblioteca Pública (Public Library)** ① *R Barroso 57, T096-3234 0588, Mon-Fri 0730-1730*. Inaugurated in 1871, this is part of the city's architectural heritage. Featuring an ornate European cast-iron staircase, it is well stocked with 19th-century newspapers, rare books and old photographs, and is worth a visit.

Nearby, on the leafy, fountain-filled Praça Heliodoro Balbi (aka Praça da Policia) is a new museum complex, the **Palacete Provincial** ① *Praça Heliodoro Balbi s/n, T092-3635 5832, Tue-Thu 0900-1900, Fri 0900-2000, Sat 0900-2000, Sun 1600-2100, free*. The *palacete* is a stately late 19th-century civic palace which was once the police headquarters. It is now home to six small museums: the **Museu de Numismática** (with a collection on Brazilian and international coins and notes); the **Museu Tiradentes** (profiling the history of the Amazon police and assorted Brazilian military campaigns); the **Museu da Imagem e do Som** (with free internet, cinema showings and a DVD library); the **Museu de Arqueologia** (preserving a handful of Amazon relics); a restoration atelier and the **Pinacoteca do Estado** (one of the best art galleries in northern Brazil, with work by important painters such as Oscar Ramos, Moacir Andrade and Roberto Burle Marx). The *palacete* is a pleasant place to while away a few hours and has a decent air-conditioned café serving tasty coffee, cakes and savouries.

What and when to visit

It may be eaten into by loggers and ranchers around the edges and along the roads but the Brazilian Amazon alone (or to give it its proper name, the Amazon Biogeographical Domain) still covers 4.2 million sq km (according to the Amazon Socioenvironmental Geo-referenced Information Network), making it roughly as big as India, Turkey and the UK combined. You will only be able to dip your toes in the rivers on a visit. So it's important to choose where you want to go carefully. Here is a guide to the best destinations:

Manaus and around (Amazonas state)

The greatest choice of forest lodges roughly split between four locations: the blackwater **Rio Negro** (two to three hours from Manaus and the best for scenery especially around the Anavilhanas archipelago), the **Lago Mamori** (two hours or so from Manaus, with a mix of secondary and primary forest, riverine communities and flooded varzea forest; good for birds and small mammals), the **Rio Urubu** (two to three hours from Manaus and a brown water tributary of the Amazon with abundant life where it is closest to the Amazon river) and **lodges close to the city** (an hour or so from Manaus, best for half or one day trips, but in secondary forest). The best operators for these areas include **Amazon Gero Tours** and **Amazon Eco Adventures** (page 143). It's good at any time but driest between June and November.

Mamirauá Ecological Reserve (Amazonas state)

This extensive reserve, a 40-minute flight from Manaus near the town of Tefé, protects a vast, pristine area of seasonally flooded, gallery and terra firme forests, extensive lakes and some beautiful backwater tributaries. There is abundant wildlife and the reserve is a world leader in conservational tourism. The floating Uakari Lodge is a delight. Visit for at least three days. It's good at any time, but driest between June and November.

Presidente Figueiredo (Amazonas state)

An easy day trip from Manaus, this area is Amazon light, with great short walks, waterfalls and rushing rivers, although little wildlife. Good at any time, it's driest between June and November.

Boa Vista (Roraima state)

For side-trips to the Amazon savannah, the Rio Branco (which has indigenous villages and abundant bird life) and the table-top mountains of the Gran Sabana,

Other museums and cultural centres

The **Palácio Rio Negro** ① *Av 7 de Setembro 1546, T096-3232 4450, www.cultura.am.gov.br, Tue-Fri 0800-1600, Sat 0900-1300, free,* was the residence of a German rubber merchant until 1917 whereupon it became the state government palace. It underwent a major refurbishment in 2010 and now has an assortment of rooms presenting potted hagiographies of Amazonas state governors, exhibition spaces and a little café.

The **Museu do Índio** ① *R Duque de Caxias 296, near Av 7 Setembro, T096-3635 1922, Tue-Fri 1130-1400, Sat, 0830-1130, US$1.50,* is managed by the Salesian missionaries who have been responsible for the ravaging of much of the indigenous culture of the upper including Mount Roraima (the inspiration for Conan Doyle's *The Lost World*), straddling the border with Venezuela. Good at any time. Driest between September and March.

Marajó Island (Pará state)
An island the size of Denmark in the Amazon mouth. Gorgeous white-sand beaches, wetlands, mangrove forests and buffalo ranches with good birdwatching and vibrant local culture. A visit to primary forest on the island requires an extensive expedition. Stay at the Casarão da Amazônia and visit with Rumo Norte Expeditions (see page 164). It's best in the dry season between June and November.

Alter do Chão (Pará state)
Extensive dry tropical, *cerrado*, terra firme, varzea and gallery forests, tens of kilometres of empty fine, white-sand beaches, a brilliant blue river and almost no mosquitoes. Trips leave from the little village of Alter do Chão for boat cruises or homestays with river communities on the Tapajoa and Arapiuns rivers. it's best to visit when the beaches are exposed between August and January.

Cristalino Rainforest Reserve (Mato Grosso state)
Cristalino Jungle Lodge (see page 121) is the best forest lodge in the lowland Amazon for dedicated birders and wildlife enthusiasts, with excellent guiding, a canopy tower and full facilities. A side trip from Cuiabá and easily visited in conjunction with the Pantanal. It's best in the driest months of April to September.

Jardim da Amazônia (Mato Grosso state)
A private ranch preserving pristine primary forest in an extensive area of soya farms. With semi-tame capybaras, ocelot, tapirs and jaguars and a comfortable ranch house lodge, this is the best destination for families with young kids. Visit from Cuiabá with Pantanal Nature (see Tours, page 109). Best in the driest months, April to September.

Xapuri (Acre state)
A sustainable development reserve set up after the death of Chico Mendes, the environmental activist and in part run by his brother. Offers fascinating insights into rubber tapper life and the chance to see some beautiful forest filled with birds and small mammals, and replete with huge Brazil nut trees. Best in the driest months between April and September.

Rio Negro. It is rather dusty and run down, and betrays a 19th-century view of indigenous culture. The displays are poorly displayed and even more poorly labelled or understood, but there are plenty of artefacts, including handicrafts, ceramics, clothing, utensils and ritual objects from the various indigenous tribes of the upper Rio Negro. There is also a small craft shop.

West of the centre
The Instituto Geográfico e Histórico do Amazonas ① *R Frei José dos Inocentes 132, T092-3622 1260, Mon-Fri 0900-1200 and 1300-1600, US$1.50*, is in the oldest part of Manaus: a cluster of streets of tiny cottages dotted with grand, rubber boom buildings. It houses a

museum and library with over 10,000 books, which thoroughly document Amazonian life through the ages.

The **zoo** ⓘ *Estrada Ponta Negra 750, T096-2125 6402, Tue-Sun 0900-1700, US$1.50, take bus No 120 from R Tamandaré by the cathedral, US$0.70, every 30 mins, get off 400 m past the 1st infantry barracks*, a big white building, is run by CIGS, the Brazilian Army Unit specializing in jungle survival. About 300 Amazonian animals are kept in the gardens, including anacondas in a huge pit.

Further afield

The **Bosque da Ciência** is an area of lush forest maintained by the **Instituto Nacional de Pesquisas da Amazônia (INPA)** ⓘ *Bosque da Ciencia, Av Otávio Cabral, s/n, Aleixo T092-3643 3192, www.bosque.inpa.gov.br, Tue-Fri 0900-1200 and 1400-1600, Sat-Sun 0900-1600, US$1.50, take bus No 519 from the Praça da Matriz*, which conducts research into all aspects of the Amazon. There is a forested park where you can see rainforest flora and fauna before you go on your jungle tour. The animals here are kept in less distressing conditions than in the city zoo. Paca (*Agouti paca*), agouti (*Myoprocta exilis*), squirrel monkeys (*Saimiri scicureus*) and tamarins (*Saguinus sp*) roam free, and among the other animals on display are Amazonian manatee (*Trichechus inunguis*) and giant otter (*Pternura brasiliensis*). A small museum within the park has displays on indigenous peoples' use of the forest, medicinal plants and bottles of pickled poisonous snakes.

INPA also part-manages one of the largest urban rainforest reserve in the world, **MUSA (Museu da Amazônia)** ⓘ *Av Margarita, Cidade de Deus, T092-3582 3188, www.museudaamazonia.org.br, Tue-Sun 0900-1700, US$2.60, US$5 to climb the canopy tower, take bus 667 from the centre*, which lies on the northeastern edge of Manaus. With extensive forest trails, a canopy observation tower and an exhibition space devoted to Amazonian natural history, this is far more interesting than the Jardim Botânico Chico Mendes, which isn't really worth visiting. **Pedro Fernandes Neto** ⓘ *T092-8831 1011, www.amazonecoadventures.com*, can organize guided tours and other activities.

The **Centro Cultural dos Povos da Amazônia** ⓘ *Praça Francisco Pereira da Silva s/n, Bola da Suframa, Centro, T096-3232 5373, www.cultura.am.gov.br, Mon-Fri 0900-1600, US$1.50, many buses run to the praça including Nos 213, 215, 355, 418, 620, 624 and 611*, is a large cultural complex devoted to the indigenous peoples of the Amazon. Outside the building there are Desano and a Yanomami *maloca* (traditional buildings), inside is the **Museu do Homem do Norte**, a modern and well-curated museum in the main building preserving many artefacts, including splendid headdresses, ritual clothing and weapons, as well as the way of life of *caboclo* river people. Explanatory displays are in Portuguese and passable English. It's a far better museum than the old-fashioned Museu do Indio. There are also play areas for children, a library and internet.

There is a curious little church, **Igreja do Pobre Diabo**, at the corner of Avenida Borba and Avenida Ipixuna, in the suburb of Cachoeirinha. It is only 4 m wide by 5 m long, and was built by a local trader, the 'poor devil' of the name. To get there, take the 'Circular 7 de Setembro Cachoeirinha' bus from the cathedral to Hospital Militar.

The **Museu de Ciências Naturais da Amazônia (Natural Science Museum)** ⓘ *Av Cosme Ferreira, Cachoeira Grande suburb, 15 km from centre, T092-3644 2799, Mon-Sat 0900-1200 and 1400-1700, US$4, best to combine with a visit to INPA (see above), and take a taxi from there*, is one of the city's little-known treasures. The remote museum is Japanese-run with characteristic efficiency, and the exhibits are beautifully displayed and clearly labelled in Japanese, Portuguese and English. The main building houses

ON THE ROAD
Responsible jungle lodges and tour operators

Increasing numbers of travellers try and choose companies and lodges who conserve both the forest and local life and culture. The Amazon is a delicate place and a little pollution – especially with plastics – goes and long way and stays an even longer time. Certain species of fish – particularly *pirarucu* – have been over-harvested over the last two decades, and communities struggle to survive often with scant or inappropriate support from local or state government. Choosing an operator like **Amazon Gero Tours** in Manaus, **Mamiraua** in Tefé or **Sabia** in Alter do Chão – who do their best to support communities, the forest and rivers or both – can make a real difference.

Here are a few questions you can ask to check if the operator you are choosing has best practice according to the declarations of the World Tourism Organisation's responsible and ecotourism guidelines and those of the UN Department of Economic and Social Affairs.

Community sensitivity
What does the operator do to:
- Minimize negative social, economic and environmental impacts
- Generate greater economic benefits for local people. Do they pay above the minimum wage, for instance?
- Improve working conditions for locals
- Involve local people in decision-making that affect their lives. Do they support education projects or schools for example?
- Make positive contributions to the conservation of natural and cultural heritage
- Provide a greater understanding of local cultural, social and environmental issues
- Encourage respect between tourists and hosts

Green tourism
What does the operator do to:
- Recycle and remove rubbish from the lodges
- Generate electricity through sustainable sources (like solar power)
- Recycle water
- Encourage tourists to remove rubbish they bring to the Amazon
- Use sustainably sourced products such as recycled timber and sustainably caught fish
- Safeguard local wildlife through monitoring and research
- Provide technical support to research centres and conservation organizations

hundreds of preserved Amazonian insects and butterflies, together with stuffed specimens of a selection of the river's bizarre fish. You can also see live versions, including the endangered pirarucu (*Arapaima gigas*), which can grow up to 3.5 m, and a primitive osteoglottid fish that breathes air.

Beaches
The **Praia da Ponta Negra**, which lies upstream of the city's pollution, is the most popular and the most heavily developed. It is backed by high-rise flats and lined with open-air restaurants, bars and areas for beach volleyball and football. Many of the better hotels, including the **Tropical**, are situated here. Nightlife is lively, especially at weekends; on most nights at least one of the bars (such as **O Laranjinha**, see page 141) will have boi bumba dance shows.

To get here, take any bus marked 'Ponta Negra' (eg No 120) from the local bus station next to the cathedral. The beach can also be reached on the **Tropical**'s shuttle bus (see Where to stay, below). Boats also leave from here for other beaches on the Rio Negro.

The meeting of the waters

About 15 km from Manaus is the confluence of the coffee-coloured **Rio Solimões** (Amazon) and the black-tea coloured **Rio Negro**, which is some 8 km wide. The two rivers run side by side for about 6 km without their waters mingling. This phenomenon is caused by differences in the temperature, density and velocity of the two rivers.

Tourist agencies run boat trips to this spot (US$30-50). The simplest route is to take a taxi, or bus No 713 'Vila Buriti', to the Porto de CEASA dock, and take the car ferry across to Careiro. Ferries leave regularly when full and there are many smaller boats too. The last departure from CEASA is at 1800 and the last return to CEASA from Careiro is 2000. Motor boats charge US$10 per person or US$60 per boat (up to five people). Boats also leave from the hotel **Tropical** (US$70 per boat, up to five people). You should see river dolphins, especially in the early morning. Alternatively, hire a motorized canoe from near the market in the city centre (about US$20; per person or US$165 per boat for up to eight people). Allow three to four hours to experience the meeting properly. A 2-km walk along the Porto Velho road from the CEASA ferry terminal leads to some ponds, some way from the road, in which huge Victoria Regia water lilies can be seen from April to September.

Listings Manaus map p130

Tourist information

The website for tourism in the Amazon, www.visitamazonas.am.gov.br, has extensive information on accommodation throughout the state in Portuguese. *A Crítica* (www.acritica.uol.com.br) newspaper lists local events in Portuguese.

Centros de Atendimento ao Turista (CAT)
Main office: 50 m south of the opera house, Av Eduardo Ribeiro 666, T092-3182 6250. Mon-Fri 0800-1700, Sat 0800-1200.
Additional offices are at the **airport** (T096-3182 9850, 24 hrs; at the **port** (regional terminal, Rua Marquês de Santa Cruz, Armazém 07, T092-3182 7950, Mon-Fri 0800-1700; and international terminal (Rua Marquês de Santa Cruz, Armazém 10, which opens only when cruise liners dock).

Where to stay

Whilst there are a number of hostels and cheap guesthouses, Manaus lacks hotels of quality in the Centro Histórico. The best establishments are in Ponta Negra, close to the airport or the commercial centre; all inconvenient for travellers here to see the sights. The best area to stay in the city centre is around the Teatro Amazonas, where the Italianate colonial houses and cobbled squares have been refurbished. Although the area around Av Joaquim Nabuco and R dos Andradas has lots of cheap hotels, this is a sketchy area at night, as is the Zona Franca, around the docks.

$$$$ Tropical
Av Coronel Teixeira 1320, Ponta Negra, T092-3659 5000, www.tropicalhotel.com.br.
A lavish though increasingly frayed 5-star hotel 20 km outside the city in a semi-forested parkland setting next to the river. The hotel has a private beach, tennis court and a large pool with wave machine. There are several restaurants including a decent *churrascaria*. The river dock is a departure point for many river cruises.

$$$ Boutique Casa Teatro
R 10 de Julho 632, T092-3633 8381,
www.casateatro.com.br.
The best place to stay in the historic centre,
in a superb location opposite the Teatro
Amazonas. Rooms are tiny but tastefully
decorated and modern, with bunk beds,
and there's a sitting room with panoramic
views of the opera house. Free Wi-Fi.

$$$ Lord Manaus
R Marcílio Dias 217, T092-3622 2844,
www.lordmanaus.com.br.
Pleasant, spacious lobby and standard a/c
rooms with writing desks and beds, all of
which are in some need of refurbishment.
Conveniently located for boats and shops,
in the heart of the Zona Franca, but it is
not safe to walk around this area at night.

$$$ Manaós
Av Eduardo Ribeiro 881, T092-3633 6148
www.hotelmanaos.com.br.
Right next to the Teatro Amazonas.
Spruce a/c rooms with marble floors
and smart bathrooms. Decent breakfast.

$$$-$$ Chez Les Rois
Travessa dos Cristais, Quadra G, 1, Conj
Manauense, Bairro Nossa Senhora Das
Graças, T092-98102 7186, www.chezlesrois.
com.br.
Family-run B&B in a mock-colonial house
with 10 homey rooms (with polished
wood or tiled floors, en suites and modest
furnishings), a pool and pleasant public
spaces. A 20-min bus ride from the colonial
centre (US$7.50 in a taxi).

$$$-$$ Go Inn
R Monsenhor Coutinho 560, Centro Histórico,
T092-3306 2600, www.atlanticahotels.com.br.
One of the very few decent, modern a/c
accommodation options in the city centre,
with undistinguished but no-nonsense
corporate-designed rooms with tiny desks,
queen-sized beds and wall-mounted TVs.

$$ Central
R Dr Moreira 202, T092-3622 2600,
www.hotelcentralmanaus.com.br.
A business hotel tucked away behind the
Palacete Provincial, with a range of rooms,
many very scruffy although some well-kept;
look at a few. Excellent large breakfast.

$$ Lider
Av 7 de Setembro 827, T092-3621 9700,
www.liderhotelmanaus.com.br.
Small modern a/c rooms with marble
floors, little breakfast tables and en suite
bathrooms. The best are at the front of the
hotel on the upper floors. Very well kept.

$ Dez de Julho
R 10 de Julho 679, T092-3232 6573,
www.hoteldezdejulho.com.
One of the better cheap options, with clean
simple rooms (some with a/c and hot water).
One of the best tour operators, **Amazon
Gero Tours**, is in the lobby. Efficient, English-
speaking staff. Great location next to Praça
São Sebastião.

$ Hostel Manaus
*R Lauro Cavalcante 231, Centro, T092-
3233 4545, www.hostelmanaus.com.*
Cheaper for HI members. HI hostel in one of
the city's original houses. Good-value dorms
and private rooms. Quiet and reasonably
central with views of the city from the
rooftop patio. Australian-run. Great place to
join a jungle tour, with a good tour operator
in the lobby. They also run **Pousada Pico
da Neblina** (www.pousadapicodaneblina.
com) in São Gabriel da Cachoeira. Not to be
confused with a non-HI hostel in the city
using a similar name.

Lodges accessible from Manaus
When reserved in advance, either direct or
through an operator (see page 143), lodges
will organize all transfers from either a
Manaus hotel or in many cases the airport.
Community homestays are also available –
often for a cheaper price than a jungle

Choosing a lodge or tour

If you are interested first and foremost in wildlife and want accurate scientific information and a designated wildlife guide then you should head either to **Mamirauá** or **Cristalino Jungle Lodge** (see page 121). Manaus and Belém (with the Ilha do Marajó and/or a side-flight to Alter do Chão) are great destinations for first-time visits and for trips which take in more than the forest. Both cities are fascinating destinations in their own right and are well worth exploring.

When choosing a tour company in Manaus don't go for the cheapest. The cut price operators pay their staff cut price salaries, use poor equipment and visit locations which are cheap and easy to get to. Splash out a little and you will end up having a far more rewarding (and comfortable) trip with a guide who even if they are not trained zoologists at least have a good working knowledge of the forest and local life.

Standard tours (especially from Manaus) involve a walk through the forest looking at plants and their usage, caiman spotting at night (many guides drag caiman out of the water, which has negative long-term effects and should be discouraged), piranha fishing and boat trips through the *igapós* (flooded forests) or the *igarapés* (creeks). They may also visit a *caboclo* (river village) or one of the newly established indigenous villages around the city. Other trips involve light adventure such as rainforest survival, which involves learning how to find water and food in the forest, and how to make a shelter and string up a hammock for a secure night's sleep. Trips out of Alter do Chão and Xapuri tend to involve homestays with local riverine communities and trail walks (and in the case of Alter river excursions) from the villages. Cristalino, Jardim Amazônia and Mamirauá are lodge-based trips focusing on seeing the animals. Boa

lodge – through **Amazon Gero Tours** (see page 143).

Most lodges do not adhere to proper ecotourism practices; this guide lists the exceptions. Good practice includes integration and employment for the local community, education support, recycling and proper rubbish disposal, and trained guides with good wildlife lodges. We have tried wherever possible to support operators who adhere to this code. We would love to receive feedback about lodges and operators you feel are (or aren't) making a difference. See also box, above, and page 135.

$$$$ Amazon Jungle Palace
Office at R Emilio Moreira 470, T092-3211 0400, www.amazonjunglepalace.com.br.
A rather ungainly floating lodge with very comfortable a/c 4-star rooms and a pool,

on a black-water tributary of the Rio Negro some 5 km from the Anavilhanas. Excellent guides and service but, as ever with lodges close to Manaus, somewhat depleted forest. The tour company that runs the lodge offers jungle cruises. Avoid these as they are in huge boats with huge crowds, offering little chance of seeing more than scenery.

$$$$ Anavilhanas Lodge
Edif Manaus Shopping Centre, Av Eduardo Ribeiro 520, sala 304, T092-3622 8996, www.anavilhanaslodge.com.
This is the nearest jungle lodges get to boutique. Minimalist rooms with high thread count cotton on the beds, low-lighting, flatscreen TVs and tasteful rustic chic hangings and decor sit in thatch-roofed cabins whose front walls are entirely glass-fronted – affording spectacular views

Vista trips focus more on light adventure, hiking up the table-top mountains and taking excursions on the Rio Branco river.

Trips from Manaus vary in length. A half-day or a day trip will usually involve a visit to the meeting of the waters and the Parque Ecológico do Lago Janauari, where you are likely to see plenty of birds, some primates and river dolphins. The reserve was set up to receive large numbers of tourists so there are captive parrots on display and the area feels very touristy. Yet ecologists agree that the reserve helps relieve pressure on other parts of the river. Boats for day trippers leave the harbour in Manaus constantly throughout the day, but are best booked at one of the larger operators. Those with more time can take the longer cruises with a company like **Amazon Clipper** (see page 144) or the **MV Tucano** or stay in one of the rainforest lodges. To see virgin rainforest, a five-day trip by boat is needed.

Prices vary but usually include lodging, guide, transport, meals (but not drinks) and activities. The recommended companies charge around US$60-100 per person per day for all food, transfers and accommodation in a private room with its own bathroom. Backpacker packages staying in shared accommodation can be cheaper.

Homestays

It is possible to stay with a riverine community in the heart of the Amazon through **Amazon Gero Tours** (see What to do, page 143) or any of the companies in Alter do Chão, a fascinating alternative to a jungle lodge offering a real glimpse of the realities of Amazon life. Homestays are based within villages and are fairly rustic. Bring a Portuguese phrasebook, your own mosquito net, toiletries, torch (flashlight) and insect repellent. What is lacking in comfort is more than made up for by a far more immersive experience in Amazon life than you will get in a lodge and often at a lower cost.

out over the Rio Negro and the adjacent Anavilhanas archipelago. There's a lodge bar serving *cupuaçu* caipirinhas, amongst other drinks, and a range of comfortable lounging areas. But bring a mosquito net. The large menu of activities includes the standard piranha fishing, community visits, hikes and dolphin spotting alongside more meditative kayaking and sunset tours of the Anavilahnas.

$$$$ Ariaú Amazon Towers
60 km and 2 hrs by boat from Manaus, on the Rio Ariaú, 2 km from Archipélago de Anavilhanas; office at R Leonardo Malcher 699, Manaus, T092-2121 5000, www.ariautowers.com.br.
With 271 rooms in complex of towers connected by walkways, a pool, meditation centre, large restaurant and gift shop, this is a

jungle hotel more than a jungle lodge. If you are after intimacy with the forest you won't find it here. But the hotel is a good option for older people or those with small children. The guided tours are generally well run, although specialist wildlife guides are not available and tame wildlife hangs around the lodge.

$$$$-$$$ Amazon Ecopark Lodge
Igarapé do Tarumã, 20 km from Manaus, 15 mins by boat, T092-3005 5536, www.amazonecopark.com.br.
The best lodge within an hour of Manaus, in a private forest that would otherwise have been deforested. The lodge makes a real effort at conservation and good practice. The apartment cabins are very comfortable (hot showers) and set in the forest. The lodge has a lovely white-sand beach and is close to the **Amazon Monkey Jungle**, an ecological

park where primate species (including white uakari) are treated and rehabilitated in natural surroundings. The **Living Rainforest Foundation**, which administers the Ecopark, also offers educational jungle trips and overnight camps (bring your own food), entrance US$10.

$$$ Amazon Eco Adventures Lodge
Rio Urubu, book through Amazon Eco Adventures (see page 143).
Lovely little floating lodge with palm-thatch walls and an attractive deck area. The lodge is set on a bend in the Urubu river close to where it meets the main stream of the Amazon. The area is rich in wildlife and luckily poor in mosquitoes.

$$$ Amazon Turtle Lodge
Paraná do Mamori, T092-3613 4683.
Run in partnership with the local community and offering simple wood huts with palm thatch roofs set in a line in a stand of secondary growth forest on the shores of Mamori lake.

$$$ Ararinha Lodge
Paraná do Araçá, exclusively through Amazon Gero Tours, www.amazongerotours.com.
One of the more comfortable lodges in the Mamori area. This lodge sits on a riverbank overlooking the Paraná do Araça – a little visited and unspoilt river running off the Lago do Mamori lake regions. Accommodation is in smart wooden chalets housing suites of individual rooms which come complete with double or single beds with mosquito nets. The area is one of the best for wildlife in the Mamori region.

$$$ Dolphin Lodge
Paraná do Mamori, T092-3663 0392, www.dolphinlodge.tur.br.
A small lodge with simple wooden cabins perched on a grassy bluff overlooking the Parana do Mamori River (off Lago Mamori). The lodge runs tours and has kayaks for guests to use.

$$$ Juma
Lago da Juma, T092-3232 2707, www.jumalodge.com.
A refurbished lodge in a beautiful location on the outer reaches of Lago Mamori at Juma. Accommodation is in comfortable wooden and palm-thatch huts on high stilts right on the riverbank. The owners have a burgeoning interest in birdwatching and run proper wildlife tours.

$$$-$$ Amazon Antônio's Lodge
Through Antonio Jungle Tours, www.antonio-jungletours.com.
A thatched roof wooden lodge with plain, fan-cooled wooden rooms and an observation tower. Set in a beautiful location overlooking a broad curve in the river Urubu 200 km from Manaus.

Restaurants

Many restaurants close Sun night and Mon. The best are a 10- to 15-min taxi ride from the Centro Histórico.

$$$ Banzeiro
R Libertador 102, Adrianópolis, T092-9204 7056, www.restaurantebanzeiro.com.br.
Chef Felipe Schaedler cooks gourmet traditional Amazonian and Brazilian dishes, served in a pretty dining room. 10-min taxi ride from the Centro Histórico. Dishes include *pato no tucupi* and *caldeirinha de tucanaré* (peacock bass fish broth). Delicious drinks include *batidas de cacau* (made with the chocolate bean fruit) and *caipiroska amazonica* (with *cupuaçu*).

$$$-$$ Himawari
R 10 de Julho 618, opposite Teatro Amazonas, T092-3233 2208.
A conveniently located a/c Japanese restaurant serving reasonable sushi, sashimi, steamed pastries and salads by Teruko Sakai who was born and spent his early years in Nagasaki. Attentive service, good sake and open Sun night when many restaurants close.

$$ Canto da Peixada
R Emílio Moreira 1677 (Praça 14 de Janeiro), T092-3234 3021.
One of the longest-established *peixadas* (simple fresh fish restaurants) in Manaus. Unpretentious, always vibrant and with excellent Amazon fishes from Jaraqui to Tambaqui. A short taxi ride from the centre.

$$ Churrascaria Búfalo
R Pará 490, Vieiralves, T092-3131 9000, www.churrascariabufalo.com.br.
The best *churrascaria* in Manaus, withan US$8 all-you-can-eat Brazilian barbecue and a vast choice of meat. Come with an empty stomach. It's 5 mins' taxi ride from the centre.

$$ Fiorentina
R José Paranaguá 44, Praça da Polícia, T092-3232 1295.
Fan-cooled traditional Italian with cheesy vegetarian dishes and even cheesier piped music. Great *feijoada* on Sat, half-price on Sun. Dishes are served with mugs of wine.

$ Senac
R Saldanha Marinho 644, T092-3633 2277. Lunch only.
Cookery school with a self-service restaurant. Highly recommended.

$ Skina dos Sucos
Eduardo Ribeiro and 24 de Maio.
A large choice of Amazonian fruit juices and bar snacks.

$ Sorveteria Glacial
Av Getúlio Vargas 161, and other locations.
Recommended for unusual ice creams such as *açaí* and *cupuaçu*.

Bars and clubs

Manaus has lively nightlife with something going on every night. **O Laranjinha** in Ponta Negra is popular any week night and has a live Boi Bumba dance show on Wed.

The scene is constantly changing and clubs and bars are often in different districts far from the centre. The cheapest way of exploring Manaus's nightlife is with a guide such as **DJ (Djalma) Oliveira** (T092-9185 4303, djalmatour@hotmail.com, or book through **Amazon Gero Tours**), who will take visitors out to sample Manaus' club life. He is cheaper than a taxi and speaks a little English.

Entertainment

Performing arts
For **Teatro Amazonas** and **Centro Cultural Palácio Rio Negro**, see pages 127 and 132. In Praça da Saudade, R Ramos Ferreira, there is sometimes a Sun funfair from 1700; try prawns and *calaloo* dipped in *tacaca* sauce. **Teatro da Instalação**, *R Frei José dos Inocentes 445, T092-3234 4096*. A performance space in a restored historic building with free music and dance (from ballet to jazz), May-Dec Mon-Fri at 1800. Charge for Sat and Sun shows. Recommended.

Festivals

6 Jan Epiphany.
Feb Carnaval in Manaus has spectacular parades in a *sambódromo* modelled on Rio's, but with 3 times the capacity. Tourists may purchase grandstand seats, but admission at ground level is free (don't take valuables). Carnaval lasts for 5 days, culminating in the parade of the samba schools.
3rd week in Apr A Semana do Indio (Indigenous Brazilian week), a festival celebrating all aspects of indigenous life. Tribal people arrive in Manaus, there are small festivals and events (contact the tourist office for details, see page 136) and indigenous handicrafts are on sale throughout the city.
Jun Festival do Amazonas, a celebration of all the cultural aspects of Amazonas life, indigenous, Portuguese and from the northeast, especially dancing. Also in Jun is the **Festival Marquesiano**, with typical dances from those regions of the world which have sent immigrants to Amazonas, performed by the students of the Colégio Marquês de Santa Cruz.

29 Jun São Pedro, boat processions on the Rio Negro.

Sep Festival de Verão do Parque Dez, 2nd fortnight, festival with music, fashion shows, beauty contests and local foods at the Centro Social Urbano do Parque Dez. In the last week of Sep is the **Festival da Bondade**, with stalls from neighbouring states and countries offering food, handicrafts, music and dancing at SESI, Estr do Aleixo, Km 5.

Oct Festival Universitário de Música (**FUM**), the most traditional festival of music in Amazonas, organized by the university students, on the university campus.

8 Dec Processão de Nossa Senhora da Conceição, from the Igreja Matriz through the city centre and returning to Igreja Matriz for a solemn Mass.

Shopping

All shops close at 1400 on Sat and all day Sun. Since Manaus is a free port, the riverfront is lined with electronics shops. This area, known as the **Zona Franca**, is the commercial centre, where the shops, banks and hotels are concentrated.

Markets and souvenirs

To buy a hammock head to the **Casa das Redes** and other shops on R dos Andradas. There are now many handicrafts shops in the area around the theatre. The souvenir shop at the **INPA** (see page 134) has some interesting Amazonian products on sale. The markets near the docks are best in the early morning. There is a very good Sun market in the **Praça do Congresso**, Av E Ribeiro. **Ponta Negra** beach boasts a small 'hippy' market, which is very lively at weekends. There is a good supermarket at the corner of Av Joaquim Nabuco and R Sete de Setembro.

Central de Artesanato Branco e Silva, *R Recife 1999, T092-3642 5458*. A gallery of arts and crafts shops and artist's studios selling everything from indigenous art to wooden carvings by renowned Manaus sculptor Joe Alcantara.

Ecoshop, *Largo de São Sebastião, T092-3234 8870, and Amazonas Shopping, T092-3642 2026, www.ecoshop.com.br*. Indigenous arts and crafts from all over the Amazon, including Yanomami and Tikuna baskets, Wai Wai necklaces and Baniwa palm work.

Galeria Amazonica, *R Costa Azevedo 272, Largo do Teatro, T092-3233 4521, www. galeriamazonica.org.br*. A large, modern space filled with Waimiri Atroari indigenous arts and crafts, from weapons, basketware, jewellery and clothing. One of the best places for buying indigenous art in Brazil.

What to do

Bus tours

Amazon Bus, *departures from CAT next to Teatro Amazonas, T092-3234 5071, www. tucunareturismo.com.br. Mon-Sat 0900 and 1430*. This double-decker bus (a/c ground floor and open-top upper deck) visits the principal attractions in Manaus on a 3-hr, drive-by tour with a guided commentary in Portuguese, US$15. However, it's not very good value for time or money. Many more interesting sights are not included (notably the Palacete Principal, the floating docks and INPA), there are some bizarre inclusions (like the Federal University) and there's only one proper stop, Ponta Negra Beach, where the bus breaks for snacks and a breath of warm air.

Swimming

Swimming is possible at **Ponta Negra** beach, 13 km from the centre (Soltur bus, US$0.50), although the beach virtually disappears beneath the water Apr-Aug.

There is good swimming at waterfalls on the Rio Tarumã, where there is lunch and shade; crowded at weekends. Take the Tarumã bus from R Tamandaré or R Frei J dos Inocentes (30 mins, US$0.50; very few Mon-Fri), getting off at the police checkpoint on the road to Itacoatiara. There is also superb swimming in the natural pools and under falls of clear water in the little streams which

Touts in Manaus

There are many hustlers at the airport in Manaus and on the street (particularly around the hotels and bars on Joaquim Nabuco and Miranda Leão), and even at hotel receptions. It is not wise to go on a tour with the first friendly face you meet. All go-betweens earn a commission so recommendations cannot be taken at face value and employing a freelance guide not attached to a company is potentially dangerous as they may not be qualified; check out their credentials. Tourist offices are not allowed by law to recommend guides, but can provide you with a list of legally registered companies. Unfortunately, disreputable companies are rarely dealt with in any satisfactory manner, and most continue to operate. Book direct with the company itself and ask for a detailed, written contract if you have any doubts. Above all avoid the cheapest tours; they are almost invariably the worst.

rush through the woods, but take locals' advice on swimming in the river as electric eels are common and there is increasing industrial pollution.

Every Sun, boats depart from the port in front of the market for beaches along **Rio Negro**, US\$2, leaving when full and returning at the end of the day. This is a real locals' day out, with loud music and food stalls on the sand.

Tours in the Amazon

When booked ahead, agencies listed here will meet visitors at the airport, book Manaus hotels and organize all transfers.
Águia Amazonas Turismo, *R 24 de Maio 440 CA-H sala 1, Vila Baipendi, T092-3231 1449, www.aguiaamazonas.com.br*. Bespoke trips, lodge stays and cruises conducted by Samuel Basilio – an experienced guide from the upper Rio Negro specializing in long expeditions (who has worked on many BBC documentaries as a location finder), and his brother-in-law Antonio João da Silva.
Amazon Antonio Jungle Tours, *c/o Hostel Manaus, R Lauro Cavalcante 231, T092-3234 1294, www.antonio-jungletours.com*. Jungle stays on the Rio Urubu, a black-water river 200 km northeast of Manaus and some of the best-value packages for backpackers and a reliable, well-run service with local, English-speaking guides.

Amazon Eco Adventures, *R 10 de Julho, 695, T092-8831 1011, www.amazonecoadventures. com*. Some of the best 1-day boat tours of the Solimões and Rio Negro available, featuring the 'meeting of the waters', *boto* encounters, river beaches, indigenous people and with options for water sports and fishing. The agency also runs spectacular ultra-light flights over the forest. Good value, excellent guiding.
Amazon Explorers, *Av Djalma Batista 2100, T092-2133 4777, www.amazonexplorers.tur.br*. Day tours including the 'meeting of the waters', Lago do Janauari, rubber collecting and lunch a number of lodges (all listed on the website) and booking and transfers for Mamirauá and the Boi Bumba and Parintins. From around US\$150 per person per day.
Amazon Gero Tours, *R 10 de Julho 679, sala 2, T092-9983 6273, www.amazongerotours.com*. Excellent tours to a series of lodges around Lago Mamori, transfers to São Gabriel for the festivals, day trips to Presidente Figueiredo and around the city of Manaus (including 'meeting of the waters'), and bookings made for lodges everywhere. Gero, the owner, is very friendly and dedicated, and one of the few operators in Manaus that genuinely contributes a share of his profits to local riverine communities. He also runs excellent volunteer projects, with homestays

at riverine communities, and has a lodge at Ararinha Lake.

Iguana Tour, *R 10 de Julho 679 (Hotel 10 de Julho), T092-3663 6507, www.amazon brasil.com.br.* Offers an extensive range of trips of various lengths. Good facilities including riverboat, **Juma** lodge and campsite in the forest.

Maia Expeditions, *T092-99983 7141, maiaexpeditions.com.* A standard package of well-organized day trips and jungle tours including trips to Presidente Figueiredo.

Manati Amazônia, *Av Getúlio Vargas 334, sala 6 at Huascar Figueiredo, T092-3234 2534, www.manatiamazonia.com.* A Franco-Brazilian company offering excursions to the Anavilhanas, riverboat cruises and tours in the forests around Mamori with accommodation at **Juma** lodge.

Viverde, *R das Guariúbas 47, Parque Acariquar, T092-3248 9988, www.viverde.com.br.* A family-run agency acting as a broker for a broad range of Amazon cruises and lodges (including the beautiful **Aldeia dos Lagos** lodge in Silves) and running their own city tours and local excursions.

Tour guides

Guides sometimes work individually as well as for tour agencies, and the best ones will normally be booked up in advance. Some will only accompany longer expeditions and often subcontract shorter trips. The easiest way to find a guide, however, is through an agency. Advance notice and a minimum of 3 people for all trips are required by the following guides, who are among the best in the city. All can organize bespoke trips (given notice) and can reserve hotels and jungle lodges.

Cristina de Assis, *T092-9114 2556, amazonflower@bol.com.br.* Cultural city tours telling the story of the city and the rubber boom with visits to the historic buildings and the Museu Seringal. Also trips to the Rio Negro to swim with pink dolphins (these need to be organized at least a week in advance), to the waterfalls at Presidente

Figueiredo, the Boi Bumba party in Parintins and the forest. Cristina speaks excellent English and has worked with the Waimiri-Artroari indigenous people.

Matthias Raymond, *T092-8115 5716, raymathias@hotmail.com.* A Waipixana indigenous guide offering trips to further reaches of the forest including the Pico da Neblina (book in advance). Many languages spoken.

Pedro Neto, *T092-8831 1011, pedroffneto@hotmail.com.* An adventure tour specialist offering light adventure trips to the large INPA rainforest reserve, the forest around Manaus and the waterfalls and rivers of Presidente Figueiredo, where there is trail-walking, abseiling and birdwatching for spectaculars such as the Guianan cock of the rock. Light-hearted but erudite.

Tours on river cruises

Amazon Clipper, *T092-3656 1246, www.amazonclipper.com.br.* The leading small boat cruise operator. Excellent trips along the Rio Negro with knowledgeable wildlife guides, including wildlife cruises, sports fishing and bespoke tours. Accommodation is in comfortable cabins, the best of which are private, with en suites and work desks. Set departure dates are listed on the company website. From US$180 per person per day.

Iberostar Grand Amazon, *www.iberostar.com.br/amazon.* This leviathan cruises the Amazon (Solimões) river from Manaus on 3- or 4-night trips. With a pool, dance hall, piped music, vast sundeck and space for 200-plus people this is hardly an intimate rainforest experience. Each day is peppered with 3 or 4 optional forest and creek excursions on smaller launches. These are often fairly crowded. Those who are environmentally concerned might like to enquire about waste management and the treatment of cruise ship's sewage before booking a trip.

Mamori Community Houseboat Tours, *through Geraldo Mesquita, T092-3232 4755, geroexpeditions@hotmail.com.* River tours on traditional wooden Amazon river boats –

some of which are over 40 years old – with accommodation in cabins or hammocks on board and the option of nights camping in the rainforest or spent in traditional riverine communities. Proceeds from the trips revert to the local people. Great value and fascinating.

Transport

Routes in Amazônia
Belém–Manaus Via **Breves**, **Almeirim**, **Prainha**, **Monte Alegre**, **Curua-Uná**, **Santarém**, **Alenquer**, **Óbidos**, **Juruti** and **Parintins** on the lower Amazon. 5 days upriver, 4 days downriver, including an 18-hr stop in Santarém (suite US$250 upriver, US$150 down; double berth US$100 upriver, US$80 down; hammock space US$50 upriver, US$40 down). *Nélio Correa* is best on this route. *Defard Vieira*, very good and clean, US$45. *São Francisco* is largest, new and modern, but toilets smelly. *Cisne Branco* of similar quality. *Cidade de Bairreirinha* is the newest on the route, a/c berths. *Lider II* has good food and pleasant atmosphere. *Santarém* is clean, well-organized and recommended. *João Pessoa Lopes* is also recommended. The Belém–Manaus route is very busy. Try to get a cabin if you can.

Manaus–Parintins–Santarém Same intermediate stops as above. 2 days upriver, 1½ days downriver, berth US$55, hammock US$14. All vessels sailing Belém–Manaus will call in Santarém and there are others operating only the Santarém–Manaus route, including: *Cidade de Terezinha III* and *IV*, good. *Miranda Dias*, family-run and friendly. Speedboats (*lanchas*) are sometimes available on this route, 16 hrs sitting, no hammock space, US$20. **Ajato** fast boats run Manaus–Parintins (**Pérola**, Thu-Fri, 7 hrs, US$50; *Princesa Lana*, Wed, 6 hrs, US$50).

Manaus–Porto Velho Via **Borba**, **Manicoré** and **Humaitá** on the Rio Madeira. 4 days upriver, 3½ days downriver (up to 7 days when the river is low), double berth US$180, hammock space US$45 per person.

Manaus–Tefé Via **Codajás** and **Coari**, 24-36 hrs, double berth US$70, 1st-class hammock space US$8 per person. *Capitão Nunes* is good. *Jean Filho* also good. Note that it is difficult to continue west from Tefé to Tabatinga without first returning to Manaus. *Ajato* fast boats run Manaus–Tefé (*Ajato 2001*, Wed and Sat, 7 hrs, US$45.

Manaus–Tabatinga Via **Fonte Boa**, **Foz do Mamaria**, **Tonantins**, **Santo Antônio do Iça**, **Amataura**, **Monte Cristo**, **São Paulo de Olivença** and **Benjamin Constant** along the Rio Solimões. Up to 8 days upriver (depending on cargo), 3 days downriver, double berth US$280, hammock space US$35 per person (can be cheaper downriver). When going from Peru into Brazil, there is a thorough police check some 5 hrs into Brazil. *Voyagers*, *Voyagers II* and *III* recommended; *Almirante Monteiro*, *Avelino Leal* and *Capitão Nunes VIII* all acceptable; *Dom Manoel*, cheaper, acceptable but overcrowded. *Ajato* fast boats run Manaus–Tabatinga (*Ajato 2000*, Tue, 30 hrs, US$90).

Manaus–São Gabriel da Cachoeira Via **Novo Airão**, **Moura**, **Carvoeiro**, **Barcelos** and **Santa Isabel do Rio Negro** along the Rio Negro. Berth US$100, hammock US$35. Boats on this route: *Almirante Martins I* and *II*, *Capricho de Deus*, *Manoel Rodrigues*, *Tanaka Netto* departing from São Raimundo dock, north of the main port.

Most locals prefer to travel by road. Small car US$180, *combi* US$250 usually including driver, other passengers extra, 4WD US$300 with 2 passengers, motorcycle US$35.

Manaus
See also box, page 125.

Air
Spruced up in 2014, the **airport**, T092-3652 1120, www.infraero.gov.br, is 10 km north of the city centre. Taxi fare to airport US$12, fixed rate, or take bus marked 'Aeroporto Internacional' from Marquês de Santa Cruz at Praça Adalberto Vale, near the

cathedral, US$1, or from Ed Garagem on Av Getúlio Vargas every 30 mins. No buses 2200-0700. It is sometimes possible to use the more regular, faster service run by the **Hotel Tropical**; many tour agencies offer free transfers without obligation. Check all connections on arrival. Allow plenty of time at Manaus airport; formalities are very slow especially if you have purchased duty-free goods.

Many flights depart in the middle of the night and while there are many snack bars there is nowhere to rest. Local flights leave from Terminal 2. Check in advance which terminal you leave from.

There are international flights to **Panama City**, **Curaçao**, **Spain**, **Portugal**, **Porlamar** on the Venezuelan island of Margarita, **Miami** and **Atlanta**. For the **Guianas**, a connection must be made in Boa Vista. Domestic flights include: **Belém**, **Boa Vista**, **Brasília**, **Cruzeiro do Sul**, **Macapá**, **Parantins**, **Porto Velho**, **Rio Branco**, **Rio de Janeiro**, **Santarém**, **São Paulo**, **Tabatinga**, **Tefé** and **Trombetas**.

Make reservations as early as possible; flights get booked up quickly.

Boat

There are boat connections with **Santarém**, **Belém**, **Parintins**, **Porto Velho**, **Tefé**, **Tabatinga** (for Colombia and Peru), **São Gabriel da Cachoeira** and intermediate ports.

The docks are open to the public 24 hrs a day. Bookings can be made up to 2 weeks in advance at the ticket sales area by the port's pedestrian entrance: bear left on entry and walk past the cafés. The names and itineraries of departing vessels are displayed here.

For boats to/from São Gabriel da Cachoeira, Novo Airão, and Caracaraí, go to **São Raimundo**, upriver from the main port. Take bus No 101 'São Raimundo', No 112 'Santo Antônio' or No 110, 40 mins. There

are 2 docking areas separated by a hill: the São Raimundo *balsa*, where the ferry to Novo Airão, on the Rio Negro, leaves every afternoon (US$10), though it has been rendered redundant by the new road bridge; and the Porto Beira Mar de São Raimundo, where the São Gabriel da Cachoeira boats dock (most departures are on Fri).

Many boat captains will allow you to sleep on the hammock deck of the boat for a day before departure or after arrival. Agencies in town can book boat tickets for a small surcharge.

See also Routes in Amazônia, above.

Bus

To get to the *rodoviária*, 5 km out of town at the intersection of Av Constantino Nery and R Recife, take a local bus from the centre, US$1, marked 'Aeroporto Internacional' or 'Cidade Nova' (or taxi, US$12). There are many daily services to **Boa Vista** on Eucatur; the best are at night leaving at 2030 and 2100 (11 hrs, US$40). Most go via **Presidente Figueiredo** (3 hrs, US$15). There are also 8 daily buses to **Itacoatiara** (4 hrs, US$15).

Other towns in the state are best visited by air or boat, especially during the Nov to May wet season when road travel is next to impossible.

Car

The Catire Highway (BR-319), from Manaus to **Porto Velho** (868 km), has been officially closed since 1990. Several bridges are out and there is no repair in sight. The alternative for drivers is to ship a car down river on a barge, others have to travel by boat (see above). To **Itacoatiara**, 285 km east on the Amazon; now paved route AM-010, 266 km, through Rio Preto da Eva.

There are car hire agencies in the airport, including major international companies such as **Localiza** and **Hertz**.

Museu do Seringal

Igarapé São João, 15 km north of Manaus up the Rio Negro, T092-3631 3632, www.cultura. am.gov.br, Tue-Sun 0800-1600, US$1.50 and US$15 round trip on a private launch from the Hotel Tropical, access only by boat. Boat rides take around 25-30 mins.

This museum, sitting at the end of a pretty *igarapé* (creek) off the Rio Negro, is a full-scale reproduction of an early 20th-century rubber-tapping mansion, with serf quarters, a factory and a shop complete with authentic products. It was built as a film set for the 2002 Portuguese feature film *A Selva*. A guided tour – especially from one of the former rubber tappers – brings home the full horror of the system of debt peonage that enslaved Brazilians up until the 1970s. The museum can be visited with **Amazon Gero Tours** or **Amazon Eco Adventures** (see page 143).

Arquipélago de Anavilhanas

Some 80 km upsteam of Manuas, this filigree of more than 350 brilliant-green islands in the jet-black Rio Negro – some fringed with white-sand beaches, others anchored only by their roots – is one of the area's most impressive sights. The scene is particularly beautiful at the end of the day when the sky looks vast and warm and the light on the trunks of the partially submerged

> **Tip...**
> Try to be at the Anavilhanas archipelago for sunset when thousands of swifts descend to roost and the light is a deep, rich gold.

trees is a thick orange-yellow. Birds fly into the Anavilhanas to roost and millions of bats leave for their night hunt. The air is silent but for bird calls, the lapping of the river and the bluster of river dolphins surfacing for air.

Several companies including **Amazon Eco Adventures** (see page 143) arrange visits to the archipelago (US$150-250, per person, one day; it takes four hours to reach the islands), as can most of the Rio Negro lodges. Rio Negro safari cruises almost always visit the Anavilhanas.

It is possible to see *botos* (pink river dolphins) at the **Boto Cor-de-Rosa** restaurant in the Anavilhanas village of Novo Airão. Visits should be booked through a Manaus tour operator in as small a group as possible.

Presidente Figueiredo

There are hundreds of waterfalls dotted through the forest and scrubby savannah that surrounds the sleepy town of Presidente Figueiredo, 117 km north of Manaus on the shores of the vast artificial lake Balbina, formed by the ill-fated Figueiredo Dam. It's possible to visit three or four on a day trip from Manaus.

With an overnight stay it's also possible to see the beautiful and (in Brazil) very rare Guianan cock of the rock (*Rupicola rupicola*). This is one of South America's most spectacular sights. Males are pigeon-sized, and brilliant tangerine, with an exuberant, almost iridescent half-moon crest which completely obscures the beak, an orange-tipped black tail and silky-orange filaments which stick out at bizarre angles around the wings and tail. Females are a dull brown with a yellow-tipped black bill. Up to 40 males at a time perform elaborate courtship dances for the females in forest clearings called *leks*, twisting and trilling and displaying their extraordinary crests until a female settles behind her chosen mate and pecks him on the rump. Cock of the rocks are usually only seen on an organized tour (see page 143).

Figueiredo has so many waterfalls and caves, it's hard to know where to begin. The most spectacular are arguably the following: **Cachoeira Gruta da Judeia**, which plummets off the lip of a gargantuan cave in the forest; **Cachoeira Arco Íris** and **Cachoeira Iracema**, which are a series of stepped falls plunging through rocky gorges and over huge boulders; and **Cachoeira Pedra Furada**, which rushes through a series of holes in an enormous rock. Activities include abseiling, canyoning and whitewater rafting and can be arranged through **Amazon Eco Adventures** (ask for Johnny; see page 143).

Presidente Figueiredo town (often called **Balbina**) is an uninteresting place, built in the 1970s as a settlers' camp for construction workers on the dam. Its grid of streets lead to a long beach which gets packed with visitors from Manaus at weekends and a small centre for rehabilitating distressed Amazonian manatees (intermittently open).

Presidente Figueiredo's attractions are spread out over a large area, and whilst even the remotest falls are no more than two hours' walk from a road, driving distances are long and there is no public transport. The only practical way to visit Figueiredo is with a hire car from Manaus, or on an organized tour. If you are passing through on the way to or from Boa Vista, trips can be organized through the **Pousada das Pedras** or the **Pousada Wal** in Balbina. There are at least six buses a day to Balbina from the Manaus *rodoviária*. Boa Vista buses will stop at Balbina on request.

Around Manaus

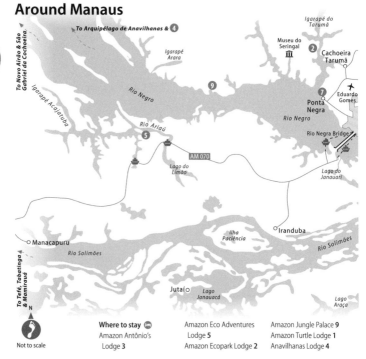

Where to stay
Amazon Antônio's
Lodge **3**

Amazon Eco Adventures
Lodge **5**
Amazon Ecopark Lodge **2**

Amazon Jungle Palace **9**
Amazon Turtle Lodge **1**
Anavilhanas Lodge **4**

Parintins

Parintins (population 90,000) is situated east of Manaus on the way to Santarém, just before the Amazonas–Pará border, on the Ilha Tupinambana. In the dry season, boats run to the river beaches and to nearby lakes.

In colonial times, this was the resting point of a group of coastal indigenous Brazilians who made an astonishing trek through thousands of miles of dense forest to escape the ravages of the Portuguese slave trade. However, they didn't evade it for long. Within a generation they had been found by slavers from Belém who took all the women and children and murdered all the men. Ironically the island is now the site of one of the country's most important and spectacular festivals, Boi Bumba, which celebrates the triumph of the indigenous and *caboclo* poor over a *coronel* (tyrannical landowner).

The **Festa do Boi Bumba** (see box, page 151) is the most vibrant in Brazil after Carnaval and draws tens of thousands of visitors to Parintins on the last three days of June each year. But since the town has only two small hotels, finding a room can be a challenge. Most people sleep in hammocks on the boats that bring them to the festival from Manaus and Santarém (a large vessel will charge US$80 per person, including breakfast).

Tefé and the Mamirauá Ecological Reserve

Tefé (population 65,000) is a sleepy riverside town roughly halfway between Manaus and west to the the Colombian border. While there are some beautiful side trips easily organized through the *pousada* Multicultura (see page 150) most visitors come en route to one of the world's most important primate and waterfowl reserves, the **Mamirauá Ecological Reserve** ① *T097-3343 4160, www.mamiraua.org.br and www.uakarilodge.com.br.* This is a **Ramsar** (www.ramsar.org) site, set up with British support to protect huge areas of terra firme, gallery, *várzea* and *igapó* forest at the confluence of the Solimões and Japurá rivers, and to manage them sustainably with the local riverine people. There are abundant birds including numerous rare trogons (*Trogoniformes*), cotingas (*Cotingidae*), curassows (*Cracidae*), hoatzin (*Opisthocomus hoazin*), harpy eagle (*Harpia harpyja*) and five species of macaw (*Arara*). There are black caiman (one of which lives under the floating lodge), both species of Amazon dolphin (*boto* and *tucuxi*), and numerous rare primates the most spectacular of which is the endemic black-headed squirrel monkey (*Saimiri vanzolinii*) and the endangered white uakari (*Cacajao calvus calvus*), known locally as the 'macaco Ingles' because of its red complexion and its genitalia. A visit is unforgettable.

To Boa Vista & Presidente Figueiredo

BR242

To Itacoatiara & 3 5
Rio Puraquequara

To Parintins

Manaus

Ceasa Ferry Dock

Encontro das Águas Meeting of the Waters

Rio Amazonas

Ilha do Careiro

Careiro

Lago do Rei

Ilha Xiborema

Ilha Machantaria

Rio Mamori

Lago Comprido

To 1 11 12 14

Lago Alvares

BR319

To Castanho

Ararinha Lodge **11**	Juma **12**
Ariaú Amazon Towers **5**	Tropical **7**
Dolphin Lodge **14**	

The reserve has a small floating lodge, the **Pousada Uakari** (see Where to stay, below) on the Mamirauá River, and visitors stay here in simple but elegant wooden rooms. Trips include walks in terra firme forest, boat and canoe trips to *igarapé* creeks, *várzea* and *igapó* forest and the vast Mamirauá Lake. Visits must be booked in advance.

Tefé is connected to Manaus six times a week and regular slow boats (at least one a day) from Manaus or from Tabatinga and fast speed boats from Manaus (see Transport, below). The town is small enough to negotiate on foot.

Listings Around Manaus *map p148*

Where to stay

Presidente Figueiredo

$$ Pousada da Wal
BR-174, T092-3324 1267,
www.pousadadawal.com.br.
A pretty little *pousada* with terracotta-tile and whitewashed bungalows set in a little garden patio off a quiet Balbina street. Rooms are very simple with TVs, fridges, simple wooden furnishings and a bed, and public areas are strung with hammocks. The hotel can help organize excursions.

$$ Pousada das Pedras
Av Acariquara 2, Presidente Figueiredo,
T092-3324 1296, www.facebook.com/
pedraspousada.
Simple tiled rooms in a tropical garden, a generous breakfast of fruit, rolls, juices and coffee and tours organized to waterfalls and caves by the enthusiastic owner.

Tefé

$$$$ Pousada Uakari
T097-3343 4672 or T097-3343 4160,
www.uakarilodge.com.br.
Together with **Cristalino Jungle Lodge** (see page 121), this is one of the best lodges for wildlife, guiding and ecotourism practice in the Brazilian Amazon. The lodge is in a magical location in the Mamirauá Reserve, floating on a river, with 10 suites of 25 sq m each linked by floating bridges. Tours are excellent. Look out for the friendly black caiman which lives in the water under the restaurant. The lodge and trips in the reserve

can be booked in Manaus via **Iguana Tours**, either at their shop or office in Manaus airport. Book well in advance.

$$ Multicultura
R 15 de Junho 136, T097-3343 6632,
www.pousadamulticultura.com.
British-Brazilian-run *pousada* with sweeping views over an Amazonian oxbow lake, and spruce rooms with huge windows letting in plenty of light. Tours of the region and trips to Mamiraua organized by the owners. Airport pick-ups.

Festivals

Parintins
Jun Festa do Boi Bumba. Huge 3-day festival attracting 40,000 people (see box, opposite).
24 Dec-6 Jan Parintins' other main festival is the **Pastorinhas**.

Transport

Parintins
Air A taxi or motortaxi to the **airport**, Estrada Odovaldo Novo s/n, Parintins, T092-3533 2700, www.parintins.am.gov.br, costs US$7. Flights to **Manaus** (1¼ hrs), **Belém**, Óbidos **and Santarém** (1 hr 20 mins) with **Azul**, www.voeazul.com.br.

Boat Boats call on the Belém–Manaus route: 60 hrs to Belém (depending on boat and if going up or down river), 10-26 passengers. There are irregular sailings to **Óbidos** (ask at the port), 12-15 hrs. A boat to **Santarém** takes 20 hrs.

FESTIVALS

Festivals in the Amazon

The Amazon has some of Brazil's best and biggest festivals, as vibrant and colourful as carnival in Rio and far less known to foreign tourists. Here is a pick of three of the best.

Círio de Nazaré, Belem
(9 October 2016, 8 October 2017, 14 October 2018)
Music, dancing and street parades in the CarnaBelem carnival following a procession with the statue of Our Lady of Nazareth, taken from the Nazaré Church and paraded around the historic centre to the cathedral.

The effigy itself has a long and fascinating history. It was discovered by Plácido José de Souza, a *caboclo*, in 1700, buried in mud on an *igarapé*. De Souza built a chapel for the image, and over the following century the statue became associated with miracles. In 1793, the Vatican authorized the first official processions in Belém.

The Boi Bumba festival, Parintins
(24-26 June 2016, 23-25 June 2017, 22-24 June 2018)
The biggest and most colourful celebration in the central Amazon takes place on a forested island in the middle of the main river next to the village of Parintins. It's a dance and music pageant, staged as a competition between two rival groups: Caprichoso (whose colour is blue) and Garantido (red).

The pageant, which originates from Braga in Portugal (heavily syncretized with indigenous and Afro-Brazilian themes) was brought to Parintins in the early 20th century by settlers from São Luís in Maranhão and tells the story of Pai Francisco and his wife Mãe Catirina who steal the prize bull from the landowner that they work for, and kill it. The landowner discovers this and threatens to kill them if they fail to resurrect his bull by midnight. The couple employ the talents of a shaman, a priest and an African *pai santo*, and these characters invoke the female spirit of rainforest fertility, the Cunhã-poranga, played by a beautiful young dancer.

The story is told to the backdrop of vast four-storey floats with moving parts and troupes of hundreds of dancers and is performed in the purpose-built *bumbódromo* stadium which holds almost 40,000 spectators.

Sairé, Alter do Chão
(Usually 1st or 2nd weekend in September)
An old festival re-modelled on the Boi Bumba, this pageant sees two rival teams re-enact the seduction of a local girl (the Cunhantã-iborari or *cabocla borari*) by a river dolphin, culminating in a passionate, balletic love-making scene, followed by the murder of the river dolphin by the girl's father and its resurrection at the hands of an Indian *pajé* shaman.

Tefé
Air The airport has a connection to **Manaus** with **Azul**, 6 times a week.

Boat If travelling on to **Tabatinga**, note that Manaus–Tabatinga boats do not usually stop at Tefé. You must hire a canoe to take you out to the main channel and try to flag down the approaching ship.

Benjamin Constant

The small town of Benjamin Constant (population 23,000), with a big sawmill and a series of little tiled houses set in bougainvillea gardens, sits on the frontier with Peru, just opposite Leticia in Colombia. There is a wonderful small Ticuna indigenous cultural centre and museum, the **Museu Magüta** ① *Av Castelo Branco 396, T096-3415 6067, www. museumaguta.com.br*, with artefacts, information panels and a gift shop. The music is haunting but sadly not for sale. Ticuna people run the museum.

There are boat services from Manaus (seven days or more), to Manaus (four days or more) and from Iquitos in Peru. There are no facilities in Benjamin Constant, but it is possible to buy supplies for boat journeys. Benjamin Constant is two hours from Tabatinga and Leticia (ferry/*recreio* US$2; 25 minutes by speedboat, US$12 per person, cheaper if more passengers). For boats to/from Manaus, see Routes in Amazônia, page 145.

Tabatinga

Tabatinga (population 38,000) is theoretically 4 km from Leticia (in Colombia) but, in reality, it is the scruffy half of the same town: a long street buzzing with mopeds, a port and some untidy houses in between. There is an important Ticuna centre here. However, there is little of interest for tourists, who are better off staying in Leticia. Flights arrive in Leticia (see below) from where a minibus to Tabatinga costs US$1.50.

The port area in Tabatinga is called Marco and the port captain is very helpful and speaks good English. There are regular boats from Manaus and from Benjamin Constant, across the water, and from Iquitos in Peru. A mosquito net for a hammock is essential if sailing upstream from Tabatinga, much less so downstream. A good hammock will cost US$22.50 in Tabatinga (try **Esplanada Teocides**).

Travel between Tabatinga and Leticia (Colombia) is very informal. Taxis between the towns charge US$7.50 (more if you want to stop at immigration offices or change money), or US$1.40 in a *colectivo* (more after 1800). Beware of taxi drivers who want to rush you expensively over the border before it 'closes'. It is not advisable to walk the muddy path between Tabatinga and Leticia as robberies occur here. Boats from Manaus normally start from Tabatinga and spend a day or two here before returning; you can stay on board. For boats to/from Manaus, see Routes in Amazônia, page 145.

Leticia (Colombia)

This riverside city is clean and modern, though run down, and is rapidly merging into one town with neighbouring Marco in Brazil. Leticia is a good place to buy indigenous products typical of the Amazon, and tourist services are better than in Tabatinga or Benjamin Constant. The best time to visit the area is in July or August, the early months of the dry season. At weekends, accommodation may be difficult to find.

The **museum** ① *Cra 11 y Calle 9*, set up by **Banco de la República**, covers local ethnography and archaeology and is set in a beautiful building with a library and a terrace overlooking the Amazon. There is a small **Amazonian zoo** ① *US$2*, and botanical garden on the road to the airport, within walking distance of town (20 minutes).

The **airport** ① *1.5 km from town*, receives flights from Manaus (three times a week with Rico) via Tefé. It is a small terminal with few facilities. A taxi to the centre costs US$1.50. There is a **tourist office** ① *Calle 10, No 9-86, Ministerio del Medio Ambiente, Cra 11, No 12-05*, for general information on national parks.

Where to stay

Benjamin Constant
There are a number of very cheap and very simple *pousadas* in town.

$$ Benjamin Constant
R Getúlio Vargas 36, beside the ferry, T092-3415 5638.
All rooms have a/c, some with hot water and TV. Good restaurant, arranges tours.

Tabatinga

$$ Pousada do Sol
General Sampaio 50, T092-3412 3987.
Simple rooms but in a hotel with a sauna and a pool. Friendly owners.

Leticia (Colombia)
The international phone code for Colombia is +57. The code for Leticia is 9819.

$$$ Anaconda
Cra 11 No 7-34, T9819-27119, www.hotelanaconda.com.co.
The plushest in town with large a/c rooms, hot water, a restaurant and pool.

Transport

Benjamin Constant
Boat Boats to **Iquitos** leave from a mudbank called Islandia, on the Peruvian side of a narrow creek, a few metres from Benjamin Constant. The journey takes a minimum of 2 days upstream, 8-36 hrs downstream, depending on the speed of the boat. On ordinary boats, fares range from US$20-30 per person, depending on the standard of accommodation, food is extra. Speedboats charge US$65 per person, 3 a week are run by **Amazon Tours and Cruises**. All boats call at Santa Rosa (2-3 days upstream to Iquitos where immigration formalities are carried out).

Tabatinga
Air The airport has a connection to **Manaus** with **Azul**.

Boat **Amazon Tours and Cruises**, T1-949 682 7745, www.amazoncruise.net, operates a luxury service between **Iquitos** and Tabatinga.

Leticia (Colombia)
Air Expect to be searched before leaving Leticia Airport, and on arrival in Bogotá from Leticia. **Trip** flies to **Manaus** (sporadically via Tefé). There are onward flights from Leticia to Bogotá.

Pará

Brazil's second largest state, Pará lies entirely within the Amazon. Virtually unknown to tourism it is nonetheless one of Brazil's most beautiful regions. The state capital Belém is an enchanting old colonial city centred on a freshly renovated river port (with one of Brazil's liveliest markets), and is vibrant with an exciting music and a burgeoning gastronomic scene. The state's interior is stunning. This is where the Amazon is at its gentlest: the clear Tapajos river is fringed by beaches of fluffy Caribbean-white sand, blue lagoons and forest free of mosquitoes.

Marajó island is the biggest of a forest-swathed archipelago which stretches across the mouth of the Amazon. As big as Denmark its dark interior is little-explored, but its outer edges are fringed with beaches of white-pepper fine sand shaded by palms sitting between little villages where locals dance *carimbo* and the police patrol on buffalo back.

Belém do Pará (1.3 million) is the great port of the eastern Amazon and has been an important Brazilian city for almost 500 years. Replete with fine Portuguese and belle époque rubber boom architecture, the city has been extensively renovated since the new millennium, an ongoing process which has transformed it from tired and tawdry into one of the country's most attractive state capitals. The broad avenues are lined with shady mango trees, the narrow streets with pretty Portuguese and late 19th-century buildings.

There are numerous pretty *praças* and little parks and a pleasant waterfront area focused on a renovated old warehouse port now turned air-conditioned restaurant and shopping centre and the Ver o Peso market where you can buy everything from Amazon Viagra and Umbanda incense to fresh fish, Marajó açai and rainforest guaraná. Belém has much of cultural interest, with a lively contemporary music and arts scene and some of the best and most unusual food in Latin America.

Belém is a good base for boat trips along the river. An archipelago of beautiful, unspoilt tropical river islands lies a short boat trip offshore. The largest island, Marajó, is as big as Denmark. With mean temperatures of 26°C, Belém is hot, but frequent showers and a prevailing breeze freshen the streets.

Sights

Belém is known to locals as the 'city of mango trees' which shade the broad avenues, leading to the the largest of the city's many attractive squares, the **Praça da República**. This square is dominated by the neoclassical **Theatro da Paz** ① *R da Paz, T091-4009 8750, www.theatrodapaz.com.br, Tue-Fri 0900-1800, Sat 0900-1200, Sun 0900-1100, tours US$2,* (1878), one of the largest theatres in Brazil. The building's handsome ballrooms, polished floors, murals, paintings and overall opulence are every bit as impressive as those of its more famous counterpart in Manaus. The building was inspired by the Scala in Milan and is stuffed full of imported materials from Europe, including an iron frame built in England, Italian marble, French bronzes and a Portuguese mosaic stone floor. There are paintings by Olinda-born painter and caricaturist Crispim do Amaral and the Italian Domenico de Angelis (see the Pálacio Lauro Sodré and the cathedral, below), who also worked in the Teatro Amazonas in Manaus. Domenico de Angelis painted a magnificent ceiling which crumbled and fell to the floor only decades after it was finished. The theatre has its own orchestra (the Orquestra Sinfônica do Theatro da Paz) and jazz band, and it stages performances by national and international stars, as well as hosting an annual opera festival (usually in August and September). There is a programme of free concerts and shows both in the building and in the *praça* itself.

West of here, at the **Estação das Docas** (www.estacaodasdocas.com.br), the abandoned warehouses and quays of the port have been restored into a waterfront complex with an air-conditioned interior with a gallery of cafés, restaurants and boutiques. It's a great place to come in the late afternoon when the sun is golden over the Baía do Guajará and locals promenade along the cobbles under the towering 19th-century cranes. There are three converted warehouses in the Estação das Docas – each a 'boulevard'. The **Boulevard das Artes** contains the **Cervejaria Amazon** (brewery), with good beer and simple meals, an archaeological museum, arts, crafts, music and fashion shops and ATMs. The **Boulevard de Gastronomia** has smart restaurants and the five-star **Cairu** ice cream

Essential Belém

Finding your feet

Val-de-Cans international airport
lies 10 km north of the city centre.
An air-conditioned 'VIP' airport bus
(daily 0730-1700, every 75 minutes,
US$0.70) leaves from outside the
terminal. Buses Nos 638 (Pratinha–
Pte Vargas), 637 (Pratinha–Ver-o-Peso)
and 634 (Estação Marex–Arsenal)
also make the journey, leaving every
15 minutes, US$0.70. A taxi costs US$14.

Interstate buses arrive at the *rodoviária*
at the end of Avenida Governor José
Malcher, 3 km from the centre. Buses
to the centre cost US$0.20; taxis charge
US$3-5. At the *rodoviária* you are given
a ticket with the taxi's number on it;
threaten to go to the authorities if the
driver tries to overcharge.

Boats from Ilha do Marajó, Macapá,
Manaus and Santarém, as well as other
parts of the Amazon region and delta,
arrive at the new Porto do Belém next
to the Estação das Docas market. See
also Transport, page 164.

Getting around

The city centre is easily explored on foot.
City buses and taxis run to sites of interest
and transport hubs.

Safety

Belém has a high crime rate. Take taxis
at night and avoid visiting the slum
communities on the city's outskirts.

parlour (try *açaí* or the *pavê de capuaçu*). In
the **Boulevard das Feiras** there are trade
fairs. Live music is transported between
the boulevards on a moving stage. Belém's
brand new boat terminal, the Terminal
Hidroviário, is for boats to Marajó island
and other destinations (see page 167). It
sits immediately to the north of the Estação
das Docas. Heading south, the 17th-century
church of **Mercês** (1640) is the oldest in
Belém. It forms part of an architectural
group known as the Mercedário, the rest of
which was heavily damaged by fire in 1978
and has now been restored.

Near the church, the Belém market,
known as **Ver-o-Peso** ① *Blvd Castilhos
França 27, T091-3212 0549*, was the
Portuguese Posto Fiscal, where goods
were weighed to gauge taxes due, hence
the name: 'see the weight'. Inside are stalls
selling all manner of items including: herbal
remedies, Brazil nuts, açaí, bead jewellery,
African-Brazilian religious charms, incense
and, in the main gallery, scores of tiled slabs
covered with bizarre river fish, from *piraiba*
as big as a man to foot-long armour-plated
cat fish. You can see them being unloaded
at around 0530, together with hundreds
of baskets of açaí. Immediately opposite
Ver-o-Peso inland is the old wrought
19th-century meat market, the **Mercado
Municipal de Carnes Francisco Bolonha**,
beautifully restored in 2015, and home to
galleries of little shops and with a viewing
platform reached by a winding stairway. A
colourful, if dirty, dock for fishing boats lies
immediately upriver from Ver-o-Peso and
whole area swarms with people (including
thieves and pickpockets).

Around Praça Dom Pedro II is a cluster
of interesting buildings. The **Palácio
Lauro Sodré** and **Museu Histórico do Estado do Pará** ① *Praça Dom Pedro II, T091-
4009 0831, Facebook: MuseuEstadoPara, Tue-Fri 1000-1800, Sat-Sun 0900-1300, US$1*, is a
gracious 18th-century Italianate building. It contains Brazil's largest framed painting,
The Conquest of Amazônia, by Domenico de Angelis. The building was the work of
the Italian architect Antônio Landi, who also designed the cathedral, and was the
administrative seat of the colonial government. During the rubber boom many new
decorative features were added.

Also on Praça Dom Pedro II is the **Palácio Antônio Lemos**, which houses the **Museu de Arte de Belém** as well as the **Prefeitura** ① *T091-3114 1028, www.culturapara.art.br, Tue-Fri 1000-1800, Sat and Sun 0900-1300*. It was originally built as the Palácio Municipal between 1868 and 1883, and is a fine example of the Imperial neoclassical style. In the downstairs rooms there are old views of Belém; upstairs, the historic rooms, beautifully renovated, contain furniture and paintings, which are all well explained.

The **cathedral** ① *Praça Frei Caetano Brandão, Mon 1500-1800, Tue-Fri 0800-1100, 1530-1800,* (1748), is also neoclassical, and contains a series of brilliantly coloured paintings by the Italian artist Domenico de Angelis, most famous for his work on the Teatro Amazonas in Manaus, but whose first visit to the Amazon was actually to Belém in 1884 to paint this cathedral and the Theatro da Paz. Directly opposite is the restored 18th-century **Santo Alexandre church** ① *Praça Frei Caetano Brandão s/n, Mon 1500-1800, Tue-Fri 0800-1100, 1530-1800*, with a fabulous rococo pediment and fine woodcarving. This was once the Jesuit headquarters in Belém – where Afro-Portuguese Father António Vieira – one of the greatest writers of the Lusitanian Renaissance, preached his hellfire sermons denouncing the indigenous slave trade. This incited the wrath of the locals, and eventually contributing to the disestablishment of the order.

Also in the old town is the **Forte do Castelo (aka Forte do Presépio)** ① *Praça Frei Caetano Brandão 117, T091-4009 8828, Tue-Fri 1000-1800, Sat and Sun 1000-1400*, which was rebuilt in 1878. The fort overlooks the confluence of the Rio Guamá and the Baía do Guajará

1 Belém orientation

⇒ Belém maps
1 Belém orientation, page 157
2 Belém, page 159

BACKGROUND

Belém

Established in 1616 because of its strategic position, Belém soon became the centre for slaving expeditions into the Amazon Basin. The Portuguese of Pará, together with those of Maranhão, treated the indigenous Brazilians abominably. Their isolation from the longer-established colonies allowed both places to become relatively lawless. In 1655, the Jesuits, under Antônio Vieira, attempted to lessen the abuses, while enticing the indigenous Brazilians to descend to the *aldeias* around Belém. *Aldeias* were set up all over South America as much to protect the indigenous people from the slave trade as to proselytize them. The *aldeias* proved disastrous for the indigenous when smallpox spread from the south, striking the Pará *aldeias* in the 1660s.

Between 1835 and 1840, just over 10 years after the country had won its independence, many of the remaining resettled indigenous people who remained in Pará joined forces with impoverished Afro-Brazilians and mixed-race *cabanos* who lived in marginalized communities along the rivers near Pará's cities, in the Caboclo uprising or **Revolta da Cabanagem**. The rebels swept through the region, occupying Belém, executing the city governor Lobo de Sousa and installing a new peasant-friendly leader, Félix Malcher. When Malcher attempted to feather his own nest by making deals with the regional governor he was assassinated by the rebels, who found a new leader in the charismatic Batista Campos. Some 30,000 were killed, a quarter of the population of Brazilian Amazônia.

Like neighbouring Amazonas, Belém boomed at the end of the 19th century when the world's demand for rubber made the city one of the wealthiest in the southern hemisphere, with a lively cultural scene and rows of fashionable shops lining the shady boulevards. At this time Belém was known as the Paris of Latin America. Many of the city's most beautiful buildings today date from this period and include the Palácio Lauro Sodré, Teatro da Paz, Palácio Antônio Lemos and the Ver-o-Peso market. The new-found wealth attracted a stream of immigrants from Spain, Japan, China and France. The Japanese left the greatest mark, turning the city into the biggest producer of black pepper in the world.

The city's strategic location became important once again during the Second World War, when Belém was used as an airbase by the Americans.

and was where the Portuguese first set up their defences. The excellent museum, **Museu do Forte do Presépio**, has interesting displays on indigenous archaeology and some artefacts. At the square on the waterfront below the fort, açaí berries are landed in the early mornings before dawn, after being picked in the jungle and sold in a lively market. Açaí berries, ground up with sugar and mixed with manioc, are a staple food in the region.

Opposite the fort across the square is the **Espaço Cultural Casa das Onze Janelas** ① *Praça Dom Pedro II s/n, T091-4009 8825, Tue-Fri 1000-1800, Sat-Sun, 1000-1400, US$1.50, Tue free*, housed in a stately 18th-century mansion and with galleries devoted to temporary exhibitions, usually of Amazonian art and photography.

East of the centre, the Italianate **Basílica de Nossa Senhora de Nazaré** ① *Praça Justo Chermont, Av Magalhães Barata, Mon-Sat 0500-1130, 1400-2000, Sun 0545-1130, 1430-2000*, was built in 1909 from rubber wealth. The interior has beautiful coloured marble, mosaics and attractive stained-glass windows. The *basílica* feels very tranquil and sacred, especially when empty. A museum here is devoted to the Círio de Nazaré, the biggest religious festival in northern Brazil (see box, page 151). The statue itself, Nossa Senhora de Nazaré, sits illuminated in a shrine in the sacristy. The botanic gardens, **Bosque Rodrigues Alves** ① *Av Almirante Barroso 2305, T091-3226 2308, Tue-Sun 0800-1700*, is a 16-ha public garden (really a preserved area of original flora), with a small animal collection. To get there, take the yellow bus marked 'Souza' or 'Cidade Nova' (any number), 30 minutes from Ver-o-Peso market, or from the cathedral.

The **Museu Emílio Goeldi** ① *Av Magalhães Barata 376, Tue-Thu 0900-1200, 1400-1700, Fri 0900-1200, Sat and Sun 0900-1700, US$1*, takes up an entire city block and consists of the museum proper (with a fine collection of indigenous Marajó pottery and an excellent

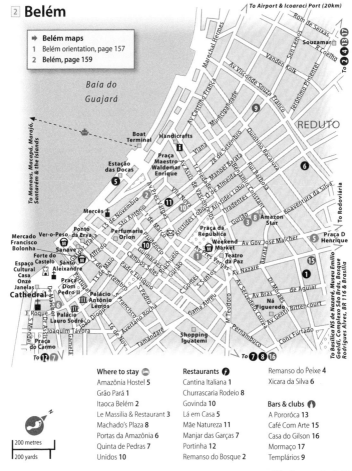

2 Belém

→ **Belém maps**
1 Belém orientation, page 157
2 Belém, page 159

Baía do Guajará

To Airport & Icoaraci Port (20km)

REDUTO

Where to stay 🛏
Amazônia Hostel 5
Grão Pará 1
Itaoca Belém 2
Le Massilia & Restaurant 3
Machado's Plaza 8
Portas da Amazônia 6
Quinta de Pedras 7
Unidos 10

Restaurants 🍴
Cantina Italiana 1
Churrascaria Rodeio 8
Govinda 10
Lá em Casa 5
Mãe Natureza 11
Manjar das Garças 7
Portinha 12
Remanso do Bosque 2

Remanso do Peixe 4
Xicara da Silva 6

Bars & clubs 🍸
A Pororóca 13
Café Com Arte 15
Casa do Gilson 16
Mormaço 17
Templários 9

exhibition of Mebengokre tribal lifestyle), a rather sad zoo and botanical exhibits including Victoria régia lilies. Buses run from the cathedral.

The **Murucutu** ruins, an old Jesuit foundation, are reached by the Ceará bus from Praça da República; entry is via an unmarked door on the right of the Ceará bus station. Also worth a visit is the **Mangal das Garças**, a little mangrove reserve some 15 minutes from the fort (see **Manjar das Garças**, page 162).

Listings Belém *maps p157 and p159*

Tourist information

See the **Instituto Chico Mendes de Conservação da Biodiversidade** (**ICMBio**) website, www.icmbio.gov.br, for information on national parks (in Portuguese only).

Belemtur
Av Presidente Vargas 158, 13º andar, T091-3230 3926, www.belem.pa.gov.br.
The municipal tourist office has a useful website (in Portuguese only) listing hotels, restaurants and tour operators.

Paratur
Praça Waldemar Henrique, Reduto, on the waterfront, T091-3224 9493, www.paraturismo.pa.gov.br.
Information on the state and city. Some staff speak English and can book hotels and tours to Marajó island.

Where to stay

The 2 best hotels in the city are operated by the **Crowne Plaza** and **Radisson** chains and while service can be slow, facilities are up to their international brand standards. All Belém's hotels are fully booked during **Círio** (see box, page 151). There are many cheap hotels close to the waterfront (none too safe) and several others near the *rodoviária* (generally OK).

$$$ Itaoca Belém
Av Pres Vargas 132, T091-4009 2400, www.hotelitaoca.com.br.
Well-kept, bright, no-nonsense a/c rooms with writing desks and en suites. The best

are on the upper floors away from the street noise, and with river views. Decent breakfast.

$$$ Machado's Plaza
R Henrique Gurjão 200, T091-3347 9800, www.machadosplazahotel.com.br.
Bright, boutique hotel with smart and tastefully decorated a/c rooms, a small business centre, plunge pool and a pleasant a/c breakfast area. Good value.

$$$ Quinta de Pedras
R Dr Assis 834, T091-3199 1616, www.atriumhoteis.com.br.
Newly opened in late 2015, this boutique hotel right in the old city sits in a converted belle époque town house 10 mins south of the centre. Local art and Marajoara pottery sits against the raw stone walls, rooms have luxurious beds and soft lighting and there's a delightful small swimming pool in the atrium.

$$ Le Massilia
R Henrique Gurjão 236, T091-3222 2834, www.massilia.com.br.
An intimate, French-owned boutique hotel with chic little duplexes and more ordinary doubles. Excellent French restaurant and a tasty French breakfast.

$$ Portas da Amazônia
R Dr Malcher 15, T091-3222 9952, www.portasdaamazoniabelempara.com.br.
This little boutique situated in an historic *azulejo*-fronted townhouse opposite the cathedral has bags of character and couldn't be better located. Rooms are simple, but elegant, all white with chunky 19th-century furniture, parquet wood floors and plenty of light from tall windows.

$$-$ Grão Pará
Av Pres Vargas 718, T091-3321 2121,
www.hotelgraopara.com.br.
Well-kept a/c rooms with contemporary
fittings and smart en suites, and a boiler for
hot water. The best have superb river views.
Excellent breakfast. Great value.

$ Amazônia Hostel
*Av Governador Jose Malcher 592, T091-3278
4355, www.amazoniahostel.com.br.*
Dorms and doubles are very simple; there's
no a/c so they can be hot when the windows
are closed, and popular with mosquitoes
when they aren't. Staff are helpful and some
speak English, there's a book exchange,
kitchen and breakfast.

$ Unidos
*Ó de Almeida 545, T091-3252 1411,
www.hotelunidos.com.*
Simple but spruce, spacious a/c rooms
with cable TV and clean en suites. There
are other cheap hotels nearby if this one is full.

Restaurants

Belém has some of the best food in Brazil,
with award-winning chefs and a unique
cuisine. Dishes to sample include *tacacá* (a
tangy, tongue-tingling prawn soup cooked
with jambu leaves that make the mouth
go numb), *pato no tucupi* (duck in manioc
and jambu leaf sauce), *maniçoba* (made
with manioc leaves and pork, the *feijoada*
of the Amazon) and river fish like *tucunaré*
(peacock bass) and *tambaqui*. There are
many decent a/c restaurant, bar and café
options in the smart **Estação das Docas**
on the riverfront and food stalls around
the centre serve *tacacá* until just after
dark. The best of these is **Dona Maria** (on
Av Nazare 902 near the Crowne Plaza hotel).

$$$ Churrascaria Rodeio
*Rodovia Augusto Montenegro, Km 4,
T091-8800 2004.*
A choice of 20 cuts of meat and 30 buffet
dishes for a set price. Well worth the short
taxi ride to eat all you can.

$$$ Remanso do Bosque
*Travessa Perebebuí 2350 (in front of
the Jardim Botânico, T091-3347 2829,
www.restauranteremanso.com.br.*
One of the best restaurants in Latin America
and a rising star on the San Pellegrino list.
20-something year old chef Thiago Castanho
and his brother Felipe have taken Amazon
ingredients and turned them gourmet. The
fixed degustation menu is a tour de force, with
Paraense flavours from tingly *jambu* leaves,
tangy tapioca balls and tart *tucupi* through
to slivers of the finest Amazon river fish.
Not to be missed unless you're vegetarian.

$$$ Remanso do Peixe
*Tv, Barão do Triunfo 2590, Marco, T091-3228
2477, www.restauranteremanso.com.br.*
The companion restaurant to the **Remanso
do Bosque** is the Castanho brothers take
on a traditional *peixaria* (an Amazon fish
restaurant), with a choice not of gourmet
but of comfort-cooked fish dishes, from
caldeirada paraense (a fish stew a little like
a *moqueca*) and *bolinhos* to fillets.

$$$-$$ Xicara da Silva
*Av Visconde de Souza Franco 978,
T091-3230 4323.*
Set in a pretty 19th-century townhouse
with *azulejo* tiles on the walls and a lovely
low-lit evening atmosphere, this restaurant
is rightfully celebrated for its pizzas, but the
local cooking and *petisco* (tapas) are as good;
try the *risoto* Paraense.

$$ Cantina Italiana
Trav Benjamin Constant 1401, T091-3325 2033.
Excellent Italian serving pasta, pizza (try
the sun-dried tomato with parmesan and
mozzarella), Hotel delivery.

$$ Lá em Casa
Estação das Docas, T091-3212 5588.
Good local cooking, especially the buffet and
the à la carte *menu paraense*. With *maniçoba*,
tacacá and *pato no tucupi*.

$$ Le Massilia
See Where to stay, above.

French-owned and run with dishes including frog's legs, *sole meunière* and *magret de canard*. Excellent cocktails.

$$ Manjar das Garças
Praça Carniero da Rocha s/n, Arsenal da Marinha, Mangal das Garças, T091-3242 1056, www.manjardasgarcas.com.br. Closed Mon.
Huge lunch and evening buffet of local dishes and river fish. The restaurant sits next to the river in a small park on the edge of town filled with scarlet ibis.

$$-$ Mãe Natureza
R Manoel Barata 889, T091-3212 8032. Lunch only.
Vegetarian and wholefood dishes in a bright clean dining room.

$ Govinda
Trav Padre Prudencio 166 (between Manoel Barata and Ó de Almeida), T091-3222 2272, www.restaurantegovinda.com.br.
Good vegetarian food including vegetarian versions of northeastern and local dishes, such as *bobó* and *maniçoba*.

$ Portinha
R Dr Malcher 436, T091-3223 0922. Thu-Sun evenings only.
Wonderful pastries, *tacacá*, *cames* and juices.

Bars and clubs

Belém has some of the best and most distinctive live music and nightlife in northern Brazil. It's well worth heading out on the town at weekends.

A Pororóca
Av Senador Lemos 3316, Sacramenta, T091-3254 5000, www.facebook.com/APororocaShows.
Bands like Calypso made their names in these vast, steaming warehouse clubs. Every Fri and Sat they are packed to the girders with scantily clad blue-collar locals dancing wildly to techno *brega* acts, usually comprising a platinum blonde with a tiny skirt and Amazonian thighs backed by a band and a troupe of male dancers. A few hours here may be as cheesy as it comes but they are immense fun and barely known even to Brazilian tourists. Take a cab to the clubs and be wary in the vicinity.

Café Com Arte
Av Rui Barbosa 1436 (between Braz de Aguiar and Nazaré), Nazaré, T091-3224 8630, www.facebook.com/CafecomArtepa.
A brightly painted colonial house-turned-bar and club and with 3 floors devoted to live Belém rock, MPB fusion and DJs – some of whom play avant garde techno *brega*. Attracts an alternative student crowd and is especially busy on Fri. At its best after 2300.

Casa do Gilson
Trav Padre Eutíquio 3172, T091-3272 1306.
A covered courtyard space decorated with arty black and white photography and with live Rio de Janeiro *samba* and *choro* on weekends. The bar owner, Gilson, often plays mandolin in the band.

Mormaço
Passagem Carneiro da Rocha s/n, next to Mangal das Garças, T091-98043 7275, www.mormaco.net.
A warehouse-sized building on the waterfront which showcases local Belém bands and *brega* acts at weekends.

Templários
R Vinte e Oito de Setembro 1155, Reduto, T091-3224 4070, www.facebook.com/templarios.restaurante.
The best place in the city to hear cutting edge Pará sounds – from Amazon *guitarrada* surf music (from guitarist Felix Robatto) to alternative rock and traditional *carimbó* with a modern twist. There are many other street bars nearby, and the whole area buzzes between Thu and Sat nights after 2200.

Entertainment

Art galleries
Debret, *R Arcipreste Manoel Theodoro 630, Batista Campos, T091-222 4046.* Contemporary painting and sculpture, also has library specializing in art and philosophy.
Espaço Cultural Casa das Onze Janelas, *see page 158.* Cultural performances and art exhibitions, panoramic view.

Cinema
There are plenty of multiplexes in the city's shopping malls, the most modern being **Shopping Boulevard** (see Shopping, below).

Festivals

Apr Maundy Thu, half-day; **Good Fri**, all shops closed, all churches open and there are processions.
9 Jun Corpus Christi.
15 Aug Accession of Pará to Independent Brazil.
7 Sep Independence Day, commemorated on the day with a military parade, and with a student parade on the preceding Sun.
Sep Festa do Çairé, Santarém and Alter do Chão. Parades in the streets in Alter do Chão with 2 teams competing to out dance and out costume each other: the Boto Cor do Rosa (pink river dolphin) and the Boto Tucuxi (gray river dolphin) teams.
30 Oct Círio. The festival of candles, based on the legend of Nossa Senhora de Nazaré whose image was found on the site of her Basílica around 1700. On the 2nd Sun in Oct a procession carries the Virgin's image from the Basílica to the cathedral; it is returned 2 weeks later. The festival attracts many artists and musicians and has become a massive national celebration with carnival performers and rock groups. Highly recommended. See www.ciriodenazare.com.br and box, page 151.

Shopping

Ver-o-Peso is a wonderful place to stock up on everything from herbal love potions and Amazon incense to handicrafts and Brazil nuts. Just across the street are a series of shops selling traditional herbal remedies; the best is **Ponto da Erva Medicinais**; see below. There is an arts and crafts market in the **Praça da República** every weekend selling attractive seed and bead jewellery, wicker, hammocks and raw cotton weave work, toys and other knick-knacks. Belém is a good place to buy hammocks: look in the street parallel to the river, 1 block inland from **Ver-o-Peso**.

Mercado de São Brás, *Praça Lauro Sodré.* Handicraft market and folkloric shows in a building dating from 1911.
Ná Figueredo, *Av Gentil Binttencourt 449, Nazaré and Estação das Docas, T091-3224 8948, www.nafigueredo.com.br.* One of the best music shops in the north of Brazil selling a wealth of local sounds from the very best bands and unusual music from throughout Brazil. Funky T-shirts and casualwear.
Perfumaria Orion, *Trav Frutuoso Guimarães 270, T091-3241 2726.* Has a wide variety of perfumes and essences from Amazonian plants, much cheaper than tourist shops.
Ponto da Erva Medicinais, *Travessia Oriental do Mercado 41, T091-3212 3903.* Herbal remedies, teas, incenses and medicines from the rainforest. Ask for Rosa.
Shopping Boulevard, *Av Visc de Souza Franco 776, T091-3299 0500, www.boulevardbelem.com.br. Daily 1000-2200.* The biggest mall in town, where you will find Brazilian and international labels, a cinema and large food court, all a/c.

What to do

Amazon Star, *R Henrique Gurjão 236, T091-3241 8624, www.amazonstar.com.br.* Offers 3-hr city tours and river tours on traditional boats. The company also books airline tickets and hotels on Marajó.

Marola Stand-up, *T091-98162 7473, www. facebook.com/Marolastandup*. Stand-up paddle boarding on the Amazon rivers. Full instruction and all equipment provided. **Rumo Norte Expeditions**, *Av Serzedelo Correa 895, T091-3225 5915, www.rumo norte.com*. The only company offering a comprehensive menu of adventure, safari and general activities in the eastern Amazon including Belém city tours, boat trips around Belém and Santarém, visits to indigenous villages near Alter do Chão and expeditions and light adventure on Marajó and Algodoal islands and the other islands in the mouth of the Amazon. Reliable and good value.

Transport

Air Val-de-Cans international airport, Av Júlio César s/n, 10 km from the city, T091-3210 6000, has flights to **Lisbon** (with TAP), **Suriname** and **Guyane** and the major Brazilian capitals. There is car rental, 2 tour operator offices, a hotel booking service, ATMs, a chemist and a very helpful tourist office booth (daily 1000-1700) in the terminal building. For transport from the airport, see box, page 156.

Boat Boats leave from the Terminal Hidróviario immediately north of the Estação das Docias to Porto de Camará near Salvaterra on **Ilha do Marajó**, Mon-Sat 0630 and 1430, Sun 1000, 3 hrs, US$5. A fast catamaran service cutting the journey

time in half began in 2016. Car ferries to Marajó (with space for passengers) run from the port at Icoaraci (20 km north of Belém, 30 mins by bus from the *rodoviária* or from the Ver o Peso market, taxi US$25), Mon-Fri 0630, 0730, Sat 1600, 1700, Sun 1600, 1700 and 1800.

Buy boat tickets for destinations further afield through **Rumo Norte Expeditions** (see What to, above). There are river services to **Santarém** via **Breves**, **Almeirim**, **Prainha**, **Monte Alegre**, **Curua-Uná**, **Santarém**, **Alenquer**, **Óbidos**, **Juruti** and **Parintins** on the lower Amazon. 2½ days upriver, 1½ days downriver, suite US$130, berth US$115, hammock US$35 upriver, US$25 down. All vessels sailing Belém–**Manaus** will call at Santarém. The larger ships berth at Portobrás/Docas do Pará (the main commercial port), either at Armazém (warehouse) No 3 at the foot of Av Pres Vargas, or at Armazém No 10, a few blocks further north (entrance on Av Marechal Hermes, corner of Av Visconde de Souza Franco). The guards will sometimes ask to see your ticket before letting you into the port area, but tell them you are going to speak with a ship's captain. Ignore the touts who approach you. Smaller vessels (sometimes cheaper, usually not as clean, comfortable or safe) sail from small docks along the Estrada Nova (not a safe part of town). Take a **Cremação** bus from Ver-o-Peso.

There is a daily service from Belém to **Macapá** (Porto Santana) with *Silja e Souza*

of **Souzamar**, Trav Dom Romualdo Seixas, corner of R Jerônimo Pimentel, T091-3222 0719, and Comandante Solon of **Sanave** (**Serviço Amapaense de Navegação**, Av Castilho Franca 234, opposite Ver-o-Peso, T091-3222 7810). To **Breves**, **ENAL**, T091-3224 5210.

Bus There are road connections to São Luís and the northeastern coast as well as a 3-day bus link from São Paulo via Brasília.

The *rodoviária* has showers (US$0.10), a good snack bar, and agencies with information and tickets for riverboats. To get to the *rodoviária* (www.rodoviariadebelem. com.br) take **Aeroclube**, Cidade Novo, No 20 bus, or **Arsenal** or **Canudos** buses, US$0.50, or taxi, US$4 (day), US$6 (night).

For information on getting from the *rodoviária* to the centre, see box, page 156.

Buses run from Belém to Marudá town for **Algodoal** island (5 a day, 3 hrs, US$7, from Belém *rodoviária*) from where you catch a ferry (around 5 ferries a day, the last at 1700, US$3, 30 mins).

There are regular bus services to **Mosqueiro** (every 30 mins, 1 hr, US$2) and further afield to **São Luís**, 6 a day, US$40, 14 hrs, interesting journey through marshlands. To **Fortaleza**, US$65-80 (24 hrs).

Car hire Avis, R Antônio Barreto 1653, T091-3230 2000, www.avis.com, also at airport, T0800-558 066. **Localiza**, Av Pedro Álvares Cabral 200, T091-3212 2700, www.localiza. com.br, and at airport, T091-3257 1541.

Islands around Belém
a forest-swathed archipelago clustered around the world's largest river island

The mouth of the Amazon, formed by the confluence of that river in the north and the Tocantins in front of Belém, is dotted with islands and mangrove lined backwaters. There are 27 islands around Belém; the largest of which, Marajó (see below), is as big as Switzerland. Many islands can be visited on a day trip from the capital, others are a longer haul. Most are lined with long beaches of fine sand broken by strands of clay and dark stones heavy with iron ores. The water that washes them looks as expansive as an ocean, stretching to a vast horizon, but even out in what is geographically the Atlantic, it is fresh water and brown.

Ilha do Cotijuba and Ilha do Mosqueiro
Ilha do Cotijuba (www.cotijuba.com) and the more built-up Ilha do Mosqueiro (portalmosqueiro.jimdo.com) are reachable from Belém in a couple of hours. Both have a number of *pousadas* and small restaurants, stretches of forest and, on Cotijuba, gorgeous beaches. The islands get very crowded at Christmas and during Carnaval. **Ilha da Mexiana** in the Marajó archipelago is more remote and less visited.

Boats run to Cotijuba from the docks in Belém (especially at the weekends), however, the quickest way to reach all the islands is from the port in **Icoaraci**, 20 km north of Belém (30 minutes bus ride from the *rodoviária* or from near the Ver-o-Peso market; taxi US$20). There are at least four boats a day from here to Cotijuba; the first at 0900. Others only leave when full. The fastest take 20 minutes, the slowest one hour.

Mosqueiro is connected to the mainland by road. At least four buses a day leave from the *rodoviária* taking around 90 minutes to get to the main towns (Praia do Paraíso, Carandaduba and Vila Mosqueiro). There are no banks on any of these islands, so bring cash from Belém.

Ilha de Maiandeua and Algodoal village

This sandy estuarine island with long sweeping beaches is more commonly known by the name of its principal village, Vila do Algodoal, a small-scale traveller resort very popular with French backpackers. The island is a semi-protected area at the junction of the sea, the Amazon and the Rio Maracanã. It is very tranquil and has sand dunes, small lakes and a number of isolated beaches lapped by an Atlantic heavy with the silt of the Amazon. The main town is tiny with a cluster of sandy streets lined with little houses, many of them *pousadas*, and fronted by a muddy beach, the **Praia Caixa d'Agua**.

Donkey carts connect it with the island's other beaches, which include (running north and clockwise from Algodoal town): **Farol** (separated from Algodoal by a fast-flowing estuary and with flat tidal sands), and its continuation, the 14-km-long **Princesa** (with dunes, the best swimming and many of the cheap beach *pousadas*); **Fortalezinha** (some 20 km from Algodoal, with grey sands and weak waves, also reached across an estuarine inlet, but with dangerously strong currents; cross on a ferry only); **Mococa** (around 23 km from Algodoal and with sharp stones and a small fishing community); and, on the other side of the bay from Algodoal town (reachable by boat – 30 minutes), **Marudá** (muddy and with a small town); and to its north **Crispim** (which has beach bars, dunes, and good windsurfing and which is very popular with Paraenses at weekends). All accommodation is low-key and simple. Be wary of stingrays on the beaches – especially in muddier areas – and of strong rip tides, sharks and strong waves on the beaches beyond Mococa, notably at Enseada do Costeiro.

Buses run from Belém to Marudá town (five a day, three hours, US$7, from Belém *rodoviária*) from where you catch a ferry (around five ferries a day, the last at 1700, US$3, 30 minutes). There are onward bus connections from Marudá to Salinópolis and from there south to Maranhão. It is easy to find a room on arrival, except during weekends and holidays. There are no banks or ATMs in Algodoal. For more information see www.algodoal.com.

Ilha de Marajó

The largest island near Belém is also the largest riverine island in the world (although some claim that as it abuts the Atlantic the title correctly belongs to Bananal in Tocantins). Like the rest of the Amazon, Marajó is partly flooded in the rainy season between January and June.

The island is home to thousands of Asian water buffalo, which are said to have swum ashore after a shipwreck. Many are now farmed and Marajó is famous throughout Brazil for its *mozarela* cheese. The island's police force use buffalo instead of horses to get around the beaches and mangroves. Buffalo-back rides with the police can be organized through **Hotel Casarão da Amazônia** (see page 169).

The island is also home to numerous bird species, including thousands of roseate spoonbills, and black caiman, river turtles and other wildlife. There is good **birdwatching** on the *fazendas*; the best of these are listed below.

Sights The capital of Marajó is **Soure** (with a handful of restaurants, crafts shops and the island's best places to stay, with the other main town being **Salvaterra** (with fine beaches and more choice of accommodation); both are on the eastern side of the island, which has the only readily accessible shore. There are many fine beaches around both towns. **Araruna** is 2 km from Soure, from where it's a beautiful walk along the shore to **Praia do Pesqueiro**, a magnificent beach 13 km from Soure (bus from Praça da Matriz at 1030, returns 1600, or on horseback from the Casarão da Amazônia, food available in

Vila do Pesqueiro village shop). **Caju-Una** and **Céu** are 15 km and 17 km from Soure, where 400-m-wide stretches are washed by a limpid sea. Both are almost deserted. At the far end Céu extends north into a seemingly interminable expanse of beach and virgin rainforest which stretches over 100 km north through rivers and swamps to the gentle mangrove-lined cape where Marajó eventually meets the ocean.

Praia de Joanes, between the point of arrival on Marajó (Porto de Camará), and Salvaterra are other popular places to stay. They have a laid-back feel, some Jesuit ruins and a beautiful long sweep of beach framed by forest and red sandstone cliffs.

In the far south of the Marajó archipelago are the little towns of **Ponta de Pedras**, with a few colonial buildings and a fine beach, and **Breves**, in the midst of towering rainforest running northwest to areas inhabited only by indigenous people.

Fishing boats make the eight-hour trip to **Cachoeira do Arari** (one hotel, $), where there is a small **Marajó Museum**. A 10-hour boat trip from Ponta de Pedras goes to the **Arari Lake** where there are two villages: **Jenipapo** and **Santa Cruz**. The former is almost unvisited, while the latter is less primitive and less interesting; a hammock and a mosquito net are essential.

Marajó has a number of *fazendas*, where traditional buffalo ranching takes place to this day. Many are situated in extensive wetlands, punctuated with gallery and terra firme forest rich with bird and animal life. Visits can easily be organized through Rumo Norte Expeditions or Casarão da Amazônia hotel (see pages 164 and 169), and some of the *fazendas* also offer homestays.

Fazenda Bom Jesus ⓘ *5 km from Soure, Facebook: Fazenda-Bom-Jesus-Marajo,* is owned by local matriarch Eva Abufaiad and

Essential Ilha de Marajó

Access

A passenger ferry from **Belém** sails twice daily (once daily at weekends), from the new boat terminal (Terminal Hidroviário) in Belem (US$3, three hours). A fast catamaran service started in 2016; contact **Hotel Casarão da Amazônia** (see page 169) for details. Car ferries (which also carry foot passengers) run from **Porto de Icoaraci**, 20 km north of Belém (30-minute bus ride from the *rodoviária* or from near the Ver-o-Peso market; taxi US$20). Boats arrive at **Porto de Camará** (25 km south of Salvaterra and 31 km south of Soure). From here, small craft wait to transfer passengers to Salvaterra village (US$7, 30 minutes), Soure (US$8, 40 minutes, including a ferry crossing) or Praia de Joanes (US$2, 15 minutes). Each is clearly marked with the destination.

There is also an aeroplane-taxi service direct to Soure from Belém, bookable through **Rumo Norte Expeditions** (see page 164).

Tip...
Bring cash because Soure and Salvaterra's Banco do Brasil ATM is unreliable.

Getting around

Bicycles and horses can be rented in both Salvaterra and Soure (US$1/US$10 per hour respectively, through hotels) to explore beaches and the interior of the island.

has a delightful colonial chapel on over 6000 ha of land, and has rehabilitated much of its land for wildlife; a visit here is a real delight. **Fazenda Sanjo** ⓘ *35 km from Soure, T091-3228 1385, www.sanjo.tur.br*, has large areas of wetland rich in birdlife, Amazonian river and a huge herd of traditionally managed buffalo. **Fazenda São Jeronimo** ⓘ *Soure, T091-3741 2093, www.marajo.tk*, has a beautiful stretch of coastal land with extensive mangroves and

BACKGROUND
Ilha de Marajó

Marajó was the site of the pre-Columbian Marajóaras civilization, celebrated for its ceramics, beautiful replicas of which can be bought from artisans in Soure. It is also a centre for *candomblé* and *umbanda*. Many of the communities here are descended from Africans who escaped slavery in Belém and fled to the forest to found their own villages or *quilombos*. A number of beaches around Soure are sacred *candomblé* and *umbanda* sites. The *quilombolas* did not remain altogether free of slavery, however. As Marajó was settled ranchers laid claim to the land, and much of the territory around Soure and Salvaterra which was originally community land is now privately owned.

Until very recently many of the *quilombolos* were employed under a system of semi-debt peonage (where wages are offset against the cost of rent and accommodation) is organized in such a way that they can never earn enough to pay off their employers. In 2007 the Ministry of Work and Employment freed a number of people from such slavery on Fazenda Santa Maria. Other *fazendas* – including Bom Jesus – stand accused of having their farm hands impede access to roads, including the PA-154 state road linking the *quilombo* community of Caju-Una with Soure.

beaches linked by a wooden walkway. The owner cooks excellent food, including soup made from coconut, coriander and naval shipworm (*turu*), which tastes like oyster, and hosts an annual gastronomy and opera festival, held on tables in the mangroves. It's quite a spectacle.

Listings Islands around Belém

Where to stay

Cotijuba

$$ Pousada Matapi
Praia do Farol, T091-3617 1172,
www.pousadamatapicotijuba.com.
Bright pink chalets set in a little garden near the beach. Good rates during the week. Friendly owners.

Mosqueiro

There are plenty of opportunities for camping on Mosqueiro and a wealth of *pousadas* in all price brackets.

$$ Farol
Praia Farol, T091-3771 2095,
www.hotelfarol.com.br.
Chunky beach hotel on the beach with 1920s architecture, small restaurant, rooms face the beach, good views.

Ilha de Maiandeua and Algodoal

$$ Jardim do Éden
Overlooking the beach on Praia do Farol,
http://onlinehotel.com.br/para/ilha-
do-algodoal/jardim-do-eden-pousada/
index.htm.
A series of bizarre neo-Gothic brick *cabañas* with kitchenettes. Well-kept and well run and with more personality than most on the island. Tours available and camping in the grounds (on the beach). Discounts online.

$$ Pousada Bela-Mar
Av Beira Mar, Vila do Algodoal Beach, T091-
3854 1128, www.belamarhotel.blogspot.com.
A very simple beachside hotel with tiny rooms, set in a garden. Close to the boat jetty.

$$ Pousada Chalés do Atlântico
Algodoal, T091-3854 1130, www.
pousadachalesdoatlantico.com.

11 simple little *cabañas* with mosquito screening, en suites and cold showers near the beach.

Ilha de Marajó
Marajó gets very busy in the Jul holiday season; be sure to reserve ahead at this time.

$$$ Canto do Frances
6 Rua, Trav 8, Soure, T091-3741 1298, www.ocantodofrances.blogspot.com.
This French/Brazilian-owned *pousada* 20 mins' walk from the centre offers well-kept but very simple whitewash and wooden-walled rooms in a pretty bungalow surrounded by a garden filled with flowers and fruit trees. Breakfast is generous and the owners organize horse riding, canoe and bike trips around Soure. Book ahead to be met at the ferry port.

$$$ Casarão da Amazônia
4 Rua 646, Soure, T091-3741 1988, www.casaraoamazonia.com.br.
Far and away the best hotel on the island and the only boutique hotel in the Pará Amazon, lovingly restored and run by Neapolitan Nello Gentile and his wife Camila. Rooms are housed in a fabulous sky-blue belle époque grand rubber boom mansion in Soure village. The building sits in its own tropical garden next to a pool and restaurant. Good Italian-Amazonian food (with crispy pizzas). Rooms are comfortable, well-appointed and cool. Wonderful horseback and boat tours around Marajó. Come for several days.

$$$ Pousada dos Guarãs
Av Beira Mar, Salvaterra, T091-4005 5656, www.pousadadosguaras.com.br.
Well-equipped little resort hotel on the beach with an extensive tour programme.

$$ Paracuary Eco Pousada
Rio Paracuary, Soure, T091-2121 2600, www.paracauary.com.br.
A/c rooms with en suites in mock-colonial chalets around a pool 3 km from Soure and on the banks of the Rio Paracuary.

$$ Ventania
Praia de Joanes, T091-3646 2067, www.pousadaventania.com.
Pretty little cliff-top *pousada* in a lawned garden a stroll from the beach. Lovely breakfast areas with beach views. Each apartment has room for 2 couples ($). Bike rental, French, Dutch, English and Spanish spoken.

Shopping

Ilha de Marajó
Carlos Amaral, *3 Rua, Trav 20.* Beautiful Marajó ceramics, made using the same techniques and materials as the Marajoara use themselves. Pieces include large pots and lovely jewellery, with pendants, bracelets and necklaces.
François Delamare, *8 Rua 2295, Soure, T091-8199 6442.* Rings and jewellery beautiful made from discarded rainforest wood and buffalo horn. François – who is French – also serves excellent crepes.
Ronaldo Guedes, *Trav 23 1069, Soure, T091-98763 1738.* Marajó ceramics to traditional and contemporary designs.

Transport

Ilha do Marajó
Air There is a taxi-plane service between Soure and **Belém**, bookable through **Rumo Norte Expeditions** (see page 164). There are regular flights at weekends and it's worth ringing ahead to see if there's any space on a plane.

Boat Boats run from Porto de Camará near Salvaterra to the Hidroviario terminal in **Belém** Mon-Sat 0630, 1500, Sun 1500 (3 hrs, US$5) and car ferries to **Porto de Icoaraci** (Mon-Fri 1600 and 1700, Sat 1600 and 1700, Sun 1600, 1700 and 1800). Timetables regularly change so check beforehand.

Santarém

The third largest city on the Brazilian Amazon, Santarém (population 294,580) sits halfway (three days by boat) between Belém and Manaus at the confluence of the blue Rio Tapajós and the milky coffee-coloured Amazon. This business and agricultural centre has little of interest for visitors, most of whom head 40 minutes south to the delightful little village of Alter do Chão.

Santarém was founded in 1661 as the Jesuit mission of Tapajós; the name was changed to Santarém in 1758. There was once a fort here, and attractive colonial squares overlooking the waterfront still remain. The city is dominated by the giant Cargill soya warehouse and port. Lorries from the vast soya plantations which have almost completely depleted the Mato Grosso Amazon forests (and are doing the same with those in Eastern Pará) rumble into the city from the BR163 Trans Amazon highway day and night.

Sights In front of the market square, the brown Amazon water swirls alongside the green blue Tapajós River at the meeting of the waters, which is nearly as impressive as that of the Negro and Solimões near Manaus (see page 136). A small **Museu dos Tapajós** ① *Centro Cultural João Fora, on the waterfront, downriver from where the boats dock*, has a collection of ancient Tapajós ceramics, as well as various 19th-century artefacts. The unloading of the fish catch between 0500 and 0700 on the waterfront is interesting.

There are good beaches nearby on the Rio Tapajós. Maracanã, b**etween the city and the airport**, has sandy bays (when the Tapajós is low) and some trees for shade (take the 'Maracanã' bus from the centre, 20 minutes).

Alter do Chão
www.alterdochao.tur.br.

Alter do Chão (population 6740) is a small, welcoming village with a relaxed hippy feel made up of *caboclo* river people, Borari Indians (a tribe formed from a conglomeration of different tribal nations) and a community of southeastern Brazilians, many of whom have a spirituality influenced by a mix of Amazonian traditions based around the taking of Ayahuasca. It lies 30 km west of Santarém further up the Tapajos river.

The village surroundings are breathtaking. In the dry season (between July and January) the town is surrounded by tens of kilometres of broad, white-pepper fine sandy beaches, lapped by the gentle blue waters of the Tapajos river (which is some 20 km wide at the point it meets the Amazon). These beaches form a lagoon (the Lago Verde) immediately in front of the town, with a long spit (cheesily known as Love Island by hoteliers), extending to a small hill (O Morro), from where there are spectacular views out over the river, the *cerrado* forests around Alter do Chão and the vast Amazon rainforests which stretch along the other side of the river.

There's plenty to do in Alter do Chão, from soaking up the atmosphere on the beaches and around the *praça* (where there is great live *carimbó* and contemporary music at weekends), to spending an hour or two browsing the indigenous artefacts in the best indigenous arts and crafts shop in Pará. Day trips include hikes up the Morro (best at dawn and sunset), boat rides to the Ponta do Cururu (a kilometre-long spit of sand sticking out into the river) and kayaking or boating on Lago Verde. Increasing numbers of tour operators offer trips into the forest from Alter do Chão into the Amazon forest proper, to the FLONA reserve (see below) and further upstream on the Tapajos to Belterra, Fordlândia and the indigenous village, and to the Arapiuns reserve (see below).

Every second week of September, Alter do Chão celebrates one of Pará's biggest festivals, the **Festa do Çairé**, which sees big-costumed processions in the sandy streets and a pageant depicting the seduction of a river dolphin by a beautiful *cabocla* (river peasant) girl (see box, page 151).

Floresta Nacional do Tapajós (FLONA)
Information from Paratur in Belém (see page 160), www.paraturismo.pa.gov.br (in Portuguese only).

The 545,000-ha FLONA reserve on the eastern banks of blue Tapajós River south of Alter do Chão, is home to 26 riverine communities who eke a living from harvesting Brazil nuts, rubber and from fishing. The protected area forms part of a larger reserve spanning both banks of the river. On the less accessible west shore is the 648,000-ha **Reserva Extrativista**

Around Santarém

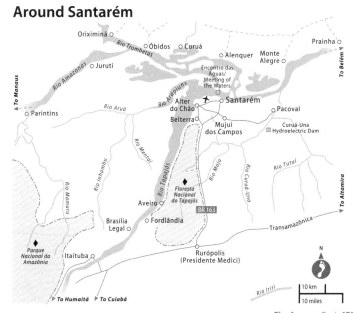

Amazon spirituality: rainforest shamanism

Shamans of the rainforest

Like most pre-Colombian religions, Amazon spirituality is rooted in shamanism, which originated in Siberia, the point of exodus for most of America's ancestors. In the rainforest, shamanism has evolved into its own, rich form. In its highest it is a journey of spiritual evolution in which the shaman is a mentor and guide whose goal is **spiritual enlightenment**. Few people opt for the tortuous, almost monastic path that takes them there. Most shamans are **holders of tradition**, ordering and organizing day-to-day events to the patterns of the spiritual world observed in the cosmos. The material world is attuned to the spiritual through the use of symbols. Everything from a hunt to the positioning of a building has to represent the higher, divine world.

Shamanic enlightenment – the true path

At the highest level, the shamanistic universe comprises two worlds that co-exist: the physical 'visible and the spiritual 'invisible'. Spiritual enlightenment involves complete, instinctual understanding of the oneness of both worlds. The 'visible' or material world is the realm of the senses and is governed by the quest for food. Underlying this is a spiritual, 'invisible' world that we share with all objects and beings in the universe. This invisible world is the realm of pure being, archetype and spirit. It is the ground of our consciousness and is where we perceive and even meet the cosmic and divine powers. Western societies tend to regard only the empirically verifiable and measureable as real. Amerindian shamans however start with the experience of consciousness itself and construct an understanding of reality from here. For example, to the Desano-Tukano people of the upper Amazon (whose philosophy is one of the best documented of all the Amazon peoples), man is known as *mári ariri kéro dohpá inyarí*, which translates 'our existence dream-like appears'. Actions in the visible world must be evaluated in terms of the invisible world, for this is where they derive their form and meaning. In other words, what we do belongs to the material world; what we are, to the spiritual. When a shaman reaches the point of realization, he is like the enlightened of Buddhism or Hinduism: the scales fall from the eyes, the two realms are perceived as one and 'what he realizes himself to be' completely informs what he does. Life is a journey from primitive understanding – life in the visible world – to sophisticated – life seen from the invisible world.

The nature of the journey is encapsulated in the Desano-Tukano understanding of the relationship between the mind and the brain. The Desano-Tukanos equate the invisible world with the left cerebral hemisphere of the brain, and the visible with the right. The left hemisphere is that of the mature, enlightened adult, the 'older brother'. It is the seat of intuition, moral authority, order, intellectual and spiritual endeavours, music, dreams and abstract thought. Its name, *ëmëkori mahsá turí*, means 'sun people dimension'. The sun is the manifestation of the power of the creator of the universe, the 'sun father'. It is also the home of the *gahí turí* or the other dimension or world, where we apprehend and interact with the archetypes and forms of the invisible world. And it is the instrument for interpreting the *bogári*, which are energy fields and 'transmissions' that emanate from nature. The right hemisphere is called *mahsá turí*, or 'human dimension'. It is subservient and is associated with the younger brother. Here lies practical knowledge and skill, tradition, customary rituals, and everything pertaining to the physical. The corpus callosum – a bundle of nerves that bridges the fissure between the two hemispheres is seen by the Desano-Tukanos as an 'anaconda river', with the dark patterns on the snake's back as stepping stones. The student learns to navigate the river, stepping on the stones to move between the left and right hemispheres. Just in front of the anaconda's head is a rock crystal symbolizing the seat of cosmic (solar) illumination.

Mind-altering tonics, such as *ayahuasca*, are used to help shift perception from the visible (right hemisphere) world to the invisible (left hemisphere). Such remedies collapse the ego and completely silence the mental voice and our tenacious regard for ourselves as separate to the external world.

Tradition – life ordered by the motion of the cosmos

Shamans are informed not only by intuition but by age-old tradition. If intuition is mystical prayer, then tradition is the text of shamanic life. It comes in the form of the myriad taboos and rituals passed down through generations, and a giant cosmological map in which positions and movements are imbued with religious significance. This map comprises the harmonic movements of the sky above and the forest around. The constellations along the path announce different harvesting and hunting seasons, ordering the physical world to the cosmic and spiritual. For the Desano-Tukano, Orion is the single most important stellar constellation. The six stars within Orion and those around the constellation are linked in a series of hexagons, as embodied by the sacred rock crystals. The rock crystal is a model of the universe; their hexagonal shape is regarded as a holy shape that infuses the rhythm of daily life. The hexagons in the sky are reconstructed in Tukanoan buildings – *malocas*. Six points mark the positions of the strongest house posts, one at each corner of the hexagon, according to the stars surrounding Orion. Six further posts delimit a central hexagon inside the *maloca*, corresponding to Orion itself. An imaginary line bisects the *maloca* through both hexagons, representing both the Equator and the belt of Orion. Ritual dances are performed within the inner hexagon, whose movements are also symbolically related to the pattern of Orion. Two groups of dancers, one male and one female, move back and forth dividing the line in triangular formations and tracing the hourglass-shape of Orion. They represent the relationship between feminine and masculine archetypes: light and darkness, sun and moon, fertility and restraint. Thus the human home for the Desano-Tukano becomes a theatre for the play of 'man within the universe', and the dances represent the eternal play that occurs within the soul.

Tapajós Arapiuns, created to allow local people to extract rubber and nuts, hunt on a small scale to reduce environmental impact on the forest. Both areas are open to tourism and agencies in Alter do Chão offer trips which include Amazon homestays with riverine communities. The forests and rivers themselves are not as wild as those in similar reserves in Acre or Amazonas, but the area is stunningly beautiful, with white-sand beaches, pink river dolphins and the forest itself, with its many towering Kapok and Brazil nut trees. Trips can be organized with tour operators in Alter do Chão, see page 176.

Fordlândia and Belterra

Both **Fordlândia** and Belterra can easily be visited from Alter do Chão. **Fordlândia**, 220 km south of Alter do Chão, was Henry Ford's first rubber plantation. He founded it in 1926 in an attempt to provide a cheaper source of rubber for his Ford Motor Company than the British and Dutch controlled plantations in Malaya. There are three shops on the town square, two bars, a restaurant and **Hotel Zebu**, in the old Vila Americana (turn right from the dock, then left up the hill). There is a little pebble beach north of town.

Closer to Santarém, 37 km south on a dirt road, is **Belterra**, where Henry Ford established his second rubber plantation. Set in the highlands overlooking the Rio Tapajós, it is nearer to Santarém than his first project, which was turned into a research station. At Belterra, Ford built a well laid-out town, where the houses resemble the cottages of Michigan summer resorts, many with white paint and green trim. The town centre has a large central plaza that includes a bandstand, the church of Santo Antônio (circa 1951), a Baptist church and a large educational and sports complex.

Ford's project, the first modern attempt to invest in the Amazon, was unsuccessful. It was difficult to grow the rubber tree in plantation conditions, where it was unprotected from the heavy rains and harsh sun, and indigenous parasites were attracted by the concentrations of trees. Boats could only come this far upriver in the rainy season and there was a series of disputes between the American bosses and the local employees. Ford sold up in 1945 and the rubber plantation is now deserted.

Monte Alegre

There's not much to this small village. It's little more than a collection of low, scruffy buildings gathered around a street on a shallow hill rising from the vast swampy expanses of the Amazon River, but it has changed ideas about the history of Brazil, and perhaps the Americas.

Outside the town, in the municipality of Campina, is the **Parque Estadual de Monte Alegre** (Monte Alegre State Park), 5800 ha of lowland forest broken by sedimentary escarpment. This was where Anna Roosevelt undertook excavations of historical importance in the 1990s at the Caverna da Pedra Pintada. The cliffs, crags and caves of this escarpment area are covered with hundreds of blood-red paintings. Some show strange figures with pyramidical bodies and bulbous heads surrounded by halos, others have symmetrical checker board designs, dancing figures and vibrant hand patterns. The civilization which produced them has been shown by Roosevelt to be at least 11,000 years old, challenging contemporaneous ideas of origins in the Americas beginning with the Clovis migrations from the North. Visiting the state park is difficult. Trips can be organized through *pousadas* in town, or with advance notice through **Gil Serique** or **Arkus Rodrigues** at **Sabiá Tour** in Alter do Chão (see What to do, below).

Tourist information

Santarém

Comtur
R Floriano Peixoto 777, T093-3523 2434.
Mon-Fri 1000-1700.
Good information in English. Also see
www.paraturismo.pa.gov.br.

Where to stay

Santarém
The city has a poor choice of hotels.

$$$ Barrudada Tropical
Av Mendonça Furtado 4120, T093-3222 2200,
http://barrudadatropicalhotel.com.br.
Large 1970s concrete hotel, 4 km from the
centre, with a pool and boxy rooms and
a restaurant. It's the best in town but is
nothing special.

$$ Tapajos Center
Av Tapajos 1827, T093-3522 5353,
www.tapajoscenterhotel.com.br.
A big concrete block well-situated in the
centre of the city. Rooms are very simple and
plain with little furnishings. A few have no
windows. The best are on the top floor and
have balconies with great river views. No lift.

Alter do Chão
Alter do Chão could do with some decent
hotels and B&Bs. Even the cheapest are
in need of a refurb or an upgrade. Arkus
Rodrigues of **Sabiá Tour** (see What to do,
below) can organize homestays.

$$$ Beloalter
R Pedro Teixeira 500, T093-3527 1230,
www.beloalter.com.br.
Beautifully situated, a stroll from the beach
and lagoon (and 15 mins' walk from the
centre of town), with a pool, pleasant
open-sided public areas and a garden
visited by monkeys in the afternoon and

early mornings, this hotel is let down by
its plain, boxy whitewash rooms with their
ugly windows and clunk a/c. But it's the
best in town.

$$ Agualinda Hotel
R Dr Macedo Costa 777, T093-3527 1314,
www.agualindahotel.com.br.
Brick floor and cream rooms (and some
suites for families), with little more than a
bed in a pleasant, airy little *pousada* in the
town centre.

$$ Belas Praias Pousada
R da Praia 507, at the praça, T093-3527 1365,
www.pousadabelaspraias.com.br.
Very simple tile and eggshell blue rooms
with balconies on the upper floor in a
townhouse with pleasant river views.
Well located in the centre of the town,
overlooking the river and lagoon, 10 m
from the beach.

$$ Terramor
Carauari Hill, Everaldo Martins Km 27,
www.terramor.com.br, or book through
Arkus Rodrigues at Sabiá Tour (see What
to do, below).
A retreat community and private ecological
reserve situated on a forested hill
overlooking the town. Stays are in chalets
or a hammock and are for a minimum of
a few days. Meditation, movement, music
and Ayahuasca sessions can be included.

$ Albergue Pousada da Floresta
T093-9921 6566, www.alberguedafloresta-
alterdochao.blogspot.co.uk.
A simple but colourful backpacker hostel
with basic cabanas and a very cheap open-
space for slinging hammocks. Facilities
include kitchen, tour booking, canoe
and bike rental. It's in a great location
surrounded by forest just south of the
village. Gets booked up well ahead.

$ Pousada do Tapajos

R Laura Soudre 100, T093-9210 2166, www.pousadadotapajos.com.br.
HI hostel with spartan tiled floors and whitewashed rooms and dorms, with attentive staff who can organize tours.

$ Pousada Ecologica

Travessa Pedro Teixeira 66, Carauari, T093-99186 9849, www.pousadado johnlennon.blogspot.co.uk.
Very simple wooden huts, set in a forested garden 10 mins' walk from the beach. Friendly staff include the owner and rainforest guide Antonio 'John Lennon' Augusto. They serve a decent breakfast.

Restaurants

Alter do Chão
There is a decent pizzeria and a fish restaurant on the main *praça*. Both host excellent live music and *carimbó* dancing on weekends.

Festivals

Alter do Chão
2nd week in Sep   Festa do Çairé, religious processions and folkloric events. Recommended.

What to do

Alter do Chão
Gil Serique, *80 R Adriano Pimentel, T093-9115 8111, www.gilserique.com.* Enthusiastic, larger-than-life, English-speaking tour guide who visits the creeks, flooded forest, primary forests and savannahs around Alter do Chão, including the Tapajos National Park and Maica wetlands. Good on conservation.
Sabiá Tour, *arkusrodrigues@hotmail.com, T093-99173 2071.* Local artist Arkus Rodrigues and partner Anamaria Freitas operate some of the best low-key boat tours in the region and can organize homestays in Alter do Chão, along the Tapajos and the Arapiuns and in their own home which is decorated with Arkus's gorgeous paintings. Trips are

excellent value. Ask ahead to include a beach barbecue at sunset.
Vento em Popa, *T093-99154 2120, receptivo. ventoempopa@gmail.com.* Boat trips around Alter do Chão in converted wooden Amazon river boats run by Idelfonso Taketomi, a fascinating half-Japanese, half-indigenous Amazonian with many stories to tell.

Transport

Santarém
Air   The bus to the **airport**, T093-3523 4328, from the centre leaves from Rui Barbosa every 80 mins, 0550-1910; taxis US$5. There are flights to **Belém**, **Manaus** and other destinations in the Amazon, **Fortaleza**, **Salvador** and **Brasília** with **Gol**, **TAM** and **Azul**.

Boats   There are local services to **Óbidos** (US$15, 4 hrs), **Oriximiná** (US$20), **Alenquer**, and **Monte Alegre** (US$20, 5-8 hrs). Boats for **Belém** and **Manaus** leave from the Cais do Porto, 1 km west of town (take 'Floresta-Prainha', 'Circular' or 'Circular Externo' bus; taxi US$5); boats for other destinations, including **Macapá**, leave from the waterfront near the centre of town.
Boats run to **Itaituba** along the Rio Tapajós, 24 hrs (a bus service on this route is making the river trip less common). For further information on services to Manaus, Belém, Macapá, Itaituba and intermediate ports, see Routes in Amazônia, page 145.

Alter do Chão
Bus   Tickets and information from the bus company kiosk opposite **Pousada Tupaiulândia**. Buses to **Santarém** leave from the bus stop on Av São Sebastião, in front of Colégio Santa Clara, US$1, about 1 hr.

Belterra and Fordlândia
Bus   Bus from Belterra to **Santarém**, Mon-Sat 1300 and 1530, US$4, about 2 hrs. There is a 1-hr time difference between Santarém and Belterra.

Boat Boats that run **Santarém–Itaituba** stop at **Fordlândia** if you ask (leave Santarém 1800, arrive 0500-0600, US$12 for first-class hammock space); ask the captain to stop for you on the return journey, about 2300. Or take a tour with a Santarém travel agent.

Practicalities

Getting there

International flights into Rio de Janeiro arrive **Tom Jobim International Airport** (also known as Galeão) on the Ilha do Governador, 16 km from the city centre.

Prices are cheapest in October, November and after Carnaval and at their highest in the European summer and the Brazilian high seasons (generally 15 December to 15 January, the Thursday before Carnaval to the Saturday after Carnaval, and 15 June to 15 August). Departure tax is usually included in the cost of the ticket.

The best deals on flights within Brazil are available through **Azul** ① *www.voeazul. com.br*; **GOL** ① *www.voegol.com.br*; and **TAM** ① *www.tam.com.br*; and **Avianca** ① *www.avianca.com.br*.

TRAVEL TIP
Packing for Brazil

Bag Unobtrusive sturdy bag (either rucksack or bag with wheels) and an inelegant day pack/bag – to attract minimal attention on the streets.

Clothing Brazilians dress casually. It's best to do likewise and blend in. Avoid flashy brands. Thin cotton or a modern wicking artificial fabric are best. Take lightweight trousers, shorts, a long-sleeved shirt, skirts, cotton or wicking socks, underwear, shawl or light waterproof jacket for evenings and a sun hat.

Footwear Light Gore-Tex walking shoes (or boots if you intend to trek) are best. Buy from a serious, designated outdoor company like Brasher or Berghaus rather than a flimsy fashion brand. Wear them in before you come. Nothing gives a tourist away more than new shoes.

Sponge bag 2% tincture of iodine; Mercurochrome or similar; athlete's foot powder; tea tree oil; antibiotic ointment; toothbrush; rehydration tablets; anti-diarrheals such as Imodium; sun protection (high factor) – this is expensive in Brazil.

Electronics UK, US or European socket adaptor; camera with case to attract minimal attention; torch (flashlight).

Miscellaneous items Ear plugs for surfing, traffic noise and cockerels at dawn; pen knife; strong string (3 m); hooks with a screw-in thread (for mosquito net); gaffer tape; sunglasses (with UV filter); money belt; a sealable waterproof bag large enough for camera and clothes (essential if taking Iguaçu's Macuco safari).

For rural and beach destinations take a mosquito net impregnated with insect repellent (the bell-shaped models are best) and a water bottle.

What not to pack – to buy there

T-shirts (local brands make you less conspicuous and they are sold everywhere); insect repellent (Johnson's Off! aerosol is best); beachwear (unless you have neuroses about your body – no one cares if their bum looks big in anything in Brazil); flip-flops (Havaianas); painkillers; shampoo and soap; toothpaste; beach sarong (*kanga*); vitamins; hammock and rope (essential for Amazon boat travel).

Air passes

TAM and GOL offer a 21-day **Brazil Airpass**, which is valid on any TAM destination within Brazil. The price varies according to the number of flights taken and the international airline used to arrive in Brazil. They can only be bought outside Brazil. Rates vary depending on the season. Children pay a discounted rate; those under three pay 10% of the adult rate. Some of the carriers operate a blackout period between 15 December and 15 January.

Baggage allowance

Airlines will only allow a certain weight of luggage without a surcharge; for Brazil this is usually two items of 32 kg but may be as low as 20 kg for domestic flights; with two items of hand luggage weighing up to 10 kg in total. UK airport staff can refuse to load bags weighing more than 30 kg. Baggage allowances are higher in business and first class. In all cases it is best to enquire beforehand.

Land

Brazil has borders with all the South American countries other than Ecuador and Chile, often in numerous locations, and many of them in the remote Amazon. Border crossings such as Tabatinga–Leticia (Amazonas Brazil–Colombia in the Amazon) are straightforward but opening hours and customs checks frequently change (sometimes as often as once a month) and it is best to check for the latest online or with the Brazilian federal police.

The Brazil–Argentina–Paraguay triple frontier at Iguaçu is a very fluid border with thousands crossing over to visit both sides of the falls. Crossings could not be easier and restrictions have not changed for years. See boxes pages 181 and 182, for details. Some remote borders (such as Ponta Porã in Mato Grosso do Sul–Paraguay; see page 89) are less used though they have been open for decades. Crossings are possible but you should be cautious as these are also smuggling routes.

Bus
Argentina Connected to the south of Brazil at Foz de Iguaçu/Puerto Iguazú (the Iguaçu Falls) in Paraná state see box, opposite.
Bolivia Connected to Brazil at Puerto Quijarro/Corumbá (see page 99) via road and rail, with onward connections to the rest of Bolivia via Santa Cruz.
Paraguay Reachable via Ciudad del Este/Foz de Iguaçu; see box, page 182.

Car
There are agreements between Brazil and most South American countries (check in the case of Bolivia) whereby a car can be taken into Brazil for a period of 90 days without any special documents. For cars registered in other countries, you need proof of ownership and/or registration in the home country and valid driving licence. A 90-day permit is given by customs or at the **Serviço de Controle Aduaneiro** ① *Ministério da Fazenda, Av Presidente Antônio Carlos, Sala 1129, Rio de Janeiro*, and the procedure is straightforward. Keep all the papers you are given when you enter, to produce when you leave.

When crossing the border into Brazil, make sure that there is an official who knows about the temporary import of cars. You must specify which border station you intend to leave by, but application can be made to the customs to change this.

River
Boats run from Iquitos in Peru to Tabatinga in Brazil. Onward travel is then on a five-day riverboat journey (or when they are available, a flight) to Manaus, the capital of

BORDER CROSSING

Brazil–Argentina

Foz de Iguaçu–Puerto Iguazú

All foreigners must get exit and entry stamps both in Brazil and Argentina every time they cross the border, even if it is only for the day. It is your responsibility to get the stamps, if riding a taxi make sure it stops at both border posts, if riding a city bus, ask for a transfer, get off at the Brazilian border post and get on the next bus through without paying again.

Argentine consulate in Foz Travessa Eduardo Bianchi 26, T045-3574 2969, Monday-Friday 1000-1500. Between October-February Brazil is one hour ahead of Argentina. It takes about two hours to get from Foz to the Argentine falls, a very tiring journey when the weather is hot.

Immigration The border is open 0700-2300. A Brazilian exit stamp is required for all foreigners leaving the country, even if only for one day. Take your passport and your entry card and make sure you get your exit stamp when you cross the bridge. The Brazilian Argentinian border at Foz do Iguaçu has a reputation for being lax, with people easily crossing, often without getting proper stamps, and then proceeding onwards to other destinations in Brazil (or Argentina). Taxis, vans and private buses often avoid the border stop if they can get away with it. However, it is very important to get the correct stamps to avoid problems on exiting Brazil or with spot checks by federal police. Penalties for improper documentation in Brazil (and Argentina) are stringent (subject to a fine of around US$200) and having the correct passport stamp is the responsibility of the individual traveller. Even if you are returning on the same day it's safer to get your exit stamp on the way out of Brazil and an entry stamp into Argentina, an exit stamp in Argentina on return and, finally, an entry stamp and entry card on the way back to Brazil again. Make sure that you receive both an entry stamp and an entry card when re-entering Brazil. Remember that Americans, Canadians and Australians are required to pay a reciprocity fee of around US$150 for entering Argentina – even if it is just for the afternoon.

There are money exchange facilities beside the Argentine immigration. If entering Brazil, be sure you also get the entry card stamped.

Transport Buses marked 'Puerto Iguazú' run every 30 minutes Monday-Saturday and every hour on Sunday and bank holidays, from the **Terminal de Transporte Urbano (TTU)**, Avenida Juscelino Kubitscheck in the center of Foz do Iguaçu. Make sure you use an international company; they are the ones that cross the bridge. Keep the ticket in case the bus driver can't wait for you at immigration, but note the ticket will be only valid with the same company. The waiting can take a long time. From the bus terminal in Puerto Iguaçu, take the bus to the Argentine falls. Taxis run from Foz do Iguaçu to the border, waiting at immigration, US$10-15.

Note Be sure you know when the last bus departs from Puerto Iguazú for Foz (usually 1930); last bus from Foz is at 1900. If visiting the Brazilian side for a day, get off the bus at **Hotel Bourbon**, cross the road and catch the bus to the falls, rather than going into Foz and out again.

BORDER CROSSING

Brazil–Paraguay

Foz de Iguaçu–Ciudad del Este

The Ponte de Amizade/Puente de Amistad (Friendship Bridge) over the Río Paraná, 6 km north of Foz, leads straight into the heart of Ciudad del Este. Paraguayan and Brazilian immigration formalities are dealt with at opposite ends of the bridge. Ask for relevant stamps if you need them. The area is intensively patrolled for contraband and stolen cars; ensure that all documentation is in order. **Paraguayan consulate in Foz**, Rua Marechal Deodoro 901, T045-3523 2768, Monday-Friday 0900-1700. Brazil is one hour ahead of Paraguay.

Transport Buses (marked Cidade-Ponte) leave from the **Terminal Urbana** on Avenida Juscelino Kubitschek in Foz, for the Ponte de Amizade (Friendship Bridge), US$1 20. To **Asunción**, **Nuestra Señora de la Asunción** (www.nsa.com.py), from the *rodoviária*, at 1205 (*ejecutivo*) and 1830 (*convencional*) (more options from Ciudad del Este). If crossing by private vehicle and only intending to visit the national parks, this presents no problems.

the Amazon. This border can also be crossed by land from Leticia in Colombia, which is alongside Tabatinga. Security is tight at these borders and Brazilian immigration occasionally refuses to allow entry to Brazil for more than 30 days. Brazil is connected to Venezuela through Puerto Ayacucho, San Carlos de Rio Negro and Cucui/São Gabriel da Cachoeira. The crossing is difficult. Exit stamps should be secured in Puerto Ayacucho. Wayumi Airlines flies to San Carlos. From here it is possible to hitch downstream to Cucui and take a bus to São Gabriel. Entry stamps must be secured in São Gabriel. Boats connect São Gabriel with Manaus (five to seven days).

Sea

Travelling as a passenger on a cargo ship to South America is not a cheap way to go, but if you have the time and want a bit of luxury, it makes a great alternative to flying. The passage is often only available for round trips.

Shipping agents

Cargo Ship Voyages Ltd ⓘ *Hemley, Woodbridge, Suffolk IP12 4QF, T01473-736265, www. cargoshipvoyages.co.uk.* Other companies include **Freighter Expeditions** ⓘ *www. freighterexpeditions.com.au*, and **Stradn** ⓘ *www.strandtravelltd.co.uk.*

Cruise ships

Cruise ships regularly visit Brazil. The website www.cruisetransatlantic.com has full details of transatlantic crossings. There are often cheaper deals off season.

Getting around

First time visitors seldom realise how big Brazil is and fail to plan accordingly. The country is the world's fifth largest, making it bigger than the USA without Alaska, or the size of Australia with France and the UK tagged on. As intercity rail is nonexistent (but for one irregular and inconsequential route), travelling within a state overland can involve long bus or car journeys: even the smaller states are as big or bigger than many European countries. The Amazon is nearly double the size of the EU.

Air

Due to the huge distances between places, flying is the most practical option to get around Western Brazil. All state capitals and larger cities in the region are linked with each other or through São Paulo with services several times a day, and all national airlines offer excellent service. Deregulation of the airlines has greatly reduced prices on some routes and low-cost airlines offer fares that can often be as cheap as travelling by bus (when booked online). Buy your internal flights before leaving home. Paying with an international credit card is not always possible online within Brazil (as sites often ask for a Brazilian social security number), but it is usually possible to buy an online ticket through a hotel, agency or willing friend without a surcharge. Many smaller airlines go in and out of business sporadically. **Avianca** ① *www.avianca.com.br*, **Azul** ① *www.voeazul.com.br*, **GOL** ① *www.voegol.com.br*, **TAM** ① *www.tam.com.br*, and **TRIP** ① *www.voetrip.com.br*, operate the most extensive routes.

River

River boat

River boats are the buses and taxis of the Amazon. Public intercity services ply between Belém, Santarém and Manaus; Belém and Macapá; from Manaus to the border with Colombia and Peru in Tabatinga; and along the Madeira and Negro rivers. Journeys are long – several days or even more than a week – especially when travelling upstream.

Tickets are available at the ports in the major cities but are most easily bought through an agent. It's also possible to get around the Amazon by private charter boat, which can be organized for short journeys at the quays or through agencies as part of a tour.

While there are cabins you'll be cooler sleeping in a hammock. But you'll need to buy your own hammock, available at shops in Manaus and Belém. Be sure to bring two lengths of rope, to tie you hammock to the rafters, and a blanket. It can be chilly at night. Central American string hammocks are too cold.

Road

Bus

Outside the Amazon (where there are almost no roads), the most reliable way of travelling is by bus. Routes are extensive, prices reasonable and buses modern and comfortable. There are three standards of intercity and interstate bus: *Comum*, or *Convencional*, are quite slow, not very comfortable and fill up quickly; *Executivo* are more expensive, comfortable (many have reclining seats), and don't stop en route to pick up passengers so are safer;

leito (literally 'bed') run at night between the main centres, offering reclining seats with leg rests, toilets, and sometimes refreshments, at double the normal fare. For journeys over 100 km, most buses have chemical toilets (bring toilet paper). Air conditioning can make buses cold at night, so take a jumper; on some services blankets are supplied.

Buses stop fairly frequently (every two to four hours) at *postos* for snacks. Bus stations for interstate services and other long-distance routes are called *rodoviárias*. They are frequently outside the city centres and offer snack bars, lavatories, left luggage, local bus services and information centres. Buy bus tickets at *rodoviárias* (most now take credit cards), not from travel agents who add on surcharges. Reliable bus information is hard to come by, other than from companies themselves. Buses usually arrive and depart in very good time. Many town buses have turnstiles, which can be inconvenient if you are carrying a large pack. Urban buses normally serve local airports.

Car hire

Car hire is competitive with mainland Europe and a little pricier than the USA and is an option around São Paulo and Iguaçu. It is less advisable in the Pantanal, where roads are often impassable after rain and where it is easy to get lost. There are no roads of consequence in the Amazon.

Roads in Western Brazil are not always well-signposted and maps are hard to come by. Use a sat nav only outside the cities. Within a city a sat nav offers the shortest routes, which can involve potentially dangerous crossings through peripheral communities. Costs can be reduced by reserving a car over the internet through one of the larger international companies such as **Europcar** (www.europcar.co.uk) or **Avis** (www.avis. co.uk). The minimum age for renting a car is 21 and it's essential to have a credit card. Companies operate under the terms *aluguel de automóveis* or *auto-locadores*. Check exactly what the company's insurance policy covers. In many cases it will not cover major accidents or 'natural' damage (eg flooding). Ask if extra cover is available. Sometimes using a credit card automatically includes insurance. Beware of being billed for scratches that were on the vehicle before you hired it.

Taxi

At the outset, make sure the meter is cleared and shows 'tariff 1', except (usually) from 2300-0600, Sunday, and in December when '2' is permitted. Check that the meter is working; if not, fix the price in advance. The **radio taxi** service costs about 50% more but cheating is less likely. Taxis outside larger hotels usually cost more. If you are seriously cheated, note the number of the taxi and insist on a signed bill; threatening to take it to the police can work. **Mototaxis** are much more economical, but many are unlicensed and there have been a number of robberies of passengers. Taxis vary widely in quality and price but are easy to come by and safe when taken from a *posto de taxis* (taxi rank).

Essentials A-Z

Accident and emergency

Ambulance T192. **Police** T190/197. If robbed or attacked, contact the tourist police. If you need to claim on insurance, make sure you get a police report.

Children

Travel with children is easy in Brazil. Brazilians love children and they are generally welcome everywhere. Facilities are often better than those back home.

Some hotels charge a cheaper family rate. Some will not charge for children under 5 and most can provide an extra camp bed for a double room. A few of the more romantic boutique beach resorts do not accept children. If you are planning to stay in such a hotel it is best to enquire ahead.

Most restaurants provide children's seats and menus as well as crayons and paper to keep them happy. Children are never expected to be seen but not heard.

Children under 3 generally travel for 10% on internal flights and at 70% until 12 years old. Prices on buses depend on whether the child will occupy a seat or a lap. Laps are free and if there are spare seats after the bus has departed the child can sit there for free.

On tours children under 6 usually go free or it may be possible to get a discount.

Disabled travellers

As in most Latin American countries, facilities are generally very poor. Problems are worst for **wheelchair users**, who will find that ramps are rare and that toilets and bathrooms with facilities are few and far between, except for some of the more modern hotels and the larger airports. Public transport is not well geared up for wheelchairs and pavements are often in a poor state of repair or crowded with street vendors requiring passers-by to brave the traffic. The metro has lifts and disabled chair lifts at some stations (but not all are operational). Disabled Brazilians obviously have to cope with these problems and mainly rely on the help of others to get on and off public transport and generally move around. Drivers should bring a disabled sticker as most shopping centres and public car parks have disabled spaces.

Disability Travel, www.disabilitytravel.com, is an excellent US site written by travellers in wheelchairs who have been researching disabled travel full-time since 1985. There are many tips and useful contacts and articles and the company also organizes group tours. **Global Access – Disabled Travel Network Site**, www.globalaccessnews.com. Provides travel information for 'disabled adventurers' and includes a number of reviews and tips. **Society for Accessible Travel and Hospitality**, www.sath.org. Has some specific information on Brazil.

Brazilian organizations include: **Sociedade Amigos do Deficiente Físico**, T021-2241 0063, based in Rio and with associate memberships throughout Brazil; and **Centro da Vida Independente**, Rio, www.cvi-rio. org.br. There are a number of specialist and general operators offering holidays specifically aimed at those with disabilities. These include: **Responsible Travel**, www.responsibletravel.com; **CanbeDone**, www.canbedone.co.uk; and **Access Travel**, www.access-travel.co.uk.

Nothing Ventured, edited by Alison Walsh (Harper Collins), has personal accounts of worldwide journeys by disabled travellers, plus advice and listings.

TRAVEL TIP
Brazilian etiquette

In his 1941 travel book, *I Like Brazil*, Jack Harding said of Brazilians that "anyone who does not get along with (them) had better examine himself; the fault is his." And perhaps the best writer on Brazil in English, Joseph Page, observed in his 1995 book *The Brazilians* that "cordiality is a defining characteristic of their behaviour. They radiate an irresistible pleasantness, abundant hospitality, and unfailing politeness, especially to foreigners." It is hard to offend Brazilians or to find Brazilians offensive, but to make sure you avoid misunderstandings, here are a few, perhaps surprising, tips.

Public nudity, even toplessness on beaches, is an arrestable offence.

Brazilians will talk to anyone, anywhere. "Sorry, do I know you?" is the least Brazilian sentiment imaginable and no one ever rustles a newspaper on the metro.

Walks in nature are never conducted in silence. This has led many Brazilians to be unaware that their country is the richest in terrestrial wildlife on the planet.

Drug use, even of marijuana, is deeply frowned upon. Attitudes are far more conservative than in Europe. The same is true of public drunkenness.

When driving it is normal, especially in Rio, to accelerate right up the bumper of the car in the lane in front of you on the highway, hoot repeatedly and flash your headlights. It is considered about as rude as ringing the doorbell in Brazil.

The phrase 'So para Ingles Ver' ('just for the English to see') is a common expression that means 'to appear to do something by the rule book whilst doing the opposite'.

This is the land of red tape. You need a social security number to buy a SIM card and fingerprint ID just to go to the dentist.

Never presume a policeman will take a bribe. And never presume he won't. Let the policeman do the presuming.

Never insult an official. You could find yourself in serious trouble.

Brazilians are very private about their negative emotions. Never moan for more than a few seconds, even with justification – you will be branded an *uruca* (harbinger of doom), and won't be invited to the party.

Never confuse a Brazilian footballer with an Argentine one.

Brazilians believe that anyone can dance samba. They can't.

Never dismiss a street seller with anything less than cordiality; an impolite dismissal will be seen as arrogant and aggressive. Always extend a polite "não obrigado".

Brazilian time. Peter Fleming, the author of one of the best travel books about Brazil, once said that "a man in a hurry will be miserable in Brazil." Remember this when you arrive 10 minutes late to meet a friend in a bar and spend the next hour wondering if they've already gone after growing tired of waiting for you. They haven't. They've not yet left home. Unless you specify 'a hora britanica' then you will wait. And wait. And everyone will be mortified if you complain.

Electricity

Generally 110 V 60 cycles AC, but occasionally 220 V 60 cycles AC is used. European and US 2-pin plugs and sockets.

Embassies and consulates

For a list of Brazilian embassies abroad, see http://embassygoabroad.com.

Gay and lesbian travellers

Brazil is a good country for gay and lesbian travellers as attitudes are fairly liberal, especially in the big cities. Opinions in rural areas are far more conservative and it is wise to adapt to this.

There is a well-developed scene in São Paulo The city's Pridemarch (usually in May) is one of the biggest in the world, with more than 2 million people, and there are many supporting cultural and musical events and parties.

Other festivals include the nationwide **Mix Brasil festival of Sexual diversity**, www.mixbrasil.uol.com.br.

Health

See your GP or travel clinic at least 6 weeks before departure for general advice on travel risks and vaccinations. Make sure you have sufficient medical travel insurance, get a dental check, know your own blood group and, if you suffer a long-term condition such as diabetes or epilepsy, obtain a **Medic Alert** bracelet (www.medicalalert.co.uk).

Vaccinations and anti-malarials

Confirm that your primary courses and boosters are up to date. It is advisable to vaccinate against polio, tetanus, typhoid, hepatitis A and, for more remote areas, rabies. Yellow fever vaccination is obligatory for most areas. Cholera, diptheria and hepatitis B vaccinations are sometimes advised. Only a very few parts of Brazil have significant malaria risk. Seek specialist advice before you leave.

Health risks

The major risks posed in the region are those caused by insect disease carriers such as mosquitoes and sandflies. The key parasitic and viral diseases are malaria, which is not widespread, South American trypanosomiasis (Chagas disease) and dengue fever. **Dengue fever** (which is present throughout Brazil) is particularly hard to protect against as the mosquitoes can bite throughout the day as well as night (unlike those that carry malaria); see box, page 188, for advice on avoiding insect bites. **Chagas disease** is spread by faeces of the triatomine, or assassin bugs, whereas sandflies spread a disease of the skin called **leishmaniasis**.

While standards of hygiene in Brazilian restaurants are generally very high, **intestinal upsets** are common, if only because many first time visitors are not used to the food. Always wash your hands before eating and be careful with drinking water and ice; if you have any doubts about the water then boil it or filter and treat it. In a restaurant buy bottled water or ask where the water has come from. Food can also pose a problem, be wary of salads if you don't know if it has been washed or not.

There is some risk of **tuberculosis** (TB) and although the BCG vaccine is available, it is still not guaranteed protection. It is best to avoid unpasteurized dairy products and try not to let people cough and splutter all over you.

Cases of **Zika** virus have been reported in Brazil and it is recommended that you check with the Foreign Office (www.gov.uk) before travelling, particularly if you're pregnant or planning to become pregnant, and seek advice from a health professional.

Websites

www.cdc.gov Centres for Disease Control and Prevention (USA).

www.fitfortravel. nhs.uk Fit for Travel (UK), A-Z of vaccine and travel health advice for each country.

www.fco.gov.uk Foreign and Commonwealth Office (FCO), UK.

TRAVEL TIP

How to avoid insect bites

Brazilian insects are vectors for a number of diseases including zika, chikungunya, dengue and, in some areas, malaria and yellow fever. These are transmitted by mosquitoes (and some by sandflies) which bite both day and night. Here are a few tips to avoid getting bitten.

- Be particularly vigilant around dawn and dusk when most diurnal and nocturnal mosquitoes bite. Cover ankles and feet and the backs of arms.
- Check your room for insects and spray insecticide before you go out for the day to ensure an insect-free night. Most hotels will have spray, otherwise it can be bought in pharmacies and supermarkets.
- Use insect repellent, especially in beach and forested areas. No repellent works 100%, but most will limit bites. Repellent is available at most pharmacies and supermarkets throughout Brazil. The Off! brand is reliable. If you wish to make your own 'industrial-chemical-free' formula, the author finds the following recipe made with essential oils effective throughout Brazil, including the Amazon: 70% jojoba oil, 30% citronella oil, 10-20 drops of Eucalyptus radiata, 10-15 drops of Wintergreen, 10-15 drops of Cajeput. Do not take this formula internally. This insect repellent also works with sandflies who cannot land on the thick jojoba oil.
- Sandflies are not as widely present in Brazil as in Central America but you will encounter them in some locations (most notably Ilhabela). Many DEET repellents and citronella-based repellents do not work on sandflies. The recipe above, jojoba oil or 'Skin so Soft' baby oil does but you need to apply it thickly.
- Bring a mosquito net. Bell nets are best. Lifesystems do treated models which repel and kill insects. Bring a small roll of duct tape, a few screw-in hooks and at least 5 m of string to ensure you can put the net up in almost all locations.
- Sleep with the fan on when you sleep. Fans are for stopping mosquitoes as much as they are for cooling.
- Consider using insect-repellent treated shirts like those in the Craghoppers Nosilife range. Avoid black clothing. Mosquitoes find it attractive.

www.itg.be Prince Leopold Institute for Tropical Medicine.
http://travelhealthpro.org.uk Useful website for the National Travel Health Network and Centre (NaTHNaC), a UK government organization.
www.who.int World Health Organization.

Books

Dawood, R, editor, *Travellers' health*, Oxford University Press, 2012.

Warrell, David, and Sarah Anderson, editors, *Oxford Handbook of Expedition and Wilderness Medicine*, Oxford Medical Handbooks2008. Wilson-Howarth, Jane. *The Essential Guide to Travel Health*, Cadogan 2009.

Insurance

Always take out travel insurance before you set off and read the small print carefully. Check that the policy covers the activities you intend or may end up doing. Also check exactly what your medical cover includes (eg ambulance, helicopter rescue or emergency flights back home). Also check the payment protocol. You may have to cough up first before the insurance company reimburses you. To be safe, it is always best to dig out all the receipts for expensive personal effects like jewellery or cameras. Take photos of these items and note down all serial numbers.

Internet

Internet usage is widespread. Most hotels offer in-room Wi-Fi (usually free but sometimes at exorbitant rates).

Language

Brazilians speak Portuguese, and very few speak anything else. Spanish may help you to be understood a little, but spoken Portuguese will remain undecipherable even to fluent Spanish speakers. To get the best out of Brazil, learn some Portuguese before arriving. Brazilians are the best thing about the country and without Portuguese you will not be able to interact beyond stereotypes and second guesses.

Cactus (www.cactuslanguage. com), **Languages abroad** (www. languagesabroad.co.uk) and **Travellers Worldwide** (www.travellersworld wide.com) are among the companies that can organize language courses in Brazil. **McGraw Hill** and **DK** (*Hugo Portuguese in Three Months*) offer the best teach-yourself books. **Sonia Portuguese** (www.sonia-portuguese.com) is a useful online resource and there are myriad free and paid-for Portuguese apps of varying quality.

Money

Currency *£1=R\$5.62; €1=R\$4.36; US\$1=R\$4 (Mar 2016).*
The unit of currency is the **real**, R\$ (plural **reais**). Any amount of foreign currency and 'a reasonable sum' in reais can be taken in, but sums over US\$10,000 must be declared.

Residents may only take out the equivalent of US\$4000. Notes in circulation are: 100, 50, 10, 5 and 1 real; coins: 1 real, 50, 25, 10, 5 and 1 centavo. **Note** The exchange rate fluctuates – check regularly.

Costs of travelling

Brazil is cheaper than most countries in South America though prices vary greatly. Rural areas can be 50% cheaper than heavily visited tourist areas in the big city. As a very rough guide, prices are about half those of Western Europe and a third cheaper than rural USA.

Hostel beds are usually around US\$8. Budget hotels with few frills have rooms for as little as US\$15, and you should have no difficulty finding a double room costing US\$30 wherever you are. Rooms are often pretty much the same price whether 1 or 2 people are staying and aside from hostels prices invariably include a large breakfast.

Eating is generally inexpensive, especially in *padarias* (bakeries) or *comida por kilo* (pay by weight) restaurants, which offer a wide range of food (salads, meat, pasta and vegetarian). Expect to pay around US\$4 to eat your fill in a good-value restaurant. Although bus travel is cheap by US or European standards, because of the long distances, costs can soon mount up. Internal flights prices have come down dramatically in the last couple of years and some routes work out cheaper than taking a bus, especially if booking online.

ATMs

ATMs, or cash machines, are easy to come by. As well as being the most convenient way of withdrawing money, they frequently offer the best available rates of exchange. They are usually closed after 2130. There are 2 international ATM acceptance systems, **Plus** and **Cirrus**. Many issuers of debit and credit cards are linked to one, or both (eg Visa is Plus, MasterCard is Cirrus). **Bradesco** and **HSBC** are the 2 main banks offering this service. **Red Banco 24 Horas** kiosks advertise that they take a long list of credit cards in their ATMs, including MasterCard and Amex, but international cards cannot always be used; the same is true of **Banco do Brasil**.

Advise your bank before leaving, as cards are usually stopped in Brazil without prior warning. Find out before you leave what international functionality your card has. Check if your bank or credit card company imposes handling charges. Internet banking is useful for monitoring your account or transferring funds. Do not rely on one card, in case of loss. If you do lose a card, immediately contact the 24-hr helpline of the issuer in your home country (keep this number in a safe place).

Exchange

Banks in major cities will change cash and, for those who still use them, traveller's cheques (TCs). If you keep the official exchange slips, you may convert back into foreign currency up to 50% of the amount you exchanged. The parallel market, found in travel agencies, exchange houses and among hotel staff, often offers marginally better rates than the banks but commissions can be very high. Many banks may only change US$300 minimum in cash, US$500 in TCs. Rates for TCs are usually far lower than for cash, they are harder to change and a very heavy commission may be charged.

Credit cards

Credit cards are widely used. Visa and Mastercard are the most widely used, with **Diners Club** and **Amex** a close second. Cash advances on credit cards will only be paid in reais at the tourist rate, incurring at least a 1.5% commission. Banks in remote places may refuse to give a cash advance: try asking for the *gerente* (manager).

Currency cards

If you don't want to carry lots of cash, prepaid currency cards allow you to preload money from your bank account, fixed at the day's exchange rate. They look like a credit or debit card and are issued by specialist money changing companies, such as **Travelex** and **Caxton FX**, as well as the **Post Office**. You can top up and check your balance by phone, online and sometimes by text.

Money transfers

Money sent to Brazil is normally paid out in Brazilian currency, so do not have more sent out than you need for your stay. Funds can ostensibly be received within 48 banking hours, but it can take at least a month to arrive, allowing banks to capitalize on your transfer. The documentation required to receive it varies according to the whim of the bank staff, making the whole procedure often far more trouble than it is worth.

Opening hours

Generally Mon-Fri 0900-1800; closed for lunch sometime between 1130 and 1400. **Banks** Mon-Fri 1000-1600 or 1630; closed at weekends. **Government offices** Mon-Fri 1100-1800. **Shops** Also open on Sat until 1230 or 1300.

Post

To send a standard letter or postcard to the USA costs US$0.65, to Europe US$0.90, to Australia or South Africa US0.65. Air mail should take about 7 days to or from Britain or the USA. Franked and registered (insured) letters are normally secure, but check that the amount franked is what you have paid, or the item will not arrive. Aerogrammes are most reliable. To avoid queues and obtain higher denomination stamps go to the stamp desk at the main post office.

The post office sells cardboard boxes for sending packages internally and abroad. Rates and rules for sending literally vary from post office to post office even within the same town and the quickest service is **SEDEX**. The most widespread courier service is **Federal Express**, www.fedex.com/br. They are often cheaper than parcel post.

Postes restantes usually only hold letters for 30 days. Identification is required and it's a good idea to write your name on a piece of paper to help the attendant find your letters. Charges are minimal but often involve queuing at another counter to buy stamps, which are attached to your letter and franked before it is given to you.

Safety

Mugging can take place anywhere. Travel light after dark with few valuables (avoid wearing jewellery and use a cheap, plastic, digital watch). Ask hotel staff where is and isn't safe; crime is patchy in Brazilian cities.

If the worst does happen and you are threatened, don't panic, and hand over your valuables. Do not resist, and report the crime to the local tourist police later. It is extremely rare for a tourist to be hurt during a robbery in Brazil. Being aware of the dangers, acting confidently and using your common sense will reduce many of the risks.

Photocopy your passport, air ticket and other documents, make a record of traveller's cheque and credit card numbers. Keep them separately from the originals and leave another set of records at home. Keep all documents secure; hide your main cash supply in different places or under your clothes. Extra pockets sewn inside shirts and trousers, money belts (best worn below the waist), neck or leg pouches and elasticated support bandages for keeping money above the elbow or below the knee have been repeatedly recommended.

Violence over land ownership in parts of the interior have resulted in a 'Wild West' atmosphere in some towns, which should therefore be passed through quickly. Red-light districts should also be given a wide berth as there are reports of drinks being drugged with a substance popularly known as 'good night Cinderella'. This leaves the victim easily amenable to having their possessions stolen, or worse.

Avoiding cons

Never trust anyone telling sob stories or offering 'safe rooms', and when looking for a hotel, always choose the room yourself. Be wary of 'plain-clothes policemen'; insist on seeing identification and on going to the police station by main roads. Do not hand over your identification (or money) until you are at the station. On no account take them directly back to your hotel. Be even more suspicious if they seek confirmation of their status from a passer-by.

Hotel security

Hotel safe deposits are generally, but not always, secure. If you cannot get a receipt for valuables in a hotel safe, you can seal the contents in a plastic bag and sign across the seal. Always keep an inventory of what you have deposited. If you don't trust the hotel, lock everything in your pack and secure it in your room when you go out. If you lose valuables, report to the police and note details of the report for insurance purposes. Be sure to be present whenever your credit card is used.

Police

There are several types of police: **Polícia Federal**, civilian dressed, who handle all federal law duties, including immigration. A subdivision is the **Polícia Federal Rodoviária**, uniformed, who are the traffic police on federal highways. **Polícia Militar** are the uniformed, street police force, under the control of the state governor, handling all state laws. They are not the same as the Armed Forces' internal police. **Polícia Civil**, also state controlled, handle local laws and investigations. They are usually in civilian dress, unless in the traffic division. In cities, the *prefeitura* controls the **Guarda Municipal**, who handles security. **Tourist police** operate in places with a strong tourist presence. In case of difficulty, visitors should seek out tourist police in the first instance.

Public transport

When you have all your luggage with you at a bus or railway station, be especially careful and carry any shoulder bags in front of you. To be extra safe, take a taxi between the airport/bus station/railway station and hotel, keep your bags with you and pay only when you and your luggage are outside; avoid night buses and arriving at your destination at night.

Sexual assault

If you are the victim of a sexual assault, you are advised firstly to contact a doctor (this can be your home doctor). You will need tests to determine whether you have contracted any STDs; you may also need advice on emergency contraception. You should contact your embassy, where consular staff will be very willing to help.

Women travellers

Most of these tips apply to any single traveller. When you set out, err on the side of caution until your instincts have adjusted to the customs of a new culture. Be prepared for the exceptional curiosity extended to visitors, especially women, and try not to overreact. If, as a single woman, you can befriend a local woman, you will learn much more about the country you are visiting. There is a definite 'gringo trail' you can follow, which can be helpful when looking for safe accommodation, especially if arriving after dark (best avoided). Remember that for a single woman a taxi at night can be as dangerous as walking alone. It is easier for men to take the friendliness of locals at face value; women may be subject to unwanted attention. Do not disclose to strangers where you are staying. By wearing a wedding ring and saying that your 'husband' is close at hand, you may dissuade an aspiring suitor. If politeness fails, do not feel bad about showing offence and departing. A good rule is always to act with confidence, as though you know where you are going, even if you do not. Someone who looks lost is more likely to attract unwanted attention.

Student travellers

If you are in full-time education you will be entitled to an **ISIC** (International Student Identity Card), which is valid in more than 77 countries. The ISIC card gives you special prices on transport and access to a variety of other concessions and services. For the location of your nearest ISIC office see www.isic.org. ISIC cards can be obtained in Brazil from **STB** agencies throughout the country; also try www.carteiradoestudante. com.br, which is in Portuguese but easy to follow (click 'pontos de Venda' for details of agencies). Remember to take photographs when having a card issued.

In practice, the ISIC card is rarely recognized or accepted for discounts outside of the south and southeast of Brazil, but is nonetheless useful for obtaining half-price entry to the cinema. Youth hostels will often accept it in lieu of a **HI** card or at least give a discount, and some university accommodation (and subsidized canteens) will allow very cheap short-term stays to holders.

Tax

Airport departure tax The amount of tax depends on the class and size of the airport, but the cost is usually incorporated into the ticket.

VAT Rates vary from 7-25% at state and federal level; the average is 17-20%. The tax is generally included in the international or domestic ticket price.

Telephone *Country code: +55.*

Ringing: equal tones with long pauses. Engaged: equal tones, equal pauses.

Making a phone call in Brazil can be confusing. It is necessary to dial a 2-digit telephone company code prior to the area code for all calls. Phone numbers are now printed in this way: 0XX21 (0 for a national call, XX for the code of the phone company chosen (eg 31 for Telemar) followed by, 21 for Rio de Janeiro, for example, and the 8 or

9-digit number of the subscriber. The same is true for international calls where 00 is followed by the operator code and then the country code and number.

Telephone operators and their codes are: **Embratel**, 21 (nationwide); **Telefônica**, 15 (state of São Paulo); **Telemar**, 31 (Alagoas, Amazonas, Amapá, Bahia, Ceará, Espírito Santo, Maranhão, most of Minas Gerais, Pará, Paraíba, Pernambuco, Piauí, Rio de Janeiro, Rio Grande do Norte, Roraima, Sergipe); **Tele Centro-Sul**, 14 (Acre, Goiás, Mato Grosso, Mato Grosso do Sul, Paraná, Rondônia, Santa Catarina, Tocantins and the cities of Brasília and Pelotas); **CTBC-Telecom**, 12 (some parts of Minas Gerais, Goiás, Mato Grosso do Sul and São Paulo state); **Intelig**, 23.

National calls

Telephone booths or *orelhões* (literally 'big ears' as they are usually ear-shaped, fibreglass shells) are easy to come by in towns and cities. Local phone calls and telegrams are cheap.

Cartões telefônicos (phone cards) are available from newsstands, post offices and some chemists. They cost US$3 for 30 units and up to US$5 for 90 units. Local calls from a private phone are often free. *Cartões telefônicos internacionais* (international phone cards) are increasingly available in tourist areas and are often sold at hostels.

Mobile phones and apps

Cellular phones are widespread and coverage excellent even in remote areas, but prices are extraordinarily high and users still pay to receive calls outside the metropolitan area where their phone is registered. SIM cards are hard to buy as users require a CPF (a Brazilian social security number) to buy one, but phones can be hired. When using a cellular telephone you do not drop the zero from the area code as you have to when dialling from a fixed line.

Some networks, eg O2, provide an app so you can use the time on your contract in your home country if you access the

app via Wi-Fi. Internet calls (eg via **Skype**, **Whatsapp** and **Viber**) are also possible if you have access to Wi-Fi.

There are many Brazilian travel guide apps available only a fraction of which are thoroughly researched. Fewer still are updated regularly. You are far better off using Google Maps and asking in the hotel or from local people.

Time

Brazil has 4 time zones: Brazilian standard time is GMT-3; the Amazon time zone (Pará west of the Rio Xingu, Amazonas, Roraima, Rondônia, Mato Grosso and Mato Grosso do Sul) is GMT-4, the State of Acre is GMT-5; and the Fernando de Noronha archipelago is GMT-2. Clocks move forward 1 hr in summer for approximately 5 months (usually between Oct and Feb or Mar), but times of change vary. This does not apply to Acre.

Tipping

Tipping is not usual, but always appreciated as staff are often paid a pittance. In restaurants, add 10% of the bill if no service charge is included; cloakroom attendants deserve a small tip; porters have fixed charges but often receive tips as well; unofficial car parkers on city streets should be tipped R$2.

Tourist information

The **Ministério do Turismo**, www.braziltour. com, is in charge of tourism in Brazil. Local tourist information bureaux are not usually helpful for information on cheap hotels, they generally just dish out pamphlets. Expensive hotels provide tourist magazines for their guests. Telephone directories (not Rio) contain good street maps.

Other good sources of information are: **LATA**, www.lata.org. The Latin American Travel Association, with useful country information and listings of all UK operators specializing in Latin America. Also has up-to-date information on public safety, health, weather, travel costs, economics and politics highlighted for each nation. Wide selection of Latin American maps available, as well as individual travel planning assistance. **South American Explorers**, T607-277 0488, www.saexplorers.org. A non-profit educational organization functioning primarily as an information network for South America. Useful for travellers to Brazil and the rest of the continent.

National parks

National parks are run by the Brazilian institute of environmental protection, **Ibama**, T061-3316 1212, www.ibama.gov.br (in Portuguese only). For information, contact **Linha Verde**, T0800-618080, linhaverde.sede@ibama.gov.br. National parks are open to visitors, usually with a permit from Ibama. See also the **Ministério do Meio Ambiente** website, www.mma. gov.br (in Portuguese only).

Useful websites

www.brazil.org.uk Provides a broad range of info on Brazilian history and culture from the UK Brazilian embassy.
www.brazilmax.com Excellent information on culture and lifestyle, the best available in English.
www.visitbrazil.com The official tourism website of Brazil, and the best.

www.gringos.com.br An excellent source of information on all things Brazilian for visitors and expats.
www.ipanema.com A quirky, informative site on all things Rio de Janeiro.
www.maria-brazil.org A wonderfully personal introduction to Brazil, specifically Rio, featuring Maria's cookbook and little black book, features and reviews.
www.socioambiental.org Invaluable for up-to-the-minute, accurate information on environmental and indigenous issues. In Portuguese only.
www.survival-international.org The world's leading campaign organization for indigenous peoples with excellent information on various Brazilian indigenous groups.
www.worldtwitch.com Birding information and comprehensive listings of rainforest lodges.

Tour operators

UK
Brazil specialists

Bespoke Brazil, T01603-340680, www. bespokebrazil.com. Tailor-made trips and private tours throughout the country, even to the lesser-known areas.
Brazil Revealed, T01932-424252, www. brazilrevealed.co.uk. A specialist, boutique and bespoke operator with excellent in-country contacts.

Journey Latin America, T020-8600 1881, www.journeylatinamerica.co.uk. An enormous range of Brazil trips, including bespoke options.
Sunvil Latin America, T020-8758 4774, www.sunvil.co.uk. Quality packages and tailor-made trips throughout the country.
Veloso Tours, T020-8762 0616, www.veloso.com. Imaginative tours throughout Brazil; bespoke options on request.

Villas
Hidden Pousadas Brazil, www.hidden pousadasbrazil.com. A choice of tasteful small hotels and homestays hand-picked from all over the country and ranging from chic but simple to luxe and languorous.

Wildlife and birding specialists
Naturetrek, T01962-733051, www.nature trek.co.uk. Wildlife tours throughout Brazil with bespoke options and specialist birding tours of the Atlantic coastal rainforests.
Ornitholidays, T01794-519445, www.ornitholidays.co.uk. Annual or biannual birding trips throughout Brazil, including the Atlantic coast rainforest, the Pantanal and Iguaçu.
Reef and Rainforest Tours Ltd, T01803-866965, www.reefandrainforest.co.uk. Specialists in tailor-made and group wildlife tours.
Wildlife World Wide, www.wildlife worldwide.com. Wildlife trips to the Amazon (on board the *Amazon Clipper*), Pantanal, safaris on the Transpantaneira, and Iguaçu; with bespoke options available.
Wildwings, T0117-965 8333, www.wildwings.co.uk. Jaguar tours around Porto Jofre in the Pantanal.

North America
Brazil For Less, T1-877-565 8119 (US toll free) or T+44-203-006 2507 (UK), www.brazilforless.com. US-based travel firm with a focus solely on South America, with local offices and operations, and a price guarantee. Good-value tours, run by

travellers for travellers. Will meet or beat any internet rates from outside Brazil.

Wildlife and birding specialists
Field Guides, T1-800-7284953, www.fieldguides.com. Interesting birdwatching tours to all parts of Brazil.
Focus Tours, T(505)216 7780, www.focus tours.com. Environmentally responsible travel throughout Brazil.

Brazil
Ambiental, T011-3818 4600, www.ambiental.tur.br. Trips to every corner of Brazil from the Pantanal to Iguaçu.
Brazil Always Summer, T061-3039 4442, www.brazilalwayssummer.com. Tour operator specializing in holidays to Brazil Services include hotel booking and excellent car rental rates. English-speaking staff.
Brazil Nature Tours, T067-3042 4659, www.brazilnaturetours.com. Individual and group tours to the Pantanal and Amazon.
Dehouche, T021-2512 3895, www.dehouche.com. Upmarket, carefully tailored trips throughout Brazil.
Matueté, T011-3071 4515, www.matuete.com. Bespoke luxury options around Brazil with a range of private house rentals.
whl.travel, T031-3889 8596, www.whl.travel. Online network of tour operators for booking accommodation and tours throughout Brazil.

Wildlife and birding specialists
Andy and Nadime Whittaker's Birding Brazil Tours, www.birdingbraziltours.com. A good company, based in Manaus. The couple worked with the BBC Natural History Unit on David Attenborough's *The Life of Birds* and are ground agents for a number of the major birding tour companies from the US and Europe.
Birding Brazil Tours, www.birdingbrazil tours.com. First-class bespoke options throughout the country.
Edson Endrigo, www.avesfoto.com.br. Bespoke options only.

Visas and immigration

Visas are not required for stays of up to 90 days by tourists from Andorra, Argentina, Austria, Bahamas, Barbados, Belgium, Bolivia, Chile, Colombia, Costa Rica, Denmark, Ecuador, Finland, France, Germany, Greece, Iceland, Ireland, Italy, Liechtenstein, Luxembourg, Malaysia, Monaco, Morocco, Namibia, the Netherlands, Norway, Paraguay, Peru, Philippines, Portugal, San Marino, South Africa, Spain, Suriname, Sweden, Switzerland, Thailand, Trinidad and Tobago, United Kingdom, Uruguay, the Vatican and Venezuela. For them, only the following documents are required at the port of disembarkation: a passport valid for at least 6 months (or *cédula de identidad* for nationals of Argentina, Chile, Paraguay and Uruguay); and a return or onward ticket, or adequate proof that you can purchase your return fare, subject to no remuneration being received in Brazil and no legally binding or contractual documents being signed. Venezuelan passport holders can stay for 60 days on filling in a form at the border.

Citizens of the USA, Canada, Australia, New Zealand and other countries not mentioned above, and anyone wanting to stay longer than 180 days, *must* get a visa before arrival, which may, if you ask, be granted for multiple entry. US citizens must be fingerprinted on entry to Brazil. Visa fees vary from country to country, so apply to the Brazilian consulate in your home country. The consular fee in the USA is US$50. Students planning to study in Brazil or employees of foreign companies can apply for a 1- or 2-year visa. 2 copies of the application form, 2 photos, a letter from the sponsoring company or educational institution in Brazil, a police form showing no criminal convictions and a fee of around US$70 is required.

Extensions

Foreign tourists may stay a maximum of 180 days in any 1 year. 90-day renewals are easily obtainable, but only at least 15 days before the expiry of your 90-day permit, from the Polícia Federal. The procedure varies, but generally you have to: fill out 3 copies of the tax form at the Polícia Federal, take them to a branch of **Banco do Brasil**, pay US$15 and bring 2 copies back. You will then be given the extension form to fill in and be asked for your passport to stamp in the extension. According to regulations (which should be on display) you need to show a return ticket, cash, cheques or a credit card, a personal reference and proof of an address of a person living in the same city as the office (in practice you simply write this in the space on the form). Some offices will only give you an extension within 10 days of the expiry of your permit.

Some points of entry, such as the Colombian border, refuse entry for longer than 30 days, renewals are then for the same period, insist if you want 90 days. For longer stays you must leave the country and return (not the same day) to get a new 90-day permit. If your visa has expired, getting a new visa can be costly (US$35 for a consultation, US$30 for the visa itself) and may take anything up to 45 days, depending on where you apply. If you overstay your visa, or extension, you will be fined US$7 per day, with no upper limit. After paying the fine to Polícia Federal, you will be issued with an exit visa and must leave within 8 days.

Officially, if you leave Brazil within the 90-day permission to stay and then re-enter the country, you should only be allowed to stay until the 90-day permit expires. If, however, you are given another 90-day permit, this may lead to charges of overstaying if you apply for an extension.

Identification

You must always carry identification when in Brazil. Take a photocopy of the personal details in your passport, plus your Brazilian immigration stamp, and leave your passport in the hotel safe deposit. This photocopy, when authorized in a *cartório*, US$1, is a legitimate copy of your documents. Be prepared, however, to present the originals when travelling in sensitive border areas. Always keep an independent record of your passport details. Also register with your consulate to expedite document replacement if yours gets lost or stolen.

Warning Do not lose the entry/exit permit they give you when you enter Brazil. Leaving the country without it, you may have to pay up to US$100 per person. It is suggested that you photocopy this form and have it authenticated at a *cartório*, US$1, in case of loss or theft.

Volunteering

Amazon Gero Tours, www.amazon gerotours.com. Offer volunteer teacher placements with riverine communities in the central Amazon.

Weights and measures

Metric.

Index

*Entries in **bold** refer to maps*

Credits

Footprint credits

Editor: Jo Williams
Production and layout: Emma Bryers
Maps: Kevin Feeney
Colour section: Angus Dawson

Publisher: Felicity Laughton
              Patrick Dawson
Marketing: Kirsty Holmes
Sales: Diane McEntee
Advertising and content partnerships:
Debbie Wylde

Photography credits

Front cover: Alex Robinson Photography
Back cover: Alex Robinson Photography
Inside front cover: Alex Robinson
Photography

Duotones
Page 24: Alex Robinson Photography
Page 70: Alex Robinson Photography
Page 122: Alex Robinson Photography

Colour section
Alex Robinson Photography

Printed in Spain by GraphyCems

Publishing information

Footprint Western Brazil
1st edition
© Footprint Handbooks Ltd
May 2016

ISBN: 978 1 910120 68 2
CIP DATA: A catalogue record for this book
is available from the British Library

® Footprint Handbooks and the
Footprint mark are a registered
trademark of Footprint Handbooks Ltd

Published by Footprint
6 Riverside Court
Lower Bristol Road
Bath BA2 3DZ, UK
T +44 (0)1225 469141
F +44 (0)1225 469461
footprinttravelguides.com

Distributed in the USA by
National Book Network, Inc.

Every effort has been made to ensure that
the facts in this guidebook are accurate.
However, travellers should still obtain advice
from consulates, airlines, etc about travel
and visa requirements before travelling.
The authors and publishers cannot
accept responsibility for any loss, injury
or inconvenience however caused.